Lament for America

Lament for America

DECLINE OF THE SUPERPOWER,
PLAN FOR RENEWAL

Earl H. Fry

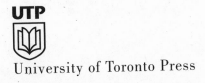

University of Toronto Press

The publisher thanks the David M. Kennedy Center for International Studies, Brigham Young University, for its assistance in the production of this book.

Library and Archives Canada Cataloguing in Publication

Fry, Earl H.

Lament for America : decline of the superpower, plan for renewal / Earl H. Fry.

Includes bibliographical references and index.

ISBN 978-1-4426-0191-8

1. United States—Politics and government—21st century. 2. United States—Foreign relations—21st century. 3. World politics—21st century—Forecasting. I. Title.

JK275.F79 2010   973.93   C2010-901361-1

We welcome comments and suggestions regarding any aspect of our publications—please feel free to contact us at news@utphighereducation.com or visit our Internet site at www.utphighereducation.com.

North America
5201 Dufferin Street
North York, Ontario, Canada, M3H 5T8

2250 Military Road
Tonawanda, New York, USA, 14150
ORDERS PHONE: 1-800-565-9523
ORDERS FAX: 1-800-221-9985
ORDERS E-MAIL: utpbooks@utpress.utoronto.ca

UK, Ireland, and continental Europe
NBN International
Estover Road, Plymouth, PL6 7PY, UK
ORDERS PHONE: 44 (0) 1752 202301
ORDERS FAX: 44 (0) 1752 202333
ORDERS E-MAIL: enquiries@nbninternational.com

The University of Toronto Press acknowledges the financial support for its publishing activities of the Government of Canada through the Book Publishing Industry Development Program (BPIDP).

Printed in Canada

Contents

Acknowledgements

I would like to thank Michael Harrison and his former colleague at the University of Toronto Press, Greg Yantz, for their special interest in this book project. Working with the University of Toronto Press publication team has been a distinct pleasure.

I am also very grateful to Jeff Ringer, director of the David M. Kennedy Center for International Studies at Brigham Young University, for his willingness to provide financial support for the preparation of the final manuscript. Lee Simons, communications manager at the Kennedy Center, and Robert H. Boden, graphic designer, went far beyond the call of duty in preparing the final polished manuscript text that was forwarded to the University of Toronto Press. Stephen Cranney, my administrative assistant, also helped in compiling the bibliography and index and providing constructive comments about the text. BYU's Political Science Department has been very accommodating in providing an administrative assistant and in assigning our very talented main-office personnel to create many of the charts used in the book.

As always, I must thank my wife, Elaine, our children and grand-children, and other family members for their unwavering support and the unparalleled joy and sense of purpose they bring into my life. Gratitude should also be expressed to the thousands of U.S. Foreign Policy students who have endured my classes and offered constructive comments over more than three decades of teaching about America's role in the world.

This book discusses very controversial themes, offers blistering criticism of various U.S. practices, and presents bold and far-reaching policy solutions. The intent is to inform, provoke much-needed debate, and generate new policy directions. Any errors in judgment, facts, scholarship, and plain-old grammar are entirely my own responsibility.

Earl H. Fry
Professor of political science and Endowed Professor of Canadian Studies
Brigham Young University
Provo, Utah
1 February 2010

Preface

The first decade of the new millennium has finally come to an end, and it has been a difficult period for many Americans:

- The unemployment rate at the beginning of 2000 was 4 percent versus 10 percent at the end of 2009;

- The number of non-farm payroll jobs was at the same level in December 2009 as it had been in January 2000, even though the U.S. population grew by almost thirty million during the decade. The number of private-sector jobs actually declined;

- The median household's real income was lower at the end of the decade than at the beginning;

- During the same period, the median price of a new home was up modestly in nominal terms but down when inflation is factored in;

- The Dow Jones Industrial Average ended the decade about one thousand points lower than at the beginning of 2000;

- The NASDAQ average plummeted by almost half during the same period;

- The poverty rate among adults and children was higher in December 2009 than in 2000, and the percentage of Americans reliant on food stamps doubled from the beginning to the end of the decade, with a record one in eight Americans, including one in four children, using food stamps at the end of 2009;

- A higher percentage and higher number of Americans were without health insurance at the end of 2009 compared with the beginning of the decade;

- The average family's premium for health-care coverage more than doubled during the decade, from $6,438 to $13,375;

- During the ten-year period, the federal government's debt more than doubled from $5.7 trillion to $12.1 trillion. Washington spent more than ever before, but its expenditures and policies did little to improve the quality of life for most Americans.

These grim statistics may actually underestimate the plight of many U.S. households. The wealth of the average family is derived from three major sources: jobs, home equity, and pension savings. Job insecurity is currently at its highest level in decades, and total unemployment and underemployment at the beginning of 2010 surpassed 17 percent. Long-term unemployment is also at levels not seen since the 1930s. Men between ages thirty and thirty-nine also earn about 12 percent less in real terms than their same age group a generation ago. Home equities have plummeted since 2007, and almost a quarter of homeowners owe more on their mortgages than their properties are worth. Pension savings are linked to the performance of the stock market, which at the beginning of the current decade was still down by almost 30 percent from its October 2007 highs. Some companies are also jettisoning their 401(k) programs for their employees or no longer offer matching funds to encourage employee retirement savings.

Furthermore, GDP and productivity gains during the decade have been siphoned into the coffers of a very small percentage of Americans. Roughly 34 percent of the private wealth in the United States is held by 1 percent of households, greater than the wealth of the bottom 90 percent of households combined. Through much of the past decade, two-thirds of all the income gains in the United States accrued to the top 1 percent of earners. This concentration of wealth and income is reminiscent of the earlier Gilded Ages of the 1880s and 1920s.

America's domestic problems are also spilling over into the international arena. Although claiming the planet's largest national economy, the U.S. share of the world's GDP fell from over 31 percent in 2000 to about 23 percent in 2009. The U.S. began the decade as the world's largest exporter of merchandise goods and ended it having been surpassed by both China and Germany. America's total share of merchandise exports fell during the period from almost 13 percent to about 8 percent, whereas China's increased from 4 percent to over 9 percent. The U.S. had the dubious honor of solidifying its position as the world's largest external debtor country, with its gross external debt increasing from $6.6 trillion in mid-2003 to $13.7 trillion near the end of 2009. Meanwhile, the U.S. proportion of global military expenditures increased from 37 percent in 2000 to about 42 percent in 2009. For fiscal year 2010, Congress authorized a military budget of $680 billion, almost double the $359 billion spent in fiscal year 2000. President Obama has requested $708 billion for fiscal year 2011.

During the first decade of the twenty-first century, Washington did little to cope with the major problems facing the country. In the eyes of most Americans, the White House and Congress have consistently favored the wealthy and the powerful special interests over the general interests of the common people. In 2010, 70 percent of the population perceived their government was either "unhealthy" or in need of major reforms. Tragically, over the past ten years, the United States has become less prosperous, less egalitarian, and less democratic. In view of its serious challenges at home and overextended commitments abroad, the United States can ill afford to be complacent about the new decade ahead.

This book tackles head-on a very troubling issue for most Americans—the realization that their nation-state is a superpower in the throes of decline. It examines fifteen major fault lines plaguing the nation at home, plus external challenges represented by the rise of competitor nations and a rapidly evolving international landscape characterized by expanding globalization, unprecedented technology change, and widespread creative destruction.

As will be emphasized in the text, it is almost inevitable that America's superpower status will experience relative decline between 2010 and 2050. However, whether that decline is steep or modest will largely depend on the willingness of U.S. leaders and the American people to embrace the substantive policy changes highlighted in this book. Failure to implement these changes will result in a significantly diminished U.S. role globally and a perpetuation of some of the "lost-decade" trends that have plagued many Americans domestically. Even more ominously, the repercussions of an "enfeebled" United States will reverberate throughout the world and precipitate major fluctuations in the global distribution of economic, military, and political power.

The twenty-first century is likely to make the dramatic changes that occurred during the previous century look both modest and insignificant. The pace and scope of future change will be without precedent in human history, and the increasingly uncertain role of the United States on the global stage should be of deep concern to Americans and those around the world who have been influenced by U.S. policies during the post–World War II superpower era.

Chapter 1

No Superpower Is Too Big to Fail

A Nation at Risk

Historians of the future will likely refer to the United States as having been the foremost superpower in human history, or at least the most powerful since the legendary Roman empire.[1]

Sadly for its own citizens and many of its allies abroad, the United States is currently a superpower in the throes of decline. America's National Intelligence Council predicts that by 2025 the international system "will be almost unrecognizable" with "an historic transfer of relative wealth and economic power from west to east."[2] The report adds that "the United States' relative strength—even in the military realm—will decline and U.S. leverage will become more constrained."[3] Financier George Soros was even more blunt when he addressed the recent collapse along Wall Street: "It's the end of an era, as far as the United States is concerned, because the prosperity was based on a false foundation. It has now collapsed, and you cannot rebuild it."[4] Kishore Mahbubani, who once wrote that the United States "has done more good for the rest of the world than any other society," now suggests that America is in danger of failing because of colossal domestic and foreign policy blunders.[5]

This downward thrust is attributable to three major factors: first, the special conditions manifested in the phenomenon known as globalization that mitigate the international influence of any individual nation-state; second, the rise of competitor nation-states or groups of nation-states; and third and most troubling, significant erosion within the United States itself.

The first is linked to the exigencies of globalization. The world is definitely becoming more globalized, with a growing interconnectedness and interdependence among countries, societies, businesses, and peoples. All countries are vulnerable to decisions rendered or events that transpire outside their borders, and this vulnerability reaches down to the neighborhood and household levels of every nation-state. For example, the U.S. industrial and transportation systems could not function efficiently without foreign sources providing over 60 percent of their petroleum requirements.

Globalization will require progressively more cross-border cooperation to solve international problems, and this trend runs contrary to the ambitions of any one nation-state to exert disproportionate unilateral influence on the international stage. Perhaps this is best illustrated by the eight years of the George W. Bush administration. President Bush engaged in a wide range of unilateral policy actions and almost doubled the total aggregate debt of the U.S. government as he pursued some of his goals, including expending nearly half of what the world spends annually on defense. As its debt mounted, the government became increasingly reliant on foreigners to buy its instruments of debt—treasury bonds, notes, and bills. Currently, foreigners hold half of the total U.S. public debt, with China surpassing Japan in September 2008 as the largest single holder of this debt.[6] The paradox is an administration that personified unilateralism in its international policies had become so dependent on the goodwill of foreign central banks and private investors to continue to buy its burgeoning debt. If these foreigner investors ever decide to stop buying U.S. government debt or, even worse, begin to liquidate their existing debt portfolios, the United States could suffer enormous economic and financial upheavals.[7]

The second factor is the rise of new competitors challenging U.S. ascendancy in an increasingly interdependent global setting.[8] China's explosive growth should permit it to surpass the U.S. as the world's largest economy in roughly two decades. The European Union, with twenty-seven nation-states and a half billion people, is also becoming a more prominent international economic and political actor, and the euro may one day challenge the U.S. dollar as the world's major trade and reserve currency. India, Japan, Brazil, Russia, and the Association of Southeast Asian Nations (ASEAN) are among the other countries or groups of countries that might exert a larger voice in international decision-making within the next few decades. Even if the U.S. economy continues to grow, its portion of the global economic pie will shrink, and it will be viewed as a major country among several major countries or blocs of countries, but not as a nation-state exerting the dominant authority of a so-called "unipolar power."

The third factor is directly linked to the challenges the United States faces within its own boundaries. America has just completed an inglorious "lost decade" with the median household's real income lower near the end of the decade than during the year 2000. In addition, the poverty rate among adults and children was higher than it had been in 2000, and the percentage of Americans reliant on food stamps doubled from the beginning to the end of the decade, with a record one in eight Americans, including one in four children, using food stamps at the end of 2009.[9] Furthermore, a higher percentage and higher number of Americans were without health insurance, and there were fewer private-sector jobs, even though many more Americans were seeking these jobs.[10] At its current rate of decline, the United States risks losing its superpower status by 2050 or perhaps even as early as 2040. Almost all observers in 2001 concurred with the accuracy of Henry R. Luce's prediction made back in 1941, prior to the U.S. entry into World War II, that the twentieth century would be known as the "American century."[11] As historians gather in 2101 and look back on the previous hundred years, will any of them be likely to respond that the twenty-first century had also been the "American century"?

Some foreign observers may revel in the dwindling influence of the United States, perceiving that America had become too powerful and its unilateral proclivities posed an imminent threat to other countries. A German Marshall Fund survey conducted in June 2008 found that only 36 percent of Europeans thought U.S. leadership in the world was "desirable."[12] In a Canadian Broadcasting Corporation opinion poll administered in January 2008, respondents were asked to identify "the country that stands out as a negative force in the world." Fifty-two percent selected the United States with Iran a distant second at 21 percent.[13] With the transition from the George W. Bush to the Barack Obama presidencies, some improvement in international perspectives of the United States has been noted, but many abroad remain highly skeptical about the "American model" and the overall U.S. role in global affairs.[14]

In historical perspective, the United States has actually been a rather benign superpower and provided an important degree of stability and predictability for the international system that will be greatly missed by many around the world as U.S. influence wanes. In other words, as the United States becomes a less powerful actor on the international stage, global uncertainty will increase and international relations will become more unpredictable and chaotic at times.

This book will chronicle why the United States is a declining superpower. It will also distinguish between "relative" decline and "absolute" decline. Relative decline is almost inevitable for a variety of reasons, but modest decline would mean that the standard of living of future Americans should continue to improve, even though the U.S. share of a much larger global economic pie would be smaller and its voice in international affairs noticeably subdued.

Absolute decline represents the most ominous scenario. Tom Brokaw labeled those Americans who fought in World War II and built the vibrant post-war domestic society and international order as the "greatest generation."[15] If absolute decline is now settling in, it would mean that the current generation of American leaders and Americans in general will be labeled with the scarlet letter "M," standing for mediocrity. Americans are beginning to suspect that this might transpire, with a plurality predicting that their own children will endure a lower standard of living than they have enjoyed, and two-thirds skeptical that the future of the U.S. will be as good or better than its past.[16] Today, men in their thirties earn about 12 percent less in real terms than the same age cohort a generation ago.[17] With the United States also suffering from a growing epidemic of obesity and a mostly sedentary lifestyle, some doctors are predicting that children risk having a shorter life span than their parents, in spite of marvelous advances in medical technology.[18] Stunningly, three-quarters of the thirty-one million Americans between the ages of seventeen and twenty-four are currently considered as unqualified for military service.[19] In the flippant terms of one journalist, those who are unqualified are "too fat, too sickly, too dumb to serve."[20]

In general, Americans are feeling a pervasive sense of malaise, as their country has struggled through the greatest economic downturn since the Great Depression, as their own asset base shrinks, and as their employers continue to reduce health-care and retirement benefits. In Washington, the government's deficit in fiscal year 2009 alone was greater in nominal dollars than the total debt accumulated from the presidency of George Washington through most of the first term of Ronald Reagan and greater than the federal government's entire budget just a decade and a half earlier.

Government debt actually doubled through the first decade of the twenty-first century, and is expected to double again during the second decade. Since 1961, the U.S. economy measured by annual GDP has grown on average nine years in every decade.[21] In contrast, during this same cumulative period of almost a half century, Congress has managed to balance the government's budget on average only once per decade. Runaway government spending and an inability to balance budgets in the nation's capital are fomenting a great deal of uncertainty concerning America's future economic and financial prospects.

Indeed, the United States, having for decades made many momentous contributions to international stability and prosperity, is at a crossroads in its history—and the global system may also be at an inflection point. The changes that will occur both domestically and internationally over the next two generations will be far more rapid and transformational than at any other time in human history. Bill Gates once declared that the key word describing the first decade of the twenty-first century would be "velocity."[22] However, the velocity of the decade just recorded in the history books will seem glacial in comparison to what is on the horizon. Globalization, when combined with unprecedented technology change and the process known as "creative destruction," will provoke many to exclaim: "Stop the roller coaster, I want to get off."[23] Rank-and-file Americans and residents around the world must buckle up for the greatest roller coaster ride in history. At the end of this stomach-churning ride, where will the United States rank, what will be its influence around the globe, and how will the average American view his or her quality of life?

Is America Doomed to Mediocrity?

Decline can occur much more rapidly than most people could ever imagine. In 1914, John Maynard Keynes dismissed the United States as a financial rival to Great Britain because the British pound was the world's dominant currency for international trade and central bank reserves, and no one used the U.S. dollar abroad.[24] But within a few short years, the U.S. would emerge as the dominant financial power and soon displace the United Kingdom as the world's superpower. Could the same scenario be playing out today in terms of the evolving global role of the United States and China?

The remainder of this book will zero in on the immense challenges facing the United States and underline that "business as usual" and wishful thinking will inevitably result in the end of America's status as a superpower. This book is not steeped in ideology—other than an overarching perspective that the problems facing the United States today are of monumental gravity and must be confronted head-on and then solved.

Republicans and Democrats have been equally responsible for America's downward thrust. In 2003, Republicans controlled the White House and both chambers of Congress and proceeded to make a mess of the country's domestic and international priorities. Democrats held most of the levers of power through various periods since World War II, and their performance has generally been tepid at best. In 2009, President Barack Obama moved into the White House and the Democrats expanded their control of both chambers of Congress. President Obama has recognized that major changes are imperative in order to revitalize the American nation-state, but congressional meanderings and powerful and deeply entrenched special interests have managed to water down many of his initiatives.

There are too many professional politicians and lobbyists within Washington's Beltway and too few statesmen and stateswomen willing to cast aside strident partisanship and self-interest in order to work for the good of the country as a whole. Wall Street and corporate boardrooms in general also deserve their share of blame, as do the other levels of government in the vast U.S. federal system. Furthermore, one must always remember the immortal words of Walt Kelly of *Pogo* comic strip fame, "We have met the enemy and he is us."[25] Within the confines of their own homes, American adults have consistently looked the other way and done little to ensure that the myriad deep-seated structural problems facing the United States would be solved. Never was this so clearly illustrated as in June 2008 when a record low 13 percent of adults surveyed approved of the job members of Congress were doing, and then less than five months later, reelected 94 percent of the incumbents in the House of Representatives and 86 percent in the Senate who had collectively been perceived as doing such a dismal job only a few months earlier.[26] As one bumper sticker says, "There is too much apathy in this country, but who cares?"

Chapter 2 will focus on governance within the famous Beltway and roundly condemn America's broken political system. Chapters 3 and 4 will pinpoint the dozen major domestic fault lines eroding America's economic and political foundations. Chapter 5 will illustrate why U.S. foreign policy has been misguided and must undergo a major transformation. Chapter 6 will examine the countries and groups of countries becoming noteworthy rivals to America's international leadership. Chapter 7 will look at the potent combination of globalization, unprecedented technology change, and creative destruction countering the efforts of any one nation-state to exert a dominant influence in international relations. Chapter 8 highlights the many positive features in American society and contemplates whether America's decline may be reversible, and, if so, what pragmatic but painful solutions must be implemented in order to reposition the ship of state. Finally, Chapter 9 asks the ultimate question: What will be the status of the United States at mid-century, and what are the odds that the twenty-first century will be known by future historians as the "American century," the "Chinese century," the "Asian century," or perhaps, simply, the "globalization century"?

Chapter 2

Beltway Follies

Introduction

The preamble of the U.S. Constitution solemnly declares:

> We the People of the United States, in order to form a more perfect union, establish justice, insure domestic tranquility, provide for the common defense, promote the general welfare, and secure the blessings of liberty to ourselves and our posterity, do ordain and establish this Constitution for the United States of America.

Forty signatures are affixed at the end of the document, including such heavyweights as George Washington, Benjamin Franklin, James Madison, and Alexander Hamilton.

The current capital of the United States was founded in 1790, with the exact area determined by President Washington. He decided to place the capital across the Potomac River from his beloved Mount Vernon in Virginia. Congress held its first session in Washington, D.C., in November 1800. Fast forwarding 210 years, cynics might refer to modern Washington, D.C., as 177 square kilometers (sixty-eight square miles) of insanity surrounded by reality. They might also question whether the government has lived up to the constitutional pledge to "promote the general welfare, and secure the blessings of liberty to ourselves and our posterity."

The district itself is beautiful in many areas, and the mall lined by all of its splendid museums is one of the finest tourist attractions in the world. For the American people, however, those institutions situated at opposite ends of Pennsylvania Avenue, Congress and the White House, have in recent decades been a bitter disappointment and the source of many of the problems now weighing down a once-mighty nation. In the Book of Matthew in the New Testament, a passage reads: "Wherefore by their fruits ye shall know them."

Some of the fruits of the federal government's labors over the past generation are bitter, indeed, and include the following: (1) the largest government
debt in human history and a miserable record of balancing the federal budget
only five times since 1961; (2) the largest external debt in human history and
a complete turnaround from being the world's largest creditor nation in the
early 1980s to being the world's largest debtor country today; (3) the only
health-care system in the Western world that does not offer universal coverage to its citizens but still spends twice as much per capita on health care as
most other major developed countries; (4) an almost incomprehensible tax
code that is tens of thousands of pages in length, costs Americans tens of
billions of dollars annually in tax preparation expenses alone, and is acting
to transform America from "a democracy of political equals into an aristocracy of wealth";[1] and (5) an overall record of making laws that often favor
the powerful special interests over the general welfare of the country and the
average man and woman living near Main Street USA.

Congress

Many of the members of Congress are generally good people. Nevertheless, as a group they epitomize mediocrity. Far too many are politicians
pure and simple, with only a handful of statesmen and stateswomen dedicated to solving the long-term problems facing the nation. Some have come
for personal enrichment of themselves and their families. For them, public
service is viewed as a route to material riches. Over 40 percent of the members, after leaving office, stay within the Beltway and generally command
high six- or even seven-figure salaries as lobbyists.[2] Tom Daschle had a
distinguished career as a senator, rising to the rank of Majority Leader. In
2004, he was defeated in his reelection bid. Instead of moving back to his
home state of South Dakota, he stayed within the Beltway and began to pull
down "consulting" and "speaking" fees adding up to $2 million per year. He
also received a free limousine and driver for which he failed to pay income
taxes, an oversight that cost him the post of Secretary of the Department of
Health and Human Services in the new Obama administration.[3] Although he
earned more money than most, Daschle exemplifies what often happens to
retired members of the House of Representatives and the Senate.

Congress is also the country club of almost all the legislatures in the
world. The Capitol building itself is a beautiful structure with many remind-
ers of America's glorious past. The 435 voting members of the House representing the fifty states have three cavernous buildings to the west of the

Capitol for their personal offices, and the hundred senators have three mammoth buildings to the east. An underground train system has been installed for the members to travel to and from their respective legislative chambers in tranquility. Members currently make over $170,000 per year and have one of the most generous pension and health-insurance plans in the nation. There are also doctors and nurses on call whenever Congress is in session, and the members have their own gymnasiums, restaurants, and television and radio studios. They enjoy generous franking privileges that permit them to send out letters and fliers to people back in their home districts or states. At times when they travel abroad on congressional business, they may insist on using executive branch or military planes. When they arrive abroad, staff at the local U.S. embassy will be available to respond to their needs. Members are also allocated staff for their personal offices on Capitol Hill and back in their home districts and additional staff for each committee or subcommittee assignment. Total staffing for members of Congress in 2001 exceeded twelve thousand.[4] The Congressional Research Service affiliated with the Library of Congress is also available to conduct research on any topic of interest to a representative or senator. In contrast, some British MPs do not have offices in Parliament, and they receive only £100,000 (about $160,000) a year to hire staff and rent office space.[5]

The Congressional Research Service has provided a profile of the members elected in November 2008 who would comprise the 111th Congress that began to meet in January 2009. The House has 541 members, because the District of Columbia, Puerto Rico, Guam, the U.S. Virgin Islands, American Samoa, and the Northern Mariana Islands each dispatch one non-voting member to that chamber. A member of the House must be at least twenty-five years old, and the average age of a representative in 2009 was fifty-seven. A senator must be at least thirty years old, and the average age for the 111th Congress was sixty-three. A record number of women (seventy-eight in the House and seventeen in the Senate) and Hispanics (twenty-eight in the House and three in the Senate) were selected by the voters in 2008, but both chambers are still dominated by older white males. The average length of service for a House member was eleven years and for a Senate member thirteen years.[6] During the average time of service for a representative, the U.S. government's debt increased by over $5 trillion through the end of 2009, and $5.5 trillion for a senator. Once again, many members in both chambers are good people, but few have manifested the necessary profiles in courage and tenacity required to solve America's deep and festering problems.

Congress, abetted at times by the White House, is responsible for America's massive federal debt that stood at just shy of $12 trillion and growing at the end of fiscal year 2009. In the Budget Enforcement Act of 1990, Congress required "pay-as-you-go," meaning that any deficit due to the creation of new programs or the expansion of existing ones had to be offset by corresponding reductions in spending elsewhere or paid by new revenues. In the early 1990s, Congress also placed a cap on its own spending.[7] In 2000, the Congressional Budget Office (CBO) predicted that the U.S. government would enjoy an official budget surplus of $5.6 trillion over the subsequent decade. With such good intentions and such rosy outlooks on the future, what went so wrong? Why is the country now mired in its most profound period of government indebtedness in history?[8]

Part of the answer lies in the fact that the United States has been fighting a war in the Middle East for several years and has increased its annual defense budget to over a half trillion dollars. During this period of war, however, there were record tax cuts while George W. Bush was president, cuts mostly benefiting the richest segment of American society. Earmarks that generally provide pork benefits to special constituents also quadrupled between 1992 and 2006, costing up to $29 billion in fiscal year 2006 alone, including the infamous bridge to nowhere in Alaska, which received an appropriation of $230 million.[9] Moreover, the tabulation of earmarks usually excludes defense-related boondoggles such as the much-maligned Air Force F-22 stealth fighter, the Marine Corps' tilt-wing V-22 Osprey, the Navy's DDG-1000 stealth destroyer, or the Virginia-class attack submarine.[10]

There is nothing inherently evil in lobbying. Indeed, the Constitution guarantees the people the right to petition and make their opinions known to their representatives in government. However, lobbying as it is currently played out in Washington, D.C., is a plague on American society and a substantial reason why the United States is in decline. The title of Robert G. Kaiser's 2009 book sums up the problem succinctly: *So Damn Much Money: The Triumph of Lobbying and the Corrosion of American Government*.[11] In the book, Kaiser traces the lobbying career of Gerald Cassidy over a period spanning almost four decades. When Cassidy retired, he had accumulated a personal fortune of more than $100 million. Kaiser's conclusion is that Washington has become "a venue for the great American pastime, which is not baseball, but making money."[12]

Far too many members of Congress have succumbed to campaign donations and other emoluments handed out by the largest lobbying corps in any country in the world, and this K Street–Capitol Hill axis is badly distorting the policy process and hindering the nation's recovery from the worst economic downturn in almost eighty years. Lobbying definitely works and proof is found in the statistics. Since the year 2000, the number of lobbyists in the Washington area has doubled to thirty thousand, and the salaries of lobbyists have increased dramatically—showing this has been a true growth industry bringing tangible results for the lobbyists' clients.[13] Expenditures by lobbyists, excluding campaign contributions, increased from $1.44 billion in 1998 to $3.27 billion a decade later.[14] When one adds public relations consultants, Internet advisers, advertising managers, policy experts, denizens of think tanks, and all supporting staff, the number of people engaged within the Beltway to influence the government may be as high as 261,000.[15] In general, these people are there "to capture public policy for private purposes."[16]

Ralph Reed, former executive director of the Christian Coalition, has commented that "in public policy, it matters less who has the best arguments and more who gets heard—and by whom."[17] He should have added, based on his own personal experience working with Jack Abramoff and some Indian tribes, that the lobbyist who gets heard is often carrying a suitcase full of campaign contributions with him.[18] Jim Hightower has suggested, only somewhat facetiously, that candidates for Congress should begin to wear patches, like NASCAR drivers, to identify their "sponsors."[19] What is even more distressing is that the government trough from which the lobbyists are feeding is now the largest ever in nominal dollars and 26 percent of GDP—the largest in U.S. history other than World War II.

Norman Ornstein, a long-time observer of Congress, has started to refer to the District of Columbia as the "District of Corruption," and points to the corrosive link between lobbying and government as the core of the problem.[20] Other long-time observers or practitioners use terms such as "culture of deception."[21] Ornstein points out that in 1969 a member of Congress made $42,500 versus over $170,000 today, about a four-fold increase. In 1969, a first-year associate in a top Beltway law firm made about $10,000 compared with $160,000 today, exclusive of bonuses. A senior partner in the same law firm now makes about ten times more annually than a member of Congress. In 1969, a new lobbyist with previous experience on Capitol Hill made little more than $10,000 compared with $250,000–300,000 today. In contrast, a congressional staffer today makes on average about $50,000.[22]

Ornstein concludes with dismay that "the corrupting influence of all that money is palpable," that there is "systemic corruption" in Congress, and too many young people are entering public service "in order to get rich."[23] Washington, D.C., and its immediate suburbs in Virginia and Maryland, an area dominated by government services, have recently emerged as one of the richest metropolises in the United States, a phenomenon hard to swallow in a nation that prides itself on entrepreneurialism, overwhelming reliance on private-sector initiatives, and *laissez-faire* economics.[24]

Convicted felon and former lobbyist Jack Abramoff has referred to Congress as the "favor factory," and others have used terms such as "pay to play" to describe the ties between the K-Street lobbyists and individual members of Congress.[25] Too many elected officials on Capitol Hill have been engaged in enriching themselves, their family members, or their staff through special linkages, or the revolving door with the lobbying community. Perhaps the most egregious example in recent years was Tom DeLay's K-Street project in which he instructed lobbyists and law firms to hire Republicans, many with prior experience on Capitol Hill, if they hoped to have any access to congressional leadership. This project was also designed "to create a loop in which former lawmakers and staffers would be placed in lucrative lobbying posts that paid two to ten times what they earned on Capitol Hill."[26]

Democrats have been equally guilty as indicated by the recent PMA Group earmark scandal involving House members Peter Visclosky from Indiana and the late John Murtha from Pennsylvania.[27] Robert Reich concludes that "the fundamental problem does not, for the most part, involve blatant bribes and kickbacks. Rather, it is the intrusion of supercapitalism into every facet of democracy—the dominance of corporate lobbyists, lawyers, and public relations professions over the entire political process; the corporate money that engulfs the system on a day-to-day basis, making it almost impossible for citizen voices to be heard."[28] The lobbying game has become such a way of life in conducting business within the Beltway that nearly one hundred foreign countries have moved away from traditional diplomacy and hired their own lobbyists in order to protect and promote their interests.[29] In 2008, these foreign governments spent $87 million for Beltway lobbyists in an effort to gain special access to officials on Capitol Hill and in the executive branch.[30]

Part of the big money influence on Capitol Hill is linked to perpetual campaigning. Members of the House serve for two years and, once they are reelected, they immediately return to raising money for their next campaign.[31] Senators have more leeway because of their six-year terms, but they all want to amass huge campaign war chests, in part to deter formidable challengers from opposing them. Frankly, unless a member messes up badly or is involved in a scandal, reelection is almost assured with incumbent retention rates easily surpassing 90 percent each election cycle and often as high as 98 percent. Joe Klein is correct when he asserts that incumbents and their staff generally assume that "the public is stupid and uncaring" when it comes to politics.[32] Nevertheless, there are enough anomalies, such as Majority Leader Tom Daschle not being reelected in South Dakota, that incumbents are prompted to raise money like there is no tomorrow. And as far as campaign costs go, no other nation comes close to the profligacy found in U.S. elections that involve hordes of campaign and media advisers, advertising agencies, event organizers, pollsters, canvassers, and a host of other functionaries. During the most expensive election cycle ever experienced on earth, House candidates spent $938 million in 2007 and 2008, Senate candidates $429 million, and presidential candidates $1.76 billion.[33] Senator Mark Hanna stated a century ago that "there are two things that are important in politics. The first is money, and I can't remember what the second one is."[34] Sifry and Watzman sum up well how money and campaigns combine to influence almost all aspects of American life:

> You may not think about it much as you go through your day, but our campaign finance system, in which special interest cash governs who runs for office, how they conduct their campaigns, and what they do (and don't do) once elected, touches on nearly every aspect of our lives. The air we breathe, the food we eat, the health care we receive (or don't receive), all of these are affected, and for the worse, by the influence of money in politics.[35]

Hacker and Pierson also observe that "over the past thirty years, American politics has become more money-centered at exactly the same time that American society has grown more unequal."[36]

In recent decades, members of Congress have created new ways to raise money and use the money for almost anything they want. Once upon a time, the members could actually pocket whatever was left in their campaign chests when they retired. Congress did pass a law in 1980 prohibiting members who took office after 8 January of that year from pocketing leftover campaign funds. They would eventually tighten the restrictions even further. Nevertheless, Representative Ed Jones, a Democrat from Tennessee, decided to take home the $140,000 in his campaign fund when he retired, explaining, "It's not the government's money, it's the candidate's friends' money."[37] Presently, most prominent members create Leadership PACs that can be spent as they wish. Often the money is ladled out to fellow members in their reelection bids, helping to build up IOUs in case the money dispenser wants to seek higher office in the future. On the other hand, John Edwards used his Leadership PAC to provide his mistress with over $100,000 in cash.[38] Fred Wertheimer, president of Democracy 21, an organization that tracks campaign donations, asserts that Leadership PACs are "a form of giant slush fund; they should be banned."[39] Instead of being banned, these types of PACs are proliferating and are being established by the newest members of Congress. They are being used to finance vacations and golfing trips, provide stipends to friends and family members, pay for clothing, pay for friends' funerals, and they are also being used after members retire from Congress.[40] As many Americans toil through the worst economic conditions in their lifetimes, members of Congress are still enjoying enviable perks, thanks in part to the proceeds from their Leadership PACs.

There is much truth in the adage: "The president proposes, Congress disposes." The problem is that Congress rarely comes up with viable alternatives to what the president may have proposed. The congressional policy-making process is disjointed and rarely very efficient. Members have long recesses, and when they are in session, they often meet from Tuesday afternoon until Thursday afternoon. Proposed bills must make their way through a labyrinth of committees and subcommittees and only a few emerge for a final vote in each chamber. If a bill is passed in each chamber, it must then proceed to a conference committee composed of selected members from the House and Senate. These conference committees can authorize significant changes to what their members originally voted for in each chamber. If a reconciled bill finally emerges, it will then be voted on one more time in each chamber. For a bill to become law, it must have the same exact wording in the House and Senate versions and then go to the White House. The president then has four options: sign the proposed legislation within ten days, veto it, allow it to become law without his signature, or "pocket" veto the bill, meaning not signing it after Congress has adjourned. A regular veto will require at least a two-thirds vote in each chamber to override the president's disapproval. A pocket veto cannot be overturned, meaning that Congress must restart the process when it comes back into session.

Although the House of Representatives has over four times more members than the Senate, it can generally pass important legislation without undue delay if the party in charge has a healthy majority and remains relatively disciplined. The Senate is a different matter altogether. The hundred senators are often referred to as free agents, or, in more derogatory terms, as prima donnas. Many want to be president, and in 2008, four of the leading contenders for the Republican and Democratic nominations for president were senators or former senators.[41] Barack Obama, a senator from Illinois, defeated John McCain, a senator from Arizona, on 4 November.

The Senate "Bermuda Triangle" is made even worse by archaic rules or customs that permit a few members, or a single member acting alone, to obstruct or block altogether proposed legislation or nominees for executive branch or judicial posts. For example, following the tragic shooting by a deranged student at Virginia Tech University in April 2007 that killed thirty-two young people, Carolyn McCarthy, whose husband had been killed by a crazed shooter on a New York commuter train, proposed a bill that would help to prevent such horrific episodes in the future.[42] The bill provided grants to state governments permitting them to put more information on the National Instant Criminal Background Check System targeting individuals with criminal backgrounds and those identified by courts as posing a potential danger because of mental illness. Both the National Rifle Association and its major ideological adversary, the Brady Campaign to Prevent Gun Violence, supported the measure. McCarthy's bill sailed through the House and was passed unanimously in June 2007. It was then sent to the Senate and leadership in that chamber asked for unanimous consent to pass the bill quickly. One senator, Tom Coburn of Oklahoma, objected and his "hold" on the legislation effectively delayed its passage for several months.[43] The hold, which is not mentioned at all in any Senate rules, is a custom permitting a single member to delay the consideration of bills or nominations for posts by denying unanimous consent. These holds may also be requested anonymously. For months, legislation to reform the awarding of government contracts was stymied in the Senate by one anonymous hold, and then later, by another anonymous hold. Good detective work by bloggers eventually determined that the secret holds were placed by Senator Robert Byrd of West Virginia and Senator Ted Stevens of Alaska.[44]

One senator or a small group of senators may also engage in filibustering, which may result in bringing a halt to all Senate business. The only way to break a filibuster is to invoke cloture, and that requires a super-majority vote of at least sixty senators. Various other delaying tactics may also be employed by a few senators and often sixty votes are needed to stymie these tactics. The Democrats have recently attained sixty seats in the Senate, but their own disunity has made it difficult to muster cloture votes on some of the most important reforms being considered by the chamber, including health-care reform. Strong ideological leanings, bitter partisanship, allegiance to special interests or major campaign contributors, and plain old incivility have all combined to complicate efforts to pass meaningful legislation even though America is now facing some of its most ominous challenges in history.[45] Linus van Pelt, one of Charles Schulz's endearing characters in his *Peanuts* comic strip, sums up Congress in the midst of national turmoil: "No problem is so big or so complicated that it can't be run away from."[46]

The tremendous influence that powerful interest groups wield over members of Congress, in contrast to the modest influence of the American public, is illustrated by the U.S. tax code and recent congressional tax legislation. The last major overhaul of the U.S. tax code occurred in 1986 during the Reagan administration. Since that time, Congress has authorized almost fifteen thousand amendments in what is now a 1.4 million-word document.[47] The number of pages in the *CCH Standard Federal Tax Reporter*, which records tax laws, regulations, and related material, has gone from 16,300 pages in 1984 to over seventy thousand pages in 2009.[48] Revisions and amendments to the tax code have often resulted in loopholes or exceptions benefiting special interests, such as foreign tax credits for the pharmaceutical industry or drilling write-offs for the oil industry. These special tax perks or exemptions are at least ten times more damaging to Washington's fiscal outlook than the spiraling costs of earmarks, and almost all are unjustified. Meanwhile, Americans in general may be spending in time and money on tax compliance up to $90 billion per year.[49] Tom Herman, a *Wall Street Journal* reporter who has focused on the tax system for sixteen years, offers this grim assessment, "Our tax system has evolved from a mess to a nightmare."[50]

As an illustration of the tax system's blatant unfairness, Congress has permitted hedge fund managers for several years to pay taxes on their commissions and fees at a 15 percent capital gains rate instead of the highest 35 percent marginal tax rate. Several enfeebled attempts have been made to revoke this special provision, but a combination of many Republican and Democratic senators, such as Charles Schumer of New York, John Kerry of Massachusetts, and Maria Cantwell of Washington, have entered an alliance to thwart any revisions. When the latest attempt to end this favoritism was made in 2007, the hedge fund industry increased its spending on lobbying from $1.7 million to $14.3 million. The private equity industry, which was also under scrutiny for special tax treatment, upped its lobbying spending from \$5.6 million in the 2005–2006 election cycle to \$31.6 million in the 2007–2008 cycle.[51] The failure to ensure tax fairness in this case has been very costly to the U.S. Treasury, because the top fifty hedge and private equity fund managers made a combined \$29 billion in 2008, yet they paid taxes at a rate below many of their own receptionists, chauffeurs, and private jet pilots.[52] This privileged treatment to powerful individuals indicates that the tax system is rigged, especially when one takes into account that the top 1 percent of earners in America takes home in income almost twice as much as the bottom 50 percent combined, yet some are still permitted to pay taxes at rates far below the top marginal category.[53]

U.S. government budgets for many years have been far larger than revenues taken in via tax payments, yet Congress engaged in the greatest corporate tax giveaway ever in a plan enacted in 2004 and signed by President Bush. At the time, United States-based multinational enterprises had parked \$300 billion in profits offshore, in part to avoid paying U.S. corporate taxes at the prescribed 35 percent rate. Congress decided to give them a "tax holiday" and bring home the money at a "one time only" rate of 5.25 percent. In return, the companies were to invest in business expansion and job creation in the United States. The money came home and taxes were paid at the very low rate, but studies now indicate that hardly any money was spent on business expansion or job creation.[54] In addition, because the corporations were aware well in advance of the tax holiday, they transferred offshore \$100 billion of profits made in the United States and then brought that money back home at the much lower tax rate, a tactic referred to as "round-tripping."[55] In total, U.S. tax revenues were \$90 billion below what they would have been if the corporations had paid at the standard 35 percent rate.

Closer to home for most Americans, Congress has also authorized homeowners to deduct interest costs on their housing mortgages, but more than half of the subsidy goes to the top 12 percent of households, and 70 percent of tax filers and about 50 percent of homeowners do not receive any benefit at all.[56] Proponents of the mortgage subsidy claim that it promotes home ownership, but the U.S. ownership rate is at or below the rates in Canada, Australia, and Great Britain, all of which deny any tax deductibility.[57] In addition, the tax subsidy actually does more to stimulate the building of larger and more expensive homes rather than first-time home ownership.[58] Tax subsidies are offered for mortgages up to a million dollars for second homes, and, frankly, for any other costly purchase having nothing to do with home ownership except it has been paid for through home-equity loans that carry a tax deductibility on loans up to $100,000.[59] Total tax breaks for home owner-ship cost the U.S. Treasury over $100 billion per year, and tax deductibility for employer-provided health insurance another $125 billion annually.[60]

Congress also provides tax relief for those who save via IRAs, 401(k)s, and other retirement accounts, but in 2003 more than 50 percent of the tax benefits for defined-contribution plans went to the top one-tenth of house-holds and 70 percent to the top one-fifth. Sixty percent of the IRA tax benefits also accrued to the top fifth of households.[61] As for the bottom two-fifths, they accounted for only 3 percent of the tax savings provided to IRA account holders.[62]

The list of preferential tax treatment and subsidies accorded by Con-gress to special groups goes on and on. Tens of billions of dollars are spent annually helping the largest agribusinesses in the country at a time when barely 2 percent of the national population even lives on a farm.[63] A vari-ant of the agricultural subsidy is the ethanol fiasco, which has proven to be environmentally damaging and economically unsustainable but still permits agribusinesses to rake in billions of dollars in subsidies every year while banning cheaper ethanol imports from Brazil.

The defense industry may be the biggest boondoggle of all, with two-thirds of the largest weapons systems running over budget in 2008 to the tune of $296 billion, yet these overruns are still meekly paid by the U.S. Treasury.[64] John Lehman, former Secretary of the Navy, labels military con-tracting as "a total mess" in a system "where no one is in charge and no one is held accountable." He adds, "I don't think in the history of the country it's been as bad as it is today."[65] In July 2009, the Obama administration attempted to kill further production of the outmoded F-22 aircraft, a plane that has never flown in combat and that the Pentagon does not want pro-duced in the future. Nevertheless, a bipartisan group in Congress restored the production of another seven planes at a cost of $1.7 billion, claiming it was needed to preserve local jobs. In his rebuttal, which initially fell on deaf ears on Capitol Hill, President Obama insisted that "to continue to procure additional F-22s would be to waste valuable resources that should be more usefully employed to provide our troops with weapons that they actually do need."[66] Eventually, Congress was shamed into rescinding its authorization to produce more of this unnecessary aircraft.

The medical sector is another glaring example of where the special interest usually prevails over the general interest.[67] Almost everyone was in agreement that Medicare should provide some of the funding for older people to purchase prescription drugs. Unfortunately, the Medicare Part D program, which went into effect in 2006, has been a financial disaster. The chief culprit consists of weak members of Congress who were convinced by the pharmaceutical industry to prohibit Medicare administrators from pooling the buying power of forty million older patients in order to negotiate lower prices for prescriptions. As a result, taxpayers have been paying at times over three times more for some pharmaceuticals than their market value, according to a study in the journal *Health Affairs*.[68] President Obama has faced similar opposition as he has attempted to put together a workable health-care plan to cover all American citizens. In this case, the president faces the opposition of some of the most formidable entrenched interests in Washington, D.C., namely the pharmaceutical and insurance industries, hospital associations, the American Medical Association, and trial lawyers.

Capitol Hill's consistent efforts to tarnish both the democratic process and market-based economics, in favor of special interests or the well-to-do, are eroding the domestic political and economic foundations upon which the American superpower was constructed. To continue to do so during a time of almost unprecedented economic and fiscal duress borders on insanity.

The White House and Executive Branch
The White House must also share much of the blame for the generally abysmal performance of government over the past two generations. The first trillion dollars of accumulated government debt was reached during the second year of the Reagan presidency. By the time he left office after serving two terms, the debt had almost tripled. Another trillion dollars was added during the one-term presidency of the first President Bush, another trillion during the eight years of the Clinton administration, and then the debt plunged to bottom-of-the-ocean levels by doubling during the eight years of George W. Bush's presidency. During the first term of that administration, Vice President Dick Cheney publicly informed the Secretary of Treasury that "deficits don't matter."[69]

The executive branch has also had its version of earmarks with a sharp acceleration in private contracting for services once provided by government workers. Such a trend is not necessarily bad, except half of these contracts have been awarded without full open and competitive bidding, and some winners tend to have close connections to or ideological affinities with top executive branch officials.[70] In total, 3.7 million private contracts were issued by the federal government in 2008, up 76 percent since 2000, and at a cost of $368 billion.[71] In his study of the federal government, Paul C. Light concludes that the true size of government has shown "continued growth," with 14.6 million total "employees" at the end of fiscal year 2005, including 1.9 million civil servants, 770,000 postal workers, 1.44 million military personnel, 7.6 million contractors, and 2.9 million federal grantees.[72]

Never has the dysfunctional nature of private contracting been as apparent as in Iraq in the period immediately after President Bush, dressed in his pilot's uniform, landed on the aircraft carrier USS Abraham Lincoln anchored off the coast of southern California. With a huge "Mission Accomplished" poster in the background, the president declared the major phase of fighting was over in Iraq, and the U.S. had been victorious. In the ensuing weeks, thousands of private contractors and government personnel streamed into Baghdad, many of whom had been interviewed by administration appointees in Washington to ascertain if they were "qualified" to participate in the post-war phase of reconstruction. In making hiring decisions, the first questions often asked were not about one's previous experience in Iraq, one's contribution to reconstruction projects in other developing countries, or one's ability to speak Arabic. Instead, the litmus-test questions, according to Rajiv Chandrasekaran of the *Washington Post*, were: who did you vote for in the 2000 presidential election, are you a Republican, and, occasionally, do you favor or oppose the 1973 *Roe v. Wade* Supreme Court decision supporting a woman's right to seek an abortion?[73]

Many Americans remember ruefully the words George W. Bush spoke in 2005 to his Federal Emergency Management Agency (FEMA) director, Michael D. Brown: "Brownie, you're doing a heck of a job!" In reality, the Bush administration messed up badly in its reaction to the Katrina catastrophe in New Orleans. Along with the Federal Reserve Board, the executive branch also tragically mishandled the meltdown on Wall Street. Government regulators were not to be found, and some of the directors of the Federal Reserve Bank of New York were figuratively in bed with the financial executives they were supposed to be supervising, with one actually holding a seat on the board of a financial institution while at the same time serving as chairman of the New York Fed.[74] This failure to regulate Wall Street has already placed American taxpayers on the hook for potentially $13 trillion in bailouts and government guarantees—a financial catastrophe without precedent in U.S. history.

Even after the meltdown on Wall Street was under way, the executive branch seemed to be more interested in helping its friends and contributors from the financial sector than protecting the interests of the American people. For example, why did the U.S. Treasury under Henry Paulson, former chairman of Goldman Sachs, give permission to the bailed-out AIG to reimburse financial institutions such as Goldman Sachs for 100 percent of their losses after AIG reneged on its insurance contracts covering losses in derivatives trading?[75] AIG had been a private company when the problems transpired, and the U.S. government bore no responsibility for AIG's actions. Nevertheless, Washington stepped in and approved full reimbursement instead of negotiating terms that might have covered 50 percent or so of AIG's commitments. The total transfer of money from the taxpayers to Wall Street in this one transaction alone was $50 billion.[76]

Placing Government Decision-Making in Proper Perspective

The framers of the U.S. Constitution were very wary of concentrating too much government authority in the hands of too few people. As a result, they established a system of government that is cumbersome and prone to gridlock. First of all, they did not accord all the authority to the national government. Instead, they created the world's first formal federal system that divided authority between the national government and the state governments. Secondly, they divided national government authority between three branches—executive, legislative, and judicial. Thirdly, they provided each branch with checks and balances over the other two branches. The U.S. Supreme Court is a very powerful judicial institution, but the executive branch nominates the members of the court, and the Senate must approve these nominations. Congress also establishes the number of justices on the Supreme Court and how much they will earn. Through the judicial review process, which is not authorized anywhere in the Constitution but has now been accepted as legal, the federal courts may render an act of Congress or the executive branch as "unconstitutional" and therefore null and void. The president may submit his own legislative proposals to Congress and may veto legislation passed by Congress. In turn, Congress may overturn the veto by a two-thirds vote in both chambers. The president may send American soldiers into battle, but only Congress may declare war, determine how many soldiers will serve, and set how large the military budget will be. Congress also has the right to impeach (bring formal charges against) members of the executive or judicial branches and to convict them on charges of high crimes or misdemeanors. Two U.S. presidents, Andrew Johnson and Bill Clinton, have been formally impeached but neither was convicted.

The U.S. president is often referred to as the most powerful person on earth, but within the context of national policy-making, he or she is much more constrained than executive leaders in many other democratic countries. In traditional parliamentary systems such as the United Kingdom, the prime minister may make policy quickly and decisively, as long as his or her party controls a majority of seats in the House of Commons. In contrast, the American president has to rely on Congress to pass laws and the federal courts to accept his or her actions as being constitutional. Barack Obama is a Democrat and the two chambers of Congress were dominated by Democrats as he assumed the presidency, but this has not translated into him being able to enact his agenda in the same manner as a British prime minister backed by a majority government. Jimmy Carter had the same advantages when he became president and early on declared energy independence to be the moral equivalent of war. Unfortunately, the energy package he sent to Congress was torn apart once it arrived on Capitol Hill, even though Democrats were firmly in charge of both the House and the Senate.

The framers of the Constitution were also suspicious of citizens having too much direct influence over what transpires within the national government. Even to this day, Americans do not vote directly for the president or vice president. Rather, they vote for electors who will cast their ballots about a month after the presidential election has taken place. Presidents were also allowed to seek reelection indefinitely, and Franklin D. Roosevelt won four terms in office. It was only after his death that the Twenty-Second Amendment was enacted in 1947 limiting a president to two terms in office or a maximum of ten years if he or she succeeds a sitting president because of death, incapacity, resignation, or impeachment. For almost 150 years, senators were not elected directly by the people but rather selected by state legislatures. Direct election finally occurred with the ratification of the Seventeenth Amendment in 1913.

Citizens have very little immediate recourse if they believe that a president or Congress has gone badly off course. In most parliamentary systems, a vote of no confidence or a defeat of a governing party on a major piece of legislation will usually provoke a new election within a couple of months. In contrast, American voters must wait four years to elect a new president and two years to vote for all the members of the House of Representatives and one-third of the senators. From time to time, Will Rogers would express frustration with this system: "On account of being a democracy and run by the people, we are the only nation in the world that has to keep government four years, no matter what it does." He added wistfully that "there ought to be one day—just one—when there is open season on senators."[77]

Nor do citizens have the right to organize and demand nation-wide referenda on key issues. The constitutional amendment process is also extremely arduous and almost always begins with Congress instead of the state legislatures or constitutional conventions convened at the state level. There are only twenty-seven amendments in the U.S. Constitution, which went into effect in 1789. The last was ratified in 1992 and simply states that members of Congress are forbidden from increasing their pay until after an election of the members of the House of Representatives has "intervened." Ten amendments were included in the new Constitution as part of the Bill of Rights, and three subsequent amendments were related to the Civil War. Fourteen additional amendments were passed between 1789 and 2010, an average of one every sixteen years. Perhaps this may reflect on the stability of the U.S. political and governmental system, even though during that long period America moved from being a predominantly rural society to an urban society, and its population increased from less than four million to more than 308 million. It may also reflect on the limited ability of the average citizen to effectuate political change other than at the ballot box every two to four years.

In spite of a system that favors gridlock and limits the capacity of the average American to bring about change, it is still possible to transform the Beltway and bring about a new American political renaissance. Specific policy proposals will be presented later in Chapter 8, but the key will be for rank-and-file citizens to become knowledgeable about the problems facing the nation and demand change from their elected representatives. Business as usual will no longer suffice. Franklin D. Roosevelt had his "hundred days" that transformed the American system in the face of the Great Depression and an unemployment rate that had skyrocketed above 25 percent. George W. Bush found Congress to be compliant to many of his domestic and foreign policy initiatives in the wake of 9/11. Tragically, many of Bush's initiatives were misguided, but at least the period indicates that policies can be passed quickly given the right circumstances. The quest will be to bring about significant change within the Beltway, which will reenergize the American system of governance and reawaken and revitalize a country that is in the doldrums.

Chapter 3

Domestic Fault Lines: Indebtedness and Inequities

Introduction

Although globalization and challenges from competitor nations are chipping away at the United States' superpower status, the most prominent danger by far is coming from within.[1] The lamentable problems related to the governance of the nation have been highlighted in the previous chapter. This chapter will analyze the first half dozen major problem areas facing America domestically, all of which are weakening its standing in the world, its ability to influence international affairs, and its capability of providing a better standard of living for future generations of Americans.

Government Debt

In nominal dollars, the United States has the world's largest government debt. The federal government's debt accumulated since 1789 did not top $1 trillion until 1981. Ronald Reagan, who became president in 1981, once quipped that "government is like a baby: an alimentary canal with a big appetite at one end and no sense of responsibility at the other."[2] Unfortunately, Washington's debt is climbing at an almost unprecedented pace, and servicing this burgeoning debt as a percentage of Washington's overall budget is expected to quadruple over the next decade.[3] Recently, U.S. public and private sector borrowing abroad has been absorbing a staggering 70 percent of the surplus savings in the rest of the world.[4] Eventually, Washington's insatiable borrowing needs will begin to crowd out investment proposals from the U.S. private sector. This sector, with its innovation, competition, and entrepreneurialism, has the potential to lead America out of its current wilderness, but huge government borrowing demands will stand in the way of progress in the business community.

The U.S. government has balanced annual budgets an anemic five times since 1961, whereas neighboring Canada had eleven consecutive years of budget surpluses up until the 2009 fiscal year. Canadian federal government debt as a percentage of GDP, which two decades ago was much higher than Washington's, has now fallen far below that of the United States. Washington's perennial deficits have often occurred in periods of significant national economic growth, and the country's policymakers are now ill prepared to face the challenges of the recent "Great Recession" of 2007–2009 or the tidal wave of financial obligations that will occur when the seventy-six million baby boomers begin to retire in 2012 and collect full Social Security and Medicare benefits.[5] In its latest report, the Board of Trustees of the Social Security system estimates that Social Security spending will exceed projected tax collections beginning in 2016 and the Social Security trust fund will be totally exhausted by 2037.[6] Medicare projections are even grimmer.

What is most troubling is that there were a series of budget surpluses in the second term of Bill Clinton, prompting the Congressional Budget Office to predict in 2001 that the United States was on course over the first decade of the twenty-first century to eliminate nearly all of its national government debt.[7] Instead, the government's debt doubled during that first decade and may well be heading toward another doubling in the second decade to more than $20 trillion. In nominal terms, government debt also multiplied by more than twelve times in just the three decades ending in 2010 (see Figure III: 1). To understand the magnitude of a "trillion," only a trillion seconds ago the planet was not even at the peak of its most recent Ice Age (a trillion seconds equals 31,688 years).

If corporations were to use the same accounting system employed by the federal government in Washington, D.C., their CEOs would be subject to arrest. The "official" yearly deficits are far below the true deficits, and even the Department of Treasury keeps two sets of ledgers reflecting the discrepancies. In fiscal year 2005, for example, the official deficit trumpeted by government leaders was $318 billion. However, government auditors issued a second set of estimates, based on standard accounting rules and net operating costs, which indicated a deficit of $760 billion. In fiscal year 2006, the official "cash-term" deficit was $248 billion, but the Treasury's accrual-accounting method used by major U.S. corporations pushed that estimate up to $450 billion.[8]

Moreover, the government fails to highlight its future financial liabilities incurred for "entitlement" programs such as Social Security, Medicare,

FIGURE III: 1
U.S. Government Debt

FISCAL YEAR	DEBT
1982	$1.1 trillion
1986	$2.1 trillion
1990	$3.2 trillion
1992	$4.1 trillion
1996	$5.2 trillion
2001	$6.2 trillion
2004	$7.4 trillion
2006	$8.5 trillion
2007	$9.0 trillion
2008	$10.1 trillion
2009	$11.9 trillion

Medicaid, and military and federal employee pension and health plans. David M. Walker, then-comptroller general of the United States and director of the U.S. Government Accountability Office (GAO), estimated that explicit liabilities of the federal government increased by 52 percent from 2000 through 2006, and implicit exposures in Social Security and Medicare were up 197 percent during the same period. Walker contends that the total fiscal exposure of the U.S. government, calculated using Generally Accepted Accounting Practices (GAAP basis), was $50.5 trillion at the end of fiscal year 2006.[9] Total household net worth that year was $53.5 trillion, so the ratio of fiscal exposure to net worth was 95 percent.[10]

The U.S. Treasury Department finances Washington's public debt by selling Treasury bonds, bills, and notes. As will be examined in the next section, the United States is becoming more dependent than ever before on foreigners to buy this debt, with overseas purchasers accounting for half of recent purchases, up from 15 percent during the Reagan presidency. With so much more debt to be issued over the next decade, will there be enough domestic and foreign buyers, or will interest rates on the debt increase significantly in order to attract sufficient buyers? If interest rates do go up markedly, this will make the cost of borrowing money within the United States much more expensive and represent another obstacle to desperately needed business expansion.

Figure III: 2 shows the total federal government debt as a percentage of GDP. During World War II this debt approached the 120 percent range.[11] Through most of the post-war period, the debt has been in the 60 percent range but is now headed up to the 80–100 percent range over the next decade.[12] In fiscal year 2009 alone, Washington's deficit exceeded 10 percent of GDP, the highest recorded since the war-impact years of 1942–1946 and about twice as high as any other year in U.S. history except for this one period of war.[13] The deficit in 2009 was greater than the entire federal government budget in fiscal year 1993 and higher than the GDP of every other nation in the world with the exception of Japan, China, Germany, France, the United Kingdom, Italy, Brazil, Russia, and Spain.[14]

In addition, through mid-2009, Washington had committed almost $13 trillion in stimulus and bailout funds and government guarantees to the distressed financial and corporate sectors, a sum almost equal to the nation's annual GDP.[15] Federal government spending is at unprecedented levels for a period of relative peace, shooting up to 26 percent of GDP. Furthermore, Washington faces huge unfunded liabilities in its entitlement obligations such as Social Security, Medicare, and Medicaid, which add up to almost $50 trillion in unfunded mandates under existing programs.[16] Combining its current fiscal mess with its future financial obligations, the federal government's triple A credit rating, which has been constantly in place since 1917, is now at risk. A lower rating would mean that Washington would have to pay higher interest rates in order to borrow money. If business expansion also remains in a lull, growth in the nation's GDP would be tepid at best, and the government debt as a percentage of GDP would increase even beyond current projections. The United States is awash in government debt, and the prospects for a robust economic recovery in the immediate future are not promising. How long can the world's largest government debtor maintain its lofty position as a superpower, especially at a time when the nation's debt clock is ticking faster than ever before?[17]

External Debt and the Dwindling Attraction of the U.S. Dollar

In nominal dollars, the United States has become the world's largest external debtor country, with $3.5 trillion in net liabilities at the end of 2008 (see Figure III: 3).[18] This stands in stark contrast to its position as the world's largest creditor country from the end of World War I until the mid-1980s. The total U.S. deficit in trade in goods and services between 2000 and 2008 exceeded $5 trillion, and this does not include the overseas borrowing by corporations and all levels of government within the United States. The total assets held by foreigners within the U.S. have increased more than tenfold from $2.1 trillion in 1990 to $23.4 trillion at the end of 2008.[19]

FIGURE III: 2
The U.S. Federal Debt (% of GDP)

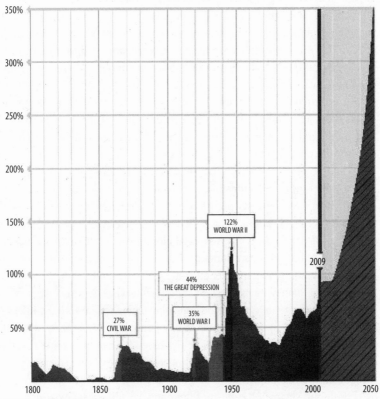

Source: Peter G. Peterson Foundation.

FIGURE III: 3
Net International Investment Position of the United States at Year End, 1983–2008

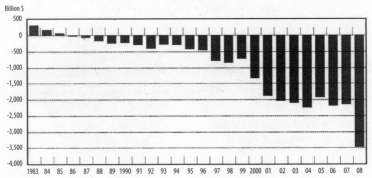

Source: U.S. Bureau of Economic Analysis, *Survey of Current Business*, July 2009.

U.S. governments, corporations, and households have all been living beyond their means, and this has resulted in unprecedented external debt obligations—obligations that will continue to grow for as far as the eye can see. Fortunately, foreign buyers, mostly governments or central banks in Asia, have been willing to step in and buy many of these IOUs, in the process helping to fan the flames of U.S. consumption and simultaneously keeping real interest rates at historically low levels. For example, foreign investors purchased two-thirds of the U.S. Treasury debt in the period 2004–2008, and foreign holdings as a percentage of U.S. government debt held by the public catapulted from just under 30 percent in 2001 to half at the end of April 2009.[20]

This growing dependency on the goodwill of foreigners to buy America's mushrooming debt, illustrated in Figure III: 4, may boomerang on the United States and limit its policy options in the international arena. With $764 billion in U.S. public debt at the end of April 2009, China is the largest holder of American IOUs, followed closely by the $686 billion held by Japan.[21] With interest-rate returns on U.S. securities being so low, and the Chinese currency gradually strengthening vis-à-vis the U.S. dollar, China is already losing money on its Treasury investments when these investments are converted back into its yuan. Some argue that China will absorb the losses so long as the United States continues to buy hundreds of billions of dollars in Chinese imports. However, as will be discussed later in this chapter, American consumers will be cutting back on their purchases, whether domestic or foreign-made. Consequently, China may begin to curtail future purchases of U.S. public-sector IOUs or, more ominously, sell off its existing inventory of Treasury and other U.S. instruments of debt. Such an action would

FIGURE III: 4
Foreign Holdings of U.S. Debt to the Public

Sources: U.S. Department of the Treasury and the Peter G. Peterson Foundation.

undoubtedly lead to higher interest rates within the U.S. in order to finance the government debt, and perhaps provoke a major run on the U.S. dollar.

Chinese officials are already very worried about present U.S. government policy, which will add several trillion dollars in debt over the next decade. In June 2009, Secretary of Treasury Timothy Geithner went hat in hand to Beijing in an effort to convince Chinese authorities to continue investing in U.S. debt instruments. When he went out of his way to assure an audience at Beijing University that Chinese investments in the United States were safe, the audience broke out in laughter.[22] Most foreign observers frankly consider that the U.S. dollar is in a downward spiral because of inappropriate fiscal and monetary policy.[23] The issuance of unprecedented amounts of government or government-guaranteed debt adds to that downward thrust, as does Federal Reserve Board policy to monetize debt through the Fed's purchases of Treasury bonds and paper issued by government-sponsored enterprises such as the Federal Home Loan Mortgage Corporation (Freddie Mac) and the Federal National Mortgage Association (Fannie Mae). As a desperate and frankly cowardly measure, Washington could permit inflation to rise in a long-term effort to pay off current debt obligations with "cheaper" dollars in the future, in the process devaluing all of the dollar-denominated savings and assets of the American people. To illustrate this point, the U.S. per capita income, when measured in euros instead of dollars, was actually down by 25 percent from the beginning of 2000 to the end of 2009.[24]

Since the end of World War II, the U.S. dollar has been the world's major currency, used in most trade transactions and as the foremost reserve currency held by central banks around the globe. Even today, the dollar accounts for almost two-thirds of all central bank reserve currencies. The high esteem held by others around the world is based primarily on America's superpower status and its dominant economic standing. Currently, however, that esteem has eroded significantly, and Chinese, Russian, Indian, and UN leaders have been among those calling for the creation of a new international currency to replace the dollar for trade and central bank purposes. Tragically, Washington has squandered the once-solid reputation of the United States, and, in the future, the federal government and other U.S. entities may have to pay their IOUs in a currency or basket of currencies other than the U.S. dollar.[25] This could greatly magnify the cost of borrowing from abroad and hasten the country's demise as a superpower.

During most of the nineteenth century and early in the twentieth century, the British pound was the dominant international currency. The dollar took over from the pound after World War I and has remained supreme ever since. Nonetheless, its hegemonic status is now at risk and may be challenged in the future by the euro; the yuan, which would first have to become internationally convertible; or a new International Monetary Fund (IMF) unit whose value would be linked to a basket of major currencies such as the euro, dollar, pound, Japanese yen, the yuan, and Swiss franc. It is quite possible that the dollar's position as the chief international currency will fall from the current 65 percent of central bank reserves to less than 50 percent within the next decade.[26] The so-called BRICs (Brazil, Russia, India, and China) have already issued a joint communiqué urging a "more diversified international monetary system" for international trade and central bank holdings.[27] The United Nations Conference on Trade and Development (UNCTAD) has also criticized the current global financial system dominated by the dollar and recommended the creation of a new global currency and a Bretton Woods-style financial system featuring managed international exchange rates.[28] C. Fred Bergsten, the director of the Peterson Institute of International Economics, contends that it is inevitable that the dollar will lose its international dominance.[29]

Bogged down in future years by the twin deficits (government and the current account) that have required it to borrow most of the surplus savings accumulated in the rest of the world, and saddled with a weakened and more erratic currency, the United States will be hard-pressed to sustain its role as the world's sole superpower.[30]

Entitlement Explosion

Trillions of dollars are currently being allocated to help bring the U.S. out of the recent Great Recession, but not a penny of this new money is being earmarked to cope with the forthcoming entitlement explosion. At the beginning of 2007, Fed Chairman Ben Bernanke was asked by a member of the Senate Budget Committee when something should be done about Social Security, Medicare, and Medicaid. He answered: "I think the right time to start is about ten years ago."[31] Actually, twenty years ago would have been preferable.

Roughly one-fourth of the entire U.S. population, the so-called baby boomers born between 1946 and 1964, are set to retire between 2012 and 2030, and many will be retiring with one-third of their lives still before them.[32] Nothing has been set aside, except a bunch of government IOUs, to prepare for the massive increase in Social Security and Medicare obligations. On the surface, it appears that Washington has been saving up the excess in

FICA payroll taxes in order to take care of the early retirees. In actuality, this is a completely false image. The surplus in what has been collected each year versus what is expended on current retirees has already been spent by the federal government. As Peter G. Peterson, former Secretary of Commerce, laments: "Social Security trust funds are a misnomer, and in fact they're an oxymoron. They shouldn't be trusted, and they're not funded."[33]

The Social Security dilemma is relatively benign when compared to the future spending obligations under Medicare, which may be six or seven times worse than the Social Security dilemma.[34] However, the trust fund that has been set aside for future Social Security recipients and contains the IOUs from Congress will likely have more money going out than coming in by 2016 and could be totally exhausted by 2037.[35] If health-care costs continue to increase far beyond the rate of inflation, total federal government spending two decades from now will be dominated by entitlements and servicing the government debt, leaving little for discretionary spending or international pursuits. In addition, the working population will be expected to shoulder a larger tax burden as the worker-to-retiree ratio dwindles from about sixteen to one when the Social Security plan was first implemented in 1935, to five to one in 1960, to 3.2 to one currently, and then down to 2.2 to one by 2030.[36]

An immediate crisis is already at hand as the Great Recession has prompted the largest spending on benefit programs ever recorded, benefits such as Social Security, food stamps, unemployment insurance, and health care.[37] This spending on entitlements and other benefits topped $2 trillion in 2009 alone. Once the U.S. economy begins to grow again, spending on such programs as food stamps and unemployment insurance will ease, but expenditures on the Social Security, Medicare, and Medicaid juggernauts will continue to expand dramatically. Initially, the Social Security program was geared to a U.S. population who would not live much beyond sixty-five years. In 1940, the life expectancy at birth was 61.4 years for men and 65.7 years for women. In 2008, however, expected longevity had increased to 75.4 and 80 years respectively.[38]

The Boards of Trustees of these trust funds acknowledge that the shortfall on spending will probably be in the range of at least $46 trillion over the next seven decades, and funds for Medicare Part A (Hospital Insurance) will be exhausted by 2017.[39] America's major safety net to protect the elderly and the poor from poverty and disease is floundering on a foundation of quicksand. Spending on these programs is absolutely unsustainable and is accentuating the unprecedented fiscal crisis now facing the U.S. government.

Health Care

Experts may differ on solutions to the problem, but few could disagree that the United States has the most costly and one of the least equitable health-care systems in the world. Among the major Western nations, U.S. health care comes from Mars while all other nations have plans that come from Venus. The United States spends on average twice as much per capita on health care as these other nations but has over forty-six million people without any health-care insurance at all, and many of those who are insured find that they do not have the coverage they thought they had when they actually seek medical treatment.[40] All the other major countries in the West, without exception, provide some form of coverage for all of their people. Each year, up to forty-five thousand Americans die unnecessarily because they lacked health insurance.[41]

President Obama has pledged to bring "affordable" health care to as many Americans as possible. This will be a formidable task. In 2007, Americans spent $2.4 trillion on health care, or $7,900 per capita. The United States currently spends about 17 percent of GDP on health care, whereas no other major nation spends over 12 percent (see Figure III: 5, which compares health spending in 2006).[42] The United States also spends over four times as much on health care as on national defense, and the typical American family spends more for health care than for housing or food.[43] Tragically, over three-fifths of American bankruptcies in 2007 were linked to medical bills, up nearly 50 percent in just six years.[44]

Annual health-care costs have consistently increased at a rate well above the overall consumer price index, and at the current rate of increase, these costs would absorb at least 20 percent of U.S. GDP by 2017, 28 percent by 2030, and 34 percent by 2040.[45] These costs represent a major impediment to the future competitiveness of the nation as U.S. businesses are asked to pay appreciably more in health-related fringe benefits than their overseas competitors. Since 2004, the Big Three automakers together produced more cars and light trucks in Ontario than in Michigan, because they could save roughly $1,000 per car just in health-care costs in Canada. The onerous health-care burden, which is part of the overall "legacy" liabilities of the Big Three, also helps explain why two of these automakers fell into bankruptcy in 2009. Because 59 percent of insured Americans under sixty-five receive health care through their employers, they sometimes forfeit the opportunity to seek better or more rewarding jobs elsewhere because of the fear of losing coverage for themselves and their families, especially

FIGURE III: 5
Health-Care Spending as a Share of GDP, 2006

Source: Organization for Economic Cooperation and Development, *OECD Health Data, 2008* (Paris: OECD, 2008).

in situations involving pre-existing medical conditions (see Figure III: 6).[46] Consequently, from the vantage point of both businesses and employees, the United States is placed at a distinct competitive economic disadvantage because of the lack of a universal, affordable, and portable health-care system.

The costs of medical care in the United States also differ dramatically from one part of the country to another, without any differences in medical outcomes. For example, expenditures in the last six months of life have been nearly twice as high for Medicare patients at certain leading academic medical facilities than at other leading centers—again with no difference in outcomes.[47] As Princeton University economist Uwe E. Reinhardt has quipped, "How can it be that 'the best medical care in the world' costs twice as much as 'the best medical care in the world?'"[48]

Debate on bringing about universal coverage often gets bogged down in the notion of socialized medicine versus a system reliant on private commercial insurance and privately run medical offices and hospitals. This debate is an absolute red herring and diverts attention from the pressing issue of providing coverage for all Americans in an effective and affordable manner. Reinhardt has shed much-needed light on this vitally important issue. He defines socialized medicine as a health system in which the government owns and operates the financing of health care and its delivery.[49] The United Kingdom has this type of system, but so does the U.S. Veterans Affairs,

FIGURE III: 6
Health Insurance Status of Non-Elderly Individuals in the United States, 2007

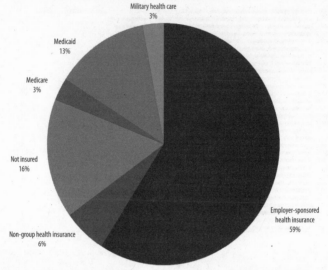

Source: U.S. Census Bureau, *Income, Poverty, and Health Insurance Coverage in the United States: 2007.*

which provides medical coverage for America's veterans. Social health insurance, according to Reinhardt, is a system "in which individuals transfer their financial risk of medical bills to a risk pool to which, as individuals, they contribute taxes or premiums based primarily on ability to pay, rather than on how healthy or sick they are."[50] This could be used in socialized medicine but is usually "coupled on the health-care delivery side with a mixture of government-owned facilities (*e.g.*, municipal hospitals), private nonprofit hospitals (roughly 90 percent of all American hospital beds) or private for-profit facilities (investor-owned hospitals, private medical practices, pharmacies, and so on)."[51] Under private commercial insurance, individuals transfer "the financial risk of bills for health care to a risk pool, but the premium the individual contributes to the risk pool reflects that individual's health status."[52] This insurance can be coupled with private or public delivery systems, or a combination of the two.

With this in mind, U.S. policymakers have the luxury of examining many models abroad that could assist in designing equitable, comprehensive, and effective spending and delivery systems. The UK has the most socialized health system in the Western world. The French provide insurance via payroll taxes through 144 independent, not-for-profit, local insurance funds.[53] Doctors in France run their own offices, and, as Atul Gawande points out, the French have a higher life expectancy, a lower infant mortality rate, more physicians proportionally, and lower costs than the United States.[54] Switzerland did not switch to universal coverage until 1994 and now requires every resident to purchase private health insurance but guarantees no one will pay more than about 10 percent of his or her income for health care.[55] The Canadians actually have fifteen separate plans divided among the ten provinces, three federal territories, natives who live on reserves, and the Canadian military.[56] Doctors are independent contractors and hospitals are also autonomous and mostly run by local health authorities. Doctors are usually paid on a fee-for-service basis. Canadians pay taxes for their health care but never receive bills for covered treatment from their doctors or hospitals.[57]

None of these other systems is close to being perfect. All face rapidly escalating health-care expenses related in part to aging populations. Patients may wait for long hours for emergency treatment and some procedures are rationed. Some do not have the best equipment or cutting-edge technologies in all of their medical facilities. Canadians normally have to pay out of pocket for most dental work, some prescription drugs, and eyeglasses.[58]

On the other hand, these systems are far less expensive than their counterpart in the United States and they cover all of their people. In a comparison of U.S. health care with systems in Canada, Germany, Japan, Sweden, the UK, and France, the U.S. Council of Economic Advisers reached this stark conclusion: all of these other countries "have better health outcomes" than the United States.[59] No one in these other nations will face bankruptcy because of a catastrophic illness or injury. If they move from a job in one part of the country to employment in another part, they and their families will always be covered by health insurance.[60]

Tremendous progress has been made in medical science in the United States and many other countries. For example, a person born in 1800 in the United States had an average life span of thirty-five years, in 1900 forty-seven years, and in 2007 an expected life span of seventy-eight years. The U.S. infant mortality rate in 1900 was roughly one hundred deaths per thousand live births; in 2007 it had decreased to below 6.8 per thousand live births. Nevertheless, it is still shocking that the CIA's *World Factbook* ranks the United States as only forty-sixth in the world in longevity, right behind Cyprus, and forty-second in infant mortality, right behind Cuba.[61] American babies are three times more likely to die in their first month than babies in Japan, and 2.5 times more likely to die than babies in Finland, Iceland, and

Norway.[62] African-American babies pass away at twice the average rate of all American infants.[63]

In 2000, the World Health Organization ranked the United States 37th in the world in overall health-system performance.[64] Horror stories abound concerning people who do not seek treatment because they feel they cannot afford it. Approximately 1.5 million families lose their homes to foreclosure every year, mainly because of unpaid medical bills.[65] In times of economic stress, companies are dropping health-care coverage for their employees or requiring their employees to pick up a higher percentage of the overall tab. Average annual premiums for family coverage obtained through an employer doubled over the past decade to more than $13,000 in 2009.[66] Ninety-six percent of U.S. firms with more than fifty employees offer health insurance to their employees compared to 43 percent of firms with fewer than fifty employees, and the number of small companies offering insurance benefits has been declining since 2001.[67] As health premiums increase, companies are also less likely to offer higher wages to their employees.[68] And, to top it all off, the huge costs of medical care are eroding the overall business competitiveness of the United States and persuading many companies to offshore their operations—much as the Big Three automakers did when they moved so much of their production north to Canada.

Plight of the American Household

The Boston Consulting Group estimates that at the end of 2006, the United States accounted for 37 percent of the $98 trillion in total wealth in the world.[69] By the conclusion of the first decade of the twenty-first century, many U.S. households were absolutely shell-shocked as a good part of their wealth had disappeared and conditions were more precarious for them than any time since the end of World War II. Even though an entire decade had passed, there were fewer private-sector jobs in September 2009 than there had been in October 1999, in spite of the overall population increasing by almost thirty million during those ten years.[70] In 2008 alone, $11 trillion in household wealth disappeared, representing 18 percent of total household wealth and a sum greater than the annual GDP of Japan, Germany, and the United Kingdom combined.[71] Adding losses in 2007 and 2008 together, households saw about a quarter of their total wealth vanish. Stunningly, the median family income in 2008, adjusted for inflation, was lower than it had been a decade earlier.[72] Forty million Americans were also living in poverty in 2008, representing almost 14 percent of the entire population, the highest in a dozen years.[73]

Household wealth in the United States is derived from three major sources: jobs, home equity, and retirement accounts. In the wake of the Great Recession, unemployment and underemployment shot up to the double-digit range, the worst since the Great Depression. Men were particularly hard hit, with double-digit unemployment hitting them by mid-2009, in part, because male workers are overwhelmingly concentrated in the devastated construction and manufacturing sectors, and, in part, because they are not as well educated as women.[74] Underemployment, which includes those too discouraged to look for jobs or those working part-time but seeking full-time employment, hovered near 18 percent, and one in eight Americans was using food stamps.[75] Housing equity had plummeted by an average of 30 percent from its 2006 peak, and retirement accounts, which are heavily invested in the stock market, suffered a similar percentage decline.[76] A quarter of homeowners were "under water," owing more on their mortgages than they could possibly receive if they were to sell their houses. In the first quarter of 2009, 67 percent of homes in Las Vegas had a negative equity, and several communities ranging from Orlando to Phoenix to Riverside, California, were above 40 percent, with the worst results found in the so-called "sand states" of California, Florida, Arizona, and Nevada.[77]

Unfortunately, household debt had also doubled to $14 trillion in the seven-year period leading up to 2008, and many homeowners had used their home equity as ATM machines. Income growth stagnated for most families, but this household debt continued to grow rapidly from a manageable 65 percent of disposable income during the period spanning the quarter century after 1960 to a staggering 130 percent by 2008.[78] The average American household was also saddled with nearly $8,400 in credit card and other revolving debt by the end of 2008.[79] In the spring of 2009, the net worth of the average American family was less than it had been in 2001.[80]

As will be discussed in the next section, most of the wealth and income accumulated in the United States over the past decade has been siphoned into the hands of a very small percentage of U.S. households. On the other hand, most homeowners at least had been on a good run in terms of rising housing values until the great collapse, which began to occur in mid-2006. The median price of an existing home in 2006 was 55 percent higher than in 2000.[81] The average home size had also increased from one thousand square feet in 1950 to twenty-four hundred square feet in 2004, and these larger houses had many more amenities than those sold in 1950.[82]

The collapse of the housing and stock markets are the most brutal manifestations of a very difficult period for many U.S. households. In public opinion surveys, upwards of 90 percent of Americans generally consider themselves as middle class, but many are struggling.[83] The average American works longer hours and takes fewer vacation days than comparable workers in the rest of the Western world but most have experienced no real income gains for many years.[84]

Roughly sixty million U.S. workers have no paid sick leave, in sharp contrast to more than 160 countries that ensure all of their citizens receive some paid sick leave and more than 110 who guarantee paid leave from the first day of illness.[85] Only about half of Americans are covered by employer-sponsored retirement plans.[86] Everyone else will have to depend solely on Social Security, which will pay someone who turns sixty-six in 2020 about $2,400 per month.[87] Many employers are now cutting back on their pension coverage and also forcing workers to pay higher premiums and co-pays for their company-sponsored health insurance plans. In 1985, roughly 80 percent of medium- and large-sized companies provided their workers with defined-benefit retirement plans, guaranteeing the workers specific cash benefits upon retirement, usually based on years of service, age, and final earnings. By 2000, that number had dwindled to 36 percent.[88]

Now, most companies that continue to offer pensions have turned to defined-contribution plans, usually in the form of 401(k)s, with the worker deciding where to invest and putting up most of the money. Companies used to provide a certain match to encourage workers to save for retirement, but as the economy tanked in recent years, many of these companies have suspended or even eliminated these matching funds, with 110 of the S&P 500 companies stating early in 2009 that they would stop matching workers' contributions.[89] Furthermore, as big corporations such as UAL, the parent of United Airlines, enter Chapter 11 bankruptcy, they jettison many of the pension and health-care obligations made to their employees.

The federal government has in place the Pension Benefit Guaranty Corporation, which insures forty-four million private pensions, but its retirement disbursements to the 1.3 million people currently receiving funds are usually less than what the bankrupt corporation had pledged to provide.[90] This quasi-independent federal agency is also deeply in the red with unfunded liabilities totaling $11 billion at the end of the 2008 fiscal year.[91] Once again, the average taxpayer may be on the hook when a corporation self-destructs and no longer fulfills its financial commitments to its employees, even though the corporation may later emerge from Chapter 11 and continue to do business.

The corporate world is not alone in the potential retirement time bomb, because many state and local government pension funds are also vastly underfunded, with state governments perhaps facing a $1.5 trillion pension shortfall within the next fifteen years.[92] In an extremely difficult job environment, workers have very little recourse other than to accept the onerous conditions placed on them by management. Unionization in the United States has been moribund in most sectors for many years, with only 7.6 percent of private-sector workers being members of unions in 2008 compared with about 35 percent in the 1950s.[93] More than half of workers now say that they would like to unionize, a sentiment up from one-third a decade ago, but very little headway has been achieved in bringing unionization to the corporate world.[94] Although corporate America has gone through its own share of trials and tribulations recently, the average U.S. worker has felt more pain and uncertainty than at any other time since the end of the Second World War.

Jacob S. Hacker and Elisabeth Jacobs sum up the problem quite well:

America's globally integrated economy means less job security, more mobility, and ever-higher skills requirements for workers. Health care and education costs are rising. With most families relying on two incomes, the cost of caregiving is a real and growing pressure on millions of families struggling to support both young children and elderly parents. The combination of these rising costs and a volatile labor market means that families need to be continually prepared for change. For too long, we've left them to go it alone, and we're seeing the disastrous consequences of that approach today.[95]

In essence, the United States has a very thin safety net for its citizens and many live within one or two paychecks of financial disaster.[96]

Almost 30 percent of American children now live in single-parent households, up from 12 percent in 1968, and poverty rates in these homes are almost five times as high as in two-parent households.[97] With so many U.S. households being battered from all sides, one should not expect the American economy will be led out of the wilderness by a huge new surge in consumer spending. Before the crash, consumer spending had actually accounted for as much as 76 percent of the nation's entire GDP, a figure far out of proportion with similar spending in other major countries.[98]

Households are beginning to deleverage and save more because of their huge debt loads, the evaporation of so much of their wealth, and concerns about job security.[99] Moreover, many of these households have seen little in income gains, when inflation is factored in, for more than thirty years.[100] For far too long, America's GDP growth was predicated on "consumptionitis" spurred on by the inflated home equity values and a willingness to chalk up huge credit-card debts. That period is now over, and with the basic unit of U.S. society, the American household, in dire straits, the road to recovery for the country as a whole has become much longer and far more difficult.

The New Gilded Age and Wall Street's Debacle

A good part of the blame for the current travails of U.S. households is linked to their own ill-considered profligacy, but Wall Street was responsible for the bloody ambush of so many families situated along Main Street, U.S.A., and in its suburbs. The biggest Ponzi scheme in global history was played out on Wall Street during the first decade of the twenty-first century, and it brought a once-mighty country's financial system to its knees. Paul Krugman labeled the period as "America the Tarnished," and added that "America is looking like the Bernie Madoff of economies."[101] Thomas Friedman chimed in by declaring that the United States had suffered "a national breakdown in financial propriety, regulations, and common sense" and needed both a financial and ethical bailout.[102] Warren Buffett referred to the U.S. as being on the verge of an "economic Pearl Harbor."[103] Nouriel Roubini declared that the United States had lived in a Ponzi bubble economy for more than a decade before the major financial downturn in 2008 and early 2009.[104]

The subprime mortgage crisis was fueled by a ridiculous assumption that housing prices would climb indefinitely, in spite of the utter impossibility of wage-earners affording such steep rises in housing costs. The situation was aggravated by offering too many mortgages to people with insufficient incomes and poor credit ratings, all rationalized by the notion that housing equity would continue to go up and this cushion would overcome the credit and income deficiencies.[105] This crisis was also abetted by Fannie Mae and Freddie Mac providing government guarantees for these subprime loans, and the concentration of mortgage lending placed in the hands of a relatively few powerful companies. In 1989, the five largest firms controlled only 7 percent of the entire mortgage servicing market, but by the time Bank of America absorbed Countrywide Financial in July 2008, the top three services—Bank of America, Wells Fargo, and Chase—controlled almost half of all residential mortgages.[106]

Too many unscrupulous mortgage companies of all sizes had granted loans to anyone who had a pulse. Securitization strategies prompted mortgages to be bundled and sold around the world, with each intermediary taking a share of the transaction fees.[107] Rating agencies such as Moody's and Standard and Poor's gave their blessings to this nefarious process by conferring triple A status on 85 percent of the bundled tranches and deeming 99 percent to be "investment grade."[108] Investment banks and other financial institutions leveraged their resources to unsustainable levels, hoping to maximize their return on each transaction. The leveraging and inordinate risk-taking were given added impetus by companies, such as AIG, that were willing to offer insurance policies called credit default swaps that were supposed to protect the financial institutions from potential losses.[109] However, once the inevitable losses began to accumulate, the insurance guarantees proved to be illusory. By the end of that turbulent decade, U.S. taxpayers had already picked up the tab for over $170 billion in bankrupt AIG's losses, and total bailouts and guarantees to the financial sector and corporate America have added up to several trillion dollars. The U.S. Treasury and, once again, the average American taxpayer have borne the brunt of Wall Street's ignominious Ponzi-style machinations.

Most Americans could not have imagined that the first decade of the twenty-first century would deteriorate into a new Gilded Age, with much in common with the original Gilded Age of the latter part of the nineteenth century and the second Gilded Age of the Roaring Twenties. All three periods were epitomized by a tremendous concentration of wealth into a small number of households, the ostentatious lifestyle flaunted by many of these wealthy families, and the inordinate influence these wealthy interests exerted over policymakers in Washington, D.C. All three also ended in calamitous economic collapse: the Panic of 1893 resulted in one of the worst depressions of the nineteenth century, the Great Depression of the 1930s, and the recent Great Recession—the deepest and most extensive economic downturn since the Great Depression.

Although economic growth occurred during part of the past decade, almost all of the gains were siphoned into relatively few American households that comprised the nation's financial and corporate plutocracy.[110] In 1985, there were thirteen billionaires in the United States, whereas in 2006 there were more than four hundred.[111] In 2004, the top 1 percent of households controlled 34 percent of the nation's total private wealth, more than the bottom 90 percent of households combined. The top 10 percent of the wealthiest households possessed 71 percent of the total wealth.[112] Deplorably, the bottom 40 percent of households together held less than 1 percent of total wealth.

Income was not quite as skewed, but in 1980 the top 1 percent of earners took home 9 percent of national income versus 22 percent in 2007.[113] Between 2002 and 2007, two-thirds of all the income gains registered in the United States went to the top 1 percent of American earners.[114] In addition, the 300,000 top income earners have recently enjoyed almost as much combined annual income as the bottom 150 million, and the rich have enjoyed the biggest slice of income since Herbert Hoover was president.[115] Tragically, in the more than half-century period covered from 1953 to 2005, the share of total family income actually decreased for four-fifths of all households, whereas the share was up dramatically for the top 5 percent of households.[116] Writing about the earlier Gilded Age, Supreme Court Justice Louis D. Brandeis warned, "We can have democracy in this country, or we can have great wealth concentrated in the hands of a few, but we can't have both."[117] In the current era, many ordinary workers have not experienced the advantages of rising U.S. productivity because of this vast increase in income inequality.[118]

The "golden rule" was also in place in the Wall Street-Beltway axis: the plutocracy that possessed the gold made the rules in Washington. For example, fifty hedge-fund managers made over $210 million each in 2007, but Congress arranged for them to pay taxes at a 15 percent rate instead of the previously stipulated 35 percent rate for high-income earners.[119] The mammoth and opaque U.S. tax code is also replete with special favors and tax exemptions for powerful individuals and corporations, all of which help to concentrate the total wealth of society into fewer and fewer hands. Many of the wealthy also took full advantage of offshore bank accounts in tax-evasion schemes that may cost the U.S. Treasury $100 billion in revenues each year.[120] Union Bank of Switzerland (UBS) admitted to seeking rich American clients from 2000 to 2007 in a blatant attempt to help them evade U.S. taxes and attracted as many as fifty-two thousand U.S. customers, who concealed their accounts through sham offshore companies in Panama, Hong Kong, the British Virgin Islands, and other tax havens.[121] More than four-fifths of the one-hundred-largest corporations in the United States have also taken full advantage of off-shore tax havens.[122] The George W. Bush administration attempted to abolish estate taxes altogether, an action that would have further entrenched the power base of the wealth-laden aristocracy.

To be fair, many financial and corporate institutions had absolutely nothing to do with Wall Street's collapse. Finance in general grew very rapidly from the late 1990s, accounting for 41 percent of all corporate profits during much of the period from 2001 through 2007, compared with an average of 16 percent in the period from 1973 to 1985 and from 21 to 30 percent during the 1990s.[123] Most of the casino-style financial wheeling and dealing was manifested in the "shadow banking" sector composed of investment banks, hedge funds, AIG's derivatives division, and the like. They eventually became more powerful financial players than the far more numerous traditional banks in the United States. Indeed, the traditional commercial banks that most Americans identify with the financial sector held only 24 percent of all financial assets by 2007, compared with 56 percent in 1977.[124]

Many leaders in the shadow banking arena were absolutely ignorant of the dangers of derivatives, which are financial instruments whose value is based on something else, such as commodities or mortgage-based securities.[125] Early on, Warren Buffett labeled derivatives as "weapons of mass destruction," but few CEOs concurred.[126] They also misjudged the "Value at Risk" financial model put together by the "quant jocks"—mainly scientists and mathematicians—that turned out to be far too complex and badly flawed.[127] This did not keep these leaders and their closest minions from reaping unparalleled short-term rewards, while they were sinking America's financial ship of state.[128] On Wall Street and among major corporations, CEO pay and compensation was 344 times higher than that of the average worker in 2007, up from 150 times in 1992.[129] Fitting for the new twenty-first century royalty, many of these CEOs also received exclusive country club memberships, the use of corporate jets, and astronomical retirement packages. Richard Fuld, who directed the 158-year-old, now-defunct Lehman Brothers, took home $484 million in salary, bonuses, and stock options from 2000 until his company's bankruptcy in 2008.[130] James "Jimmy" Cayne of Bear Stearns pocketed $173 million in the six years prior to his firm being "rescued" by J. P. Morgan, initially for $2 a share.[131] Franklin Raines was CEO of Fannie Mae, a government-sponsored enterprise, and he extracted $90 million in compensation over a five-year period before he was forced to resign in 2004 because of a major accounting scandal at the corporation.[132] Joseph Cassano, former head of AIG's financial products division, squeezed out in excess of $300 million prior to the U.S. government's takeover of the company.[133] In

2008, as AIG was sinking faster than the *Titanic*, seventy-three executives were still awarded that year with at least $1 million each in bonuses.[134] Citigroup was being taken over by the U.S. government, but its executives still attempted to buy a $50 million corporate jet.[135] Just before Merrill Lynch was absorbed by the Bank of America, its CEO, John Thain, tried to ladle out $3.6 billion in bonuses and ordered a $1 million renovation of his own office, including $35,000 for a toilet.[136] In almost all of these cases, bonuses were paid largely on the basis of massive risk taking and short-term profits, provided within an environment of unprecedented greed and hubris and with little concern for the long-term viability of the firms—many of which folded or were taken over at the last minute by more viable companies.

A post-mortem of Wall Street's collapse indicates that many individuals and entities were at fault: government regulators, the Federal Reserve, elected officials, rating agencies, shadow banking, mortgage providers, real-estate brokers and speculators, and others. As outlined in the previous chapter, the reputation of representative government in the United States became increasingly sullied, because money was allowed to sway the votes of so many politicians in Washington, D.C. Elected officials were constantly raising money for their campaigns and dispensing favors to those who contributed great sums either individually or by "bundling" donations among powerful groups with shared agendas. Although numerically weak, these well-heeled and well-organized special interests almost always won the battle in the corridors of political power over the numerically strong but organizationally weak American citizenry. Never was this pattern so clear as in the past few years when a largely discredited financial sector, which had precipitated the Great Recession, nonetheless blocked most attempts in Washington to effectuate meaningful Wall Street reform, including efforts to end forever the "too-big-to-fail" mantra that had potentially cost taxpayers trillions of dollars in bailouts and subsidies. Stephen Friedman, chair of the board of directors of the New York Federal Reserve Bank, a powerful institution that was supposed to ensure what transpired on Wall Street was in the country's interest, actually sat at the same time on the Goldman Sachs board of directors and held large amounts of stock in the company he was expected to regulate.[137] This spectacle within the Beltway and among regulators is also responsible for eroding public support for what had been a very vibrant and robust market system in the United States.[138] For a growing number of Americans, United States-style capitalism has become synonymous with corporate welfare and the notion that powerful corporate interests are entitled to privatize their profits but socialize their losses at the expense of the American public.[139]

Shoshana Zuboff, the retired Charles Edward Wilson Professor of Business Administration at the Harvard Business School, expresses quite adroitly the outrage felt by many Americans. Zuboff asserts the financial crisis shows "mounting evidence of fraud, conflict of interests, indifference to suffering, repudiation of responsibility, and systemic absence of individual moral judgment" that "produced an administrative economic massacre of such proportion that it constitutes an economic crime against humanity."[140] Most Americans pay their bills and mortgages on time and live prudently and within their means, but they are the ones who will bear the financial burden of the greed and reckless gambling in the financial sector, both in the form of higher taxes to pay off the massive government debt and in lower interest rates on their savings because of the Fed's zero interest rate policy.[141] What will happen to Richard Fuld, Joseph Cassano, and the others who precipitated the crisis? They will keep their billions of dollars "looted" from Wall Street and maintain their palatial homes, summer villas and yachts in Florida and Monaco, winter retreats in Aspen and St. Moritz, along with their other material splendor.[142] What will happen to the staggering $592 trillion over-the-counter derivatives market that continues to function in a very private and opaque fashion?[143] Will Wall Street remain in a funk for years or possibly decades? After all, the Dow Jones Industrial Average did not return to its 1929 high until thirty-four years later.[144] Frankly, the vast amount of welfare checks sent to Wall Street is abhorrent, and it is even more odious because of the general lack of transparency, accountability, and admissions of culpability. More ominous is what will happen to the United States if politicians in Washington, D.C., actually try to run Wall Street and parts of corporate America.

Chapter 4

Domestic Fault Lines: The Comfort Zone of Mediocrity

Introduction

This chapter will highlight the final half dozen domestic fault lines, ranging from a serious deterioration in the U.S. educational system to widespread complacency among the American people concerning the true nature of democracy and representative government.

Education

Brainpower will dominate the twenty-first century, as the human information base doubles every half dozen years or so, and a premium will be placed on those who can use their minds and adapt to rapid and unprecedented change in the workplace and in society as a whole. To illustrate this supersonic rate of information accumulation, the U.C. Berkeley School of Information Management and Systems estimates that in 2002 alone about five exabytes of new information were produced, the equivalent of thirty-seven thousand new libraries the size of the Library of Congress (containing seventeen million books). On a per-capita basis, the equivalent of almost ten meters of books is being added each year for every inhabitant of the earth.[1]

The United States once led the world in the quality of its K–12 public schools. By being the first to educate its masses and provide public schools, the U.S. made great economic progress through the latter half of the nineteenth century and most of the twentieth century, with education playing the key role in wedding together human capital and individual productivity.[2] However, in 1982, the National Commission on Excellence in Education released a highly publicized report entitled *A Nation at Risk*. The report warned that U.S. public schools were beginning to fall behind, and they were ill prepared to meet the needs of a competitive workforce. More than a quarter of a century later, almost all observers would conclude that the U.S. public school system was in much better shape in 1982 than in 2010, and "America is at a crossroads with education flagging both relatively and absolutely."[3] In the twenty-first century where brainpower is more important than ever before, one will need "a very high level of preparation in reading, writing, speaking, mathematics, science, literature, history, and the arts" in order to build "an indispensable foundation for everything that comes after to most members of the workforce. It is a world in which comfort with ideas and abstractions is the passport to a good job, in which creativity and innovation are the key to the good life. . . ."[4] So far in this brainpower century, U.S. students as a whole are trailing their counterparts in most other developed and in some developing societies.

In 2003, the U.S. ranked fourteenth out of twenty-one among the Organization for Economic Cooperation and Development (OECD) countries that participated in a survey with respect to high school graduation rates.[5] In comparative Program for International Student Assessment (PISA) testing, a program affiliated with the OECD, 2003 results showed fifteen-year-old U.S. students ranking fifteenth among students from twenty-nine OECD countries in reading, twentieth in science, and twenty-fourth in math.[6] In the 2006 Progress in International Reading Literacy Study (PIRLS), Russian fourth graders were on top and Americans in the middle. In the 2007 Trends in International Mathematics and Science Study (TIMSS) exam, U.S. fourth and eighth graders were about in the middle in math but well below average in science.[7] Disappointingly, comparative international tests usually display this pattern: U.S. fourth graders rank relatively high, eighth graders in the middle, and eleventh or twelfth graders in the bottom third to half, in spite of the United States spending a higher percentage of GDP on education than all other major nations.[8] Roughly a million young people in the U.S. are dropping out of school on an annual basis, and a third of high school graduates are not prepared to tackle a college curriculum or a challenging work environment.[9] Bill Gates has labeled U.S. high schools as "obsolete" and has rendered this chilling assessment: "When I compare our high schools with what I see when I'm traveling abroad, I am terrified for our work force of tomorrow."[10]

Forty years ago, the United States was the global leader in high school graduation rates, but now it ranks only eighteenth out of twenty-four major industrial countries.[11] Only 71 percent of all U.S. students graduate from high school within four years, and this rate falls to 58 percent for Hispanics and 55 percent for African-Americans.[12] The United States has a greater inequality of educational outcomes than perhaps any other major developed country, and the inequalities linked to income and wealth carry over to the schools that young people attend.[13] Jonathan Kozol refers to apartheid schooling that creates "separate worlds of education."[14] He goes on to assert that there are "cheap children" and "expensive children," with most of the latter found in the suburbs attending modern schools in safe neighborhoods, where per pupil funding is far higher than in many inner-city or rural school districts.[15] In effect, too many youngsters born into poverty also attend very poor schools.[16] The results of a substandard education and dropping out of school are absolutely catastrophic for the individual and society as a whole. Betty Yee, former deputy director for the budget in the California Department of Finance, made this observation about the 120,000 annual high school dropouts in California, who through their lifetimes "are more likely to be unemployed and pay no taxes, resort to criminal activity,.and rely on publicly funded programs for basic subsistence and healthcare. . . . A high school graduate is 68 percent less likely to be on any public assistance than a high school dropout."[17] In 2005, almost one-quarter of all California adults aged eighteen to sixty-four never graduated from high school, and an estimated $46 billion is lost in productive economic activity for each annual cohort of 120,000 twenty-year-olds who never complete high school.[18] Currently, California is spending as much on its prisons as on its university system, allocating $46,000 each year for an inmate versus $11,000 a year for a California State or University of California student.[19]

Many minority groups, recent immigrants, and low-income families from all ethnic backgrounds are the most vulnerable to receiving inferior educations and dropping out of school before graduating. Fourth graders who grow up in low-income communities tend to be three grade levels behind their peers in high-income communities. More than thirteen million children live in poverty in the United States, and about half will not graduate from high school by age eighteen, and those who do will perform on average at the eighth grade level. Only 10 percent of them will go on to graduate from college.[20] Unless these young people receive better educational opportunities, America is very much at risk. Currently, 34 percent of the U.S. population is nonwhite, but 48 percent of all new babies were nonwhite in 2008. Eventually, due to the rapid growth in the number of minority children and a decline in the number of white children, whites will become another minority "in the American melting pot."[21] All young people, regardless of ethnicity, income, or wealth, must receive quality K–12 educations, or America is destined to lose the all-important brainpower derby.

American colleges and universities are still ranked highly in comparison to their counterparts around the world, although there has been some slippage. For example, the annual *Times of London* survey of universities around the world in 2009 ranked thirty-two U.S. institutions in the top hundred globally and fifty-four in the top two hundred, down modestly in both categories from five years earlier.[22] U.S. institutions of higher learning are experiencing some of the long-term effects of shortcomings in primary and secondary schools, plus the escalating costs of a college education are beyond the reach of many low and moderate-income families.[23] In addition, relatively few Americans pursue post-graduate degrees in areas of critical importance for the twenty-first century, including the so-called "STEM"— science, technology, engineering, and math. Foreign students and immigrants currently account for half of all science researchers in the United States.[24] In 2006, they received 40 percent of the doctorates in science and engineering and 65 percent in computer science.[25] This trend is extremely worrisome for Silicon Valley and other U.S. research centers because there are few American-born PhDs available for their advanced projects, and visa restrictions limit the number of young foreign graduates who can be hired. In one lab at Hewlett-Packard specializing in nanotechnology, only eighteen of seventy-five scientists were born in the U.S.A. and only six of the U.S. scientists were under the age of thirty-five.[26] Moreover, America is doing a comparatively poor job in making it possible for adults who are employed full-time or are raising families to obtain the continuing education and training needed to survive in a rapidly evolving working environment.[27]

Tragically, 70 percent of U.S.-based students who reach college age are not actually graduating from college.[28] Unless major changes are made in how the United States educates its more than 104 million young people aged five to twenty-nine years who enroll in school every year, the following will occur:

> If we continue on our current course, and the number of nations outpacing us in the education race continues to grow at its current rate, the American standard of living will steadily fall relative to those nations, rich and poor, that are doing a better job.[29]

Infrastructure Deterioration

The U.S. government has added trillions of dollars to its overall debt, but little of this spending has gone toward modernizing its infrastructure so that the nation would become more competitive over the next several decades. Indeed, quite the opposite has occurred as the infrastructure continues to deteriorate at a time when many of the competitor nations are moving forward with massive infrastructure projects.

The Obama stimulus package has targeted some infrastructure projects proposed by state and local governments. The problem is determining how many of these projects will be critical to the future economic competitiveness of the nation as a whole. These programs are also short on guidelines, oversight, and transparency, compounded by endemic pork-barrel politics and cronyism. Japan tried this route to recovery during the 1990s, spending twice as much on infrastructure projects (as a percentage of GDP) as the United States. Several of the Japanese projects, such as construction of the Ibaraki airport and New Tomei Expressway, were wasteful, and during this period of huge Japanese infrastructure spending, the total GDP gap between the United States and Japan actually widened.[30]

As he travels around the world and observes what is occurring in various countries, Thomas Friedman has often criticized all levels of the U.S. government for the growing obsolescence of America's aging infrastructure. Friedman once related how he was visiting Hong Kong and borrowed a cell phone from a local friend and spoke clearly and without static to his wife back in the United States. He then boarded a high-speed train and used Wi-Fi without any problems as he traveled to the ultra-modern Hong Kong airport. Arriving back home, he landed at an aging and rather decrepit terminal at JFK airport in New York City, labeling his experience as "going from the Jetsons to the Flintstones."[31] The next day he was driven to the old and dingy Pennsylvania train station in Manhattan, where he boarded a train to Washington. Even the relatively fast Acela trains are not in the same league as their European, Japanese, or Chinese counterparts in terms of speed and comfort. He also kept losing cell-phone service as he traveled along the route to the nation's capital. Friedman's conclusion: "We as a country have become General Motors."[32]

Americans are aware of some of the most egregious infrastructure problems—the failure of the levees in New Orleans as a result of Hurricane Katrina and the collapse of the Interstate 35W bridge over the Mississippi River in Minneapolis. In terms of the nation's overall infrastructure, the American Society of Civil Engineers asserts that it is "dreadful" and recommends $2.2 trillion be spent over the next half decade just to bring the infrastructure back to decent shape.[33] More than a quarter of U.S. bridges are structurally deficient or functionally obsolete. Public transportation and dams and levees are generally in sorry shape. Leaks in pipes carrying drinking water cause an estimated loss of seven billion gallons of clean drinking water everyday.[34]

Bridges, roadways, railways, airports, seaports, and the vast electrical grid network are among the notable infrastructure projects requiring major renovations. Intermodal transportation networks to facilitate national and international commercial linkages are also in desperate need of modernization. Furthermore, after having taken the initial lead, the U.S. has fallen far behind several other nations in Internet access for homes, standing only twentieth in broadband penetration and thirty-third in broadband speed.[35] Cell-phone technology and coverage also rank behind many European countries and Japan. In sum, the comparative deterioration in the U.S. infrastructure mirrors many of the problems discussed earlier: gradual erosion with sporadic expressions of concern diluted by persistent wishful thinking that America must still be number one and, miraculously, will always be number one. In surveying the overall high-technology landscape and infrastructure, Craig R. Barrett, the chair of Intel Corporation, offered this chilling assessment: "We are watching the decline and fall of the United States as an economic power—not hypothetically, but as we speak."[36]

Intergenerational Strife and Festering Cleavages

Could the following be a plausible scenario for the future?

When voters cast their ballots in the presidential election of 7 November 2028, most were resigned to the fact that the United States was no longer respected globally as a superpower. The period between 2000 and 2028 had been agonizing for the nation. With only one exception, presidents had been elected for one term from 2008 onward. 2028 added a new twist, because on the first Tuesday of November, Louise Rodriguez had been elected as the first Latina president. Even more stunning, this was the first time that a president had been selected who was neither a Democrat nor Republican since the Whig Party's Millard Fillmore succeeded Zachary Taylor in 1850.

If anything is going to break the monopoly that Democrats and Republicans have had over the U.S. political system since the 1850s, it may be growing intergenerational strife within the United States. More than seventy-six million baby boomers will begin to retire beginning in 2012 with full Social Security and Medicare benefits. Instead of recognizing the precarious financial condition of their country and making some concessions, they have used their voting clout and influence in organizations such as the American Association of Retired Persons (AARP) to cower members of Congress into maintaining full benefits. Consequently, not only are younger workers being asked to bear the burden of higher taxes linked to the Wall Street rescue package, and the rapidly growing federal debt, but they will also be forced to support financially the massive wave of new retirees. This phenomenon could lead to "downward mobility," condemning future generations to smaller disposable incomes.[37]

Through the first half century following World War II, federal spending averaged around 20 percent of GDP and federal tax collections about 18 percent of GDP. The CBO is now predicting, based on a very low unemployment rate, that federal spending will represent 26 percent of GDP by 2020, but tax collections, under current rules, would only bring in the equivalent of 19 percent of GDP.[38] Unless the U.S. economy grows at a robust rate of 4 percent or more in real terms during that period, individual taxes will have to increase dramatically. Just to fill the gap between expenditures and revenues in 2020, personal taxes would have to go up by at least 44 percent, and that does not take into account any efforts to decrease Washington's huge pile of accumulated debt.[39] Furthermore, workers will have to contend with the major changes in demographics with only 2.5 active workers per retiree in 2020 and 2.2 in 2030, compared with the current 3.2.[40]

The situation among workers may become so bleak that many may decide to abandon the Democrats and Republicans, whose members on Capitol Hill have become known collectively as the "Incumbency Party" driven by the overriding ambition to be reelected rather than solve the vexing problems facing the nation. These younger voters could opt to support a new populist-oriented party promising wholesale changes in the tax system and a reduction in benefit packages paid to older Americans.

The American dream linked to meritocracy and rags-to-riches' success is at risk. Nearly half of all American children, including a staggering 90 percent of African-American children, will at some point before age twenty live in a household that receives food stamps.[41] The combined fear of poverty and food insecurity represents a major threat to the "overall health and well-being of American children."[42] In addition, social mobility, the "ability to move up the economic ladder," is eroding: "Social mobility is now less fluid in the United States than in other affluent nations. Indeed, a poor child born in Germany, France, Canada, or one of the Nordic countries has a better chance to join the middle class in adulthood than an American child born into similar circumstances."[43] If the U.S. economic and fiscal situation stagnates over much of the next decade, the intergenerational schism may be accompanied by growing ethnic and racial tensions. The worst schools are in areas dominated by ethnic and racial minorities. College graduation rates are far lower among most of these minority groups, as are home-ownership rates. The unemployment rate is also much higher among most minorities. As the next section will highlight, new immigrants and their children and grandchildren are expected to account for 82 percent of all U.S. population growth through 2050.[44] Whites will constitute 47 percent of the total population in 2050 versus 85 percent in 1960.[45] As minorities perceive they are being discriminated against and as their numbers swell, they will demand tangible improvements, hopefully, through working within the system and voting. However, if the political system is unresponsive and sclerotic, some may resort to more disruptive methods in an effort to bring about desired change.

Immigration and the Quest to Attract the Best and the Brightest

The United States is in the midst of its greatest boom since the late nineteenth century, and this wave will have a dramatic impact on the composition of American society and America's global standing in the twenty-first century. The Pew Hispanic Center estimates that at the end of 2006, 37.5 million residents of the United States were foreign born, representing 12.5 percent of the entire U.S. population.[46] The peak level as a percentage of inhabitants occurred in the 1890 census at 14.8 percent and was almost matched in the 1910 census when 14.7 percent of residents came from other countries. Then began a steady decline to a low of 4.8 percent in 1970, only to reverse and begin to climb again to 7.9 percent in 1990 and 11.1 percent in 2000. In the period 1960–2005, new immigrants and their children and grandchildren born in the United States accounted for 51 percent of the nation's total population growth.[47] In the shorter period 1980–2005, immigration accounted for 58 percent of U.S. population growth. Between 2005 and 2050, the U.S. population is expected to expand from 296 million to 438 million, and immigration will account for 82 percent of this growth.[48] Of the 117 million new residents of the United States, sixty-seven million will be immigrants and fifty million will be their United States-born children and grandchildren.[49] By mid-century, 19 percent of all U.S. residents will be foreign born.[50]

The United States has more residents born in another country than any other nation in the world.[51] The Immigration Act of 1990 allows for an annual inflow of from 416,000 to 675,000 legal immigrants per year, exclusive of those who enter for humanitarian reasons.[52] Nearly 1.1 million immigrants were granted permanent residence status in 2008, but this includes those who had been in the country for several years and finally qualified for this new status. Approximately 65 percent of immigrants enter for family reunification reasons, 15 percent for employment reasons, and another 20 percent or so for humanitarian and other reasons. On an annual basis, the United States allows in more immigrants than any other nation, but as a percentage of the overall population, Canada and Australia have in recent years maintained higher immigration quotas.

The most contentious issue in the field of immigration is tied to those who come to the U.S. illegally or come with legal visas but then stay on after their visas have expired. Roughly twelve million unauthorized immigrants were living in the United States at the end of 2008, constituting 4 percent of the U.S. population and 5.4 percent of the U.S. labor force.[53] There are a record 12.7 million Mexican immigrants in the U.S.—a seventeen-fold increase since 1970.[54] Mexicans constitute 32 percent of all immigrants in America, the highest concentration since the wave of Irish and German immigrants during the nineteenth century.[55] Eleven percent of everyone born in Mexico now live in the United States, and about 55 percent of these Mexican immigrants are undocumented.[56]

State and local leaders want help from Washington to help defray the significant health, education, infrastructure, and other costs associated with this dramatic rise in illegal immigrants, pointing out that immigration is exclusively in the domain of the national government and that Washington should ultimately bear the financial burden for its failure to keep these immigrants out of the country. Most undocumented immigrants are hard workers, but the group as a whole presents major challenges for the United States in view of the overwhelming problems now facing the nation. In 2007, among adults, 21 percent of the illegal immigrants were poor, compared with 13 percent of legal immigrants and 10 percent of United States-born residents.[57] One in three children of undocumented immigrants also lives in poverty. Fifty-nine percent of the unauthorized adults had no health insurance in 2007, more than double the rate of legal immigrants and four times the rate of United States-born adults.[58] Forty-five percent of the children of undocumented parents were also without any health insurance during 2007.[59] As a whole, illegal immigrants and their children account for 17 percent of all U.S. residents without health insurance.[60] Mexican immigrants, whether legal or undocumented, "have lower levels of education, lower incomes, larger households, and higher poverty rates than other groups."[61]

Immigration has already helped the United States to have a much better age profile than almost every other major Western nation—in plain English, they are getting much older as a society than is the United States. Immigrants may also assist significantly in making sure that there are sufficient working-age people to take care of the retiring baby boomers. On the other hand, the lack of educational attainment by most illegal immigrants is a major drawback for the United States in an increasingly competitive global landscape. Undocumented immigration must be halted as much as practicable, and this will be attained more easily through careful scrutiny of business hiring than through building huge fences along the Mexican border. All immigrants who are allowed to remain in the U.S. must also be given access to the best K–12 and post-secondary education possible.

In terms of educational attainment, America is not taking advantage of the world's brainpower because of inane immigration and visa policies. Over half of high-tech companies created in Silicon Valley between the mid-1990s and the first five years of the twenty-first century had at least one immigrant founder or co-founder, mainly from China and India.[62] A Hungarian immigrant was a major contributor to Intel's success, a Taiwanese immigrant co-founded Yahoo, Indian and German immigrants co-founded Sun Microsystems, and a Russian immigrant co-founded Google.[63] Among high-tech start-up companies across the United States, 16 percent have at least one foreign-born person as part of the founding team.[64] These immigrants who have established so many viable businesses are among the world leaders in innovation and have furnished millions of jobs for American workers directly or indirectly.

In spite of this, Washington persists in placing very strict limits on the number of highly skilled people and their immediate family members who can enter the U.S. or stay in the country after having received advanced technical degrees at American universities. One of Google's most brilliant engineers lives in Toronto because his wife has been denied a visa.[65] H-1B visas that provide company sponsorship for highly skilled workers from abroad have been pared from 195,000 annually in 2001 to sixty-five thousand since 2004.[66] In 2008, U.S. high-tech companies made 163,000 applications for the sixty-five thousand slots.[67] There is also an O-1 category of visas for geniuses. No limit has been placed on the number that may be offered every year, but the process is very rigorous and only nine thousand were awarded in 2008, many to artists, writers, and musicians.[68] Even some athletes seem to qualify, including professional basketball players.[69] As for green cards, a maximum of 9,800 are available per year for residents of any particular country. Because India and China are providing so many skilled immigrants to the U.S., their annual quotas are filled very quickly, and immigrants on H-1B visas must continue to work for the same company that initially sponsored them if they want to remain in the green-card queue.[70] This frustrates many of these talented young people from India and China at a time when research and professional development opportunities are opening up back in their homelands.[71]

The U.S. government should limit family reunification qualifications to immediate family members and substantially increase the number of permanent immigration slots set aside for the highly educated and those who could fill vitally important employment slots. Without a marked change in U.S. immigration and visa criteria, many of the best and brightest around the globe will simply refuse to come to the United States, opting instead for lucrative opportunities and generous immigration provisions in Europe, Canada, and other countries. The United States still has the allure to attract these best and brightest if Congress and the executive branch will get their acts together. Some may argue that a brain drain favoring the United States will not serve the interests of other countries, especially developing nations who lose their most capable people to the United States. This is an inaccurate assessment. The best and brightest can come and receive high-quality graduate and post-graduate training in a climate of free expression within the United States and then establish their businesses on American soil using venture-capital funding and other abundant resources. As they prosper, and as the Silicon Valley experience clearly attests, many will later open subsidiaries in their home countries and strengthen transnational linkages that will ultimately benefit both their homelands and the United States.

The United States of 2050 will look far different from the United States of 2010. Even today, there is a "majority-minority" in Hawaii, California, Texas, New Mexico, New York City, Houston, and almost 10 percent of U.S. counties. In 2050, there will be no majority race in the nation as a whole, and Americans must learn to prepare for a post-racial, multicultural landscape.[72] The United States is truly an immigrant nation and will become even more so over the next several decades. Some, such as Patrick Buchanan, believe that waves of illegal immigration and short-sighted immigration policies in general will transform the U.S. into a Third World country and be the death knell for America's superpower status.[73] Others are more sanguine, believing that immigration will keep the United States relatively young, dynamic, and outward looking.[74] How governments and civil society react to this immigration phenomenon, and how well prepared these new immigrants are to adapt to life in the U.S. and contribute to the country's competitiveness, will go a long way toward determining the global status of the United States in 2050.

Federalism

An oft-repeated aphorism states: "As California goes, so goes the nation." Long perceived as a trendsetter for America as a whole, California has now fallen on hard times, experiencing a double-digit unemployment rate during the Great Recession and governance reminiscent of the silent-film era's Keystone Cops. The same label may also be applied to New York, Illinois, New Jersey, Nevada, and several other state and local governments.[75] Governance at the state level is critical for the future success, or lack of success, of the entire nation. California, for example, was the eighth largest "national" economy in the world in 2008 measured by the production of goods and services, and the state government's 2009 budget of $145 billion was only slightly smaller than Mexico's and significantly larger than most of the one hundred largest nation-states in the world. New York's budget in 2009 was $132 billion, even though its population of 19.3 million was only half the size of California's. As will be examined in more detail in Chapter 8, state governments are potentially significant economic players on the global stage, but they must maintain vibrant political and economic systems in order to remain competitive.

Attention so far in this book has been focused on the national government in Washington, D.C. However, the United States is included among the two dozen nations in the world that have federal systems dividing authority constitutionally between the national and regional governments. In addition to the fifty states, there are almost eighty-eight thousand distinct governmental units within the U.S. federal system, ranging from the national government headquartered in Washington, D.C., to mosquito abatement special districts in rural Nevada. Included in this list are more than three thousand county and 19,400 municipal governments.

In political terms, only the state governments may formally share authority with Washington, D.C., with the Tenth Amendment to the Constitution stipulating that all power not explicitly delegated to the national government be "reserved" to the states and the people. From its beginnings as a relatively small nation with thirteen states sequestered along the Atlantic seaboard, the United States grew immensely in territory through wise expenditures such as the Louisiana and Alaska purchases, through exploration and claiming of new lands to the west, and, at times, through the threatened or actual use of military force such as stripping Mexico of half of its land and then annexing it into the United States. Arkansas entered the Union as the twenty-fifth state in 1836, and the final territory of the contiguous or continental United States to become a formal "state," able to share governmental authority with Washington, D.C., was Arizona in 1912. Ironically, Arizona was once part of Mexico, as were Texas, California, Utah, Colorado, and New Mexico. In 1959, Alaska and Hawaii, the latter being a group of Pacific islands that late in the nineteenth century had been taken over by an armed band of Americans and later annexed by Washington, became the forty-ninth and fiftieth states respectively. Even though Alaska and Hawaii are situated far from the continental portion of the country, they are accorded the same rights and privileges as the "lower forty-eight" states.

The U.S. federal system is complicated even further by the presence of over 560 officially recognized tribal governments, each exercising some degree of sovereignty and autonomy and many being formally recognized as "domestic dependent nations."[76] As Erich Steinman asserts, "Tribal governments are now visible and active as a category of government within the boundaries of the United States," even though "tribes have long been anomalies within American governance."[77] The U.S. Bureau of Indian Affairs, which has a mostly checkered history in representing the interests of Native Americans, helps to manage fifty-six million acres of land held in trust for American Indians, Indian tribes, and Alaska natives. Occasionally, the interests of tribal and state governments conflict and U.S. federal courts will normally render the final decision in these intergovernmental disputes.

Arguably, the American system of federalism and representation does not always optimize true democratic practices. If democracy is based on the premise of "one person, one vote" and the equality of each vote, then the U.S. system has fallen short, and not just in historical terms, of denying suffrage to African-Americans and all women for so many decades. In blunt terms, the founding fathers never did trust the average citizen who was without property and lacked a formal education. As a result, the Electoral College was created, giving the ultimate authority to select a president and vice president to a group of electors who were presumably both propertied and educated. This system remains in effect today even though conditions among the general voting population have changed dramatically. A voter in Wyoming now has much more political clout than a voter in California because of the continued existence of the Electoral College, which determines the allocation of electors on the basis of the number of senators and representatives from each state. If true equality of voting had existed in 2000 and the winner had been selected on the basis of receiving the most votes nationwide, Al Gore would have become president instead of George W. Bush. Instead, what many critics consider an antiquated system remains in place, in part because of federalism. Surveys consistently indicate that many Americans would prefer a voting system based on the direct election of the president and vice president, but this would require a constitutional amendment and sparsely populated states, which benefit disproportionally from the Electoral College, would likely reject any such effort.[78]

In recent decades, many governors have felt that federalism has tilted too much in favor of Washington, D.C. In 1995, two moderate governors, Republican Michael Leavitt of Utah and Democrat Ben Nelson of Nebraska, attempted to organize a Conference of the States that would demand the strengthening of the Tenth Amendment and push for a transfer of some authority away from Washington and toward the state capitals. The meeting was to be convened in Philadelphia, with each state represented by its governor and four legislators. Ironically, this meeting would have been the first full conference of the states to discuss constitutional issues since the historic 1787 meeting in Philadelphia. Initially, momentum seemed to be on the side of these governors, because many leaders in the states and some in Washington were advocating a "devolution revolution." However, both the left and the right on the political spectrum began to have second thoughts about the conference, and eventually the governors had to scale back their expectations and agree to a watered-down States' Federalism Conference that met in Cincinnati in the autumn of 1995. Critics worried that the proposed Philadelphia meeting, which would bring together the fifty constituent state governments, could be transformed into a real constitutional convention resulting in major changes to the supreme governing document, much as had occurred in 1787 when the Articles of Confederation was torn up and replaced by an entirely new constitution. Municipal government representatives were also unhappy, because they were not invited to take part in the proceedings.

Today, most governors and state legislative leaders continue to insist that Washington has usurped too much authority that should rightfully belong to the states in education, health care, the environment, regulatory issues, control over the National Guard, and several other areas.[79] They also continue to complain about unfunded mandates in which Washington orders the state governments to do something without sufficient financial compensation to carry out the mandates. In addition, they argue that the explosive immigration issue is a federal responsibility, but state and local governments are being saddled with most of the financial burden for educating and providing medical and other services to the millions of undocumented immigrants residing in the country. One of the most vitriolic rebukes by state officials of the federal government came when Congress and the White House worked together in 2006 to change the two-hundred-year-old Insurrection Act and give the president greater control over the use of state-level National Guard units for emergencies within the United States. All fifty governors, joined by the governor of Puerto Rico, lambasted the action and condemned it as "a dramatic expansion of federal authority."[80] Republican Governor Mike Huckabee of Arkansas, acting as co-chair of the National Governors' Association, claimed the legislation "violates two hundred years of American history" and is symptomatic of a larger federal effort to make states no more than "satellites of the national government."[81] Iowa Democratic Governor Tom Vilsack added that the legislation is "one step away from a complete takeover of the National Guard, the end of the Guard as a dual-function force that can respond to both state and national needs."[82]

The National Guard episode is also emblematic of the diminishing voice of state leaders within the Beltway. Many ruefully observe that state governments are treated as just another interest group by members of Congress, even though they are co-equal with Washington according to the Constitution. Prior to the passage of the Seventeenth Amendment in 1913, the two U.S. senators for each state were selected by the state legislature and not directly by the people. Knowing that they were answerable to the state legislature, senators listened very intently to the demands of their state capitals. Currently, however, many senators are considered more as free agents or national political figures. They are not reliant on state legislatures or governors for support, and frequently they raise more money out of state than in state for their reelection campaigns. Both governors and state legislative leaders wonder whether the states have any clout within Washington, D.C., and if true federalism ends whenever one enters the Beltway's boundaries.

The United States in the second decade of the twenty-first century manifests only sporadic episodes of cooperative federalism. On the other hand, are the state governments also at fault? In an ideal federal system, state governments act as laboratories of democracy and successful best practices in one state may then be carried over to other states or to the national government. The recent fiscal and governance disasters in California, New York, Illinois, Louisiana, and some other states are reminiscent of the mess in Washington, D.C. Are there mini-Beltways scattered across the vast expanse of the U.S.A.?

For example, how can California be considered as governable when budgets and tax increases must both be passed by a two-thirds vote in the bicameral legislature and where well-financed special interest groups can ignore Sacramento entirely by having their pet projects approved through the initiative process?[83] Why is California stuck with a constitution that is eight times longer than the U.S. Constitution? How can the part-time legislators in Albany be truly responsive to New York residents when they gerrymander their election districts, set aside almost $200 million for a legalized form of vote-buying known as "member items," and pad their own staff at a cost of $230 million per year?[84] From 1980 through 2002, only thirty-eight incumbents seeking re-election in both New York state chambers were not returned to office during the entire twenty-two-year period, and from 2002 through 2006, the re-election rate of incumbents was at least 96 percent or above.[85] How can Illinois function effectively if the governor is openly selling his influence to the highest bidder and where four governors have been convicted of major crimes since 1973?[86] Louisiana may have the most tarnished reputation of all, and one need only recall the famous line of ex-governor and now-convicted felon Edwin Edwards, who once quipped that the only way he could ever lose re-election "is if I were found in bed with a dead girl or live boy."[87]

State and local governments are also engaged in their own internal competition wars that often come at the expense of sound economic policy for the nation as a whole. Almost all U.S. state, county, and municipal governments have established economic development agencies to attract domestic and foreign-owned companies to their areas of jurisdiction or keep them from closing existing facilities within their boundaries.[88] In particular, each state goes it alone in an effort to attract Foreign Direct Investment (FDI) from abroad, and this spawns bidding wars among the states and in local communities, helping major foreign auto companies in particular to reap hundreds of millions of dollars in incentives. In one case, the executives of a German auto company and the German chancellor requested that governors from southeastern states travel to Germany and, while there, present their final incentive packages to the German auto-maker.[89] This is a very serious game, because the United States at the end of 2008 had been the recipient of $2.6 trillion in FDI, and foreign central banks and other overseas investors controlled over $23 trillion in U.S. assets.[90] Roughly six million Americans also work for foreign-controlled companies on U.S. soil, and these subsidiaries of foreign corporations are much more likely to export than their American-owned counterparts and pay higher hourly wages.[91] State and local governments distribute roughly $50 billion in incentives to domestic and foreign-owned companies every year, and their right to do so was upheld in a Supreme Court decision rendered in May 2006.[92] Although the decision was a victory for states' rights, it is regrettable that so many incentives are handed out by these constituent governments because (1) in almost all cases, FDI will come to the United States without any incentives in order for foreign businesses to secure or expand their positions in the world's largest national market, (2) incentives invariably favor one company over other companies in the same or related business sectors, (3) incentives are given at the expense of taxpayers and public-sponsored programs such as education, and (4) government incentives clearly distort the market system that most Americans consider to be the hallmark of the U.S. economy.

The federal system may also be giving short shrift to the immense urban problems facing the United States. For the first time in human civilization, a majority of the planet's inhabitants now live in urban areas, compared with only 10 percent in 1900.[93] In the United States, more than four of every five residents are urban dwellers, up dramatically from less than one in three in 1900.[94] Three-quarters of Americans also live in metropolitan regions with populations exceeding a quarter of a million people.

As illustrated in Figure IV: 1, metropolitan areas account for almost 86 percent of total U.S. employment, 90 percent of labor income, and 87 percent of GDP. Figure IV: 2 indicates that the major urban areas in the United States produce more in goods and services annually than most of the world's nation-states. Indeed, forty-two U.S. metro areas, measured by GDP, would have ranked among the hundred largest national economies in the world in 2005.[95] In addition, the major metropolitan areas also produce far more than many of the U.S. states. For example in 2005, the top ten metro regions together produced more than the combined GDP of thirty-five states.[96]

FIGURE IV: 1

U.S. Metro Areas' Share of U.S. Total Employment, Income, and GDP, 2006

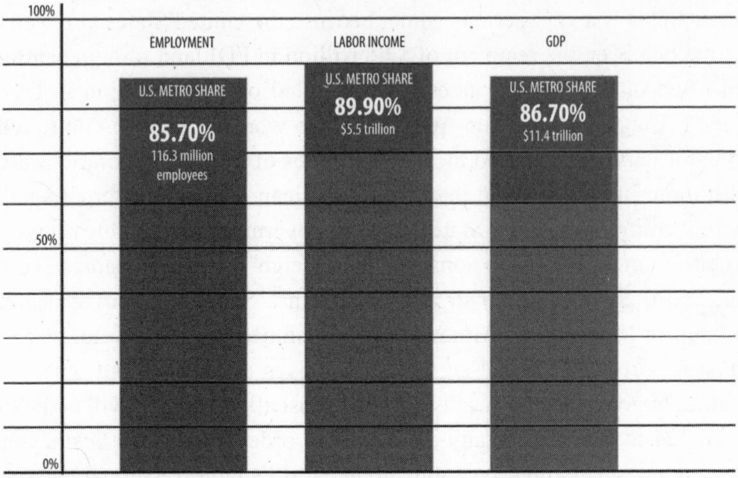

	EMPLOYMENT	LABOR INCOME	GDP
	U.S. METRO SHARE **85.70%** 116.3 million employees	U.S. METRO SHARE **89.90%** $5.5 trillion	U.S. METRO SHARE **86.70%** $11.4 trillion

Sources: U.S. Conference of Mayors and *Global Insight.*

Although all parts of the country will need to contribute, the future competitiveness of the United States will largely be determined within its urban surroundings. The vast American landscape is a study in contrasts. In their important study, Burd-Sharps, Lewis, and Martins apply a Human Development Index (HDI) to the United States, mostly linked to health, knowledge, and income indicators.[97] Using longitudinal data, the authors estimate that there is a thirty-year gap in the Human Development Index for Connecticut and Mississippi, meaning that Mississippi will take three decades to catch up to Connecticut's current HDI.[98] Residents in the congressional district with the highest HDI, located on the upper east side of Manhattan, earn over three times as much, live 4.5 years longer, and are ten times more likely to have college degrees than residents of the district with the lowest HDI, which is located around Fresno, California.[99] Even more astonishing, another congressional district in New York City, located in the Bronx only five kilometers or five subway stops from the Manhattan district, is estimated to be fifty-six years behind its Manhattan counterpart in terms of HDI development.[100]

Most of the K–12 educational problems are in urban areas, especially core cities within major metropolitan regions. Many of the infrastructure deficiencies are also urban-based. Much of the nation's poverty is concentrated in cities, as are many of its health-care problems. One in six city

Figure IV: 2 If U.S. Metro Areas Were Nations: Comparative Production of Goods and Services, 2005		
Metro Area	Billions of Dollars	(Billions of Dollars)
New York	953	10th behind Canada (1114)
Los Angeles–Long Beach	605	17th behind the Netherlands (624)
Chicago	422	17th ahead of Belgium (371)
Washington, D.C.	300	24th behind Poland (303)
Dallas	285	26th behind Indonesia (287)
Philadelphia	265	26th behind Indonesia (287)
Houston	244	27th behind Denmark (259)
Boston	241	27th behind Denmark (259)
San Francisco	214	29th behind Greece (225)
Atlanta	212	29th ahead of Ireland (202)
Miami	206	29th ahead of Ireland (202)
Detroit	178	36th behind Thailand (177)
Seattle	158	36th behind Thailand (177)
Phoenix–Mesa	153	36th behind Thailand (177)
Minneapolis–St. Paul	152	36th behind Thailand (177)
San Diego	143	36th ahead of Venezuela (140)
Riverside–San Bernardino	133	37th behind Venezuela (140)
Baltimore	122	41st behind Israel (123)
Denver	116	43rd behind Singapore (117)
Tampa–St. Petersburg	111	44th behind Chile (115)
St. Louis	109	47th behind Hungary (109)
Pittsburgh	96	51st behind Romania (99)
San Jose	94	51st behind Romania (99)
Sacramento	92	51st ahead of Egypt (89)
Cleveland	87	52nd behind Egypt (89)
Portland	86	52nd behind Egypt (89)
Orlando	84	52nd ahead of Ukraine (83)
Cincinnati	82	53rd behind Urkraine (83)
Las Vegas	79	55th behind Peru (79)
Virginia Beach–Norfolk	79	55th behind Peru (79)

Sources: World Bank, U.S. Conference of Mayors, and *Global Insight*.

dwellers has chosen to live in private ownership cooperatives or home associations, often with guarded gates or personnel at front desks who screen entrants, in part to shield the occupants from what is going on around them in the topsy-turvy urban environment.[101] Metropolitan-wide planning is in short supply in most urban regions, and intergovernmental cooperation among cities, states, and Washington, D.C., is sporadic at best. America's federal system faces perhaps its biggest test since the Civil War as all levels of government confront the myriad challenges linked to globalization and growing competition from abroad.

General Apathy and a Paucity of Civic Engagement

The most decisive battle of the U.S. Civil War was fought 1–3 July 1863 at Gettysburg, Pennsylvania. During that conflict, Union and Confederate casualties may have exceeded fifty thousand. If he had won the battle, Robert E. Lee would have had an open road to Washington, D.C., and the outcome of the Civil War may have changed dramatically.

Abraham Lincoln traveled to Gettysburg on 19 November 1863 and rendered homage to those who had paid the ultimate price during this famous battle. In his very short but poignantly eloquent Gettysburg Address, Lincoln said the following:

> It is rather for us to be here dedicated to the great task remaining before us—that from these honored dead we take increased devotion to that cause for which they gave the last measure of devotion—that we here highly resolve that these dead shall not have died in vain—that this nation, under God, shall have a new birth of freedom—and that government of the people, by the people, for the people, shall not perish from the earth.

Today, Americans need to ask themselves if they have the government alluded to in Lincoln's famous address. Are they far too apathetic and complacent to demand the changes needed to right the ship of state and experience a "new birth of freedom?"[102]

The presidential election of 2008 was historic in that the first African-American was selected as the president of the United States. If Barack Obama had not won the Democratic nomination, then it was highly likely that the first woman, Hillary Clinton, would have been elected to the Oval Office. More Americans than ever before cast ballots, and 65.2 percent of eligible voters turned out on election day compared with 60.3 percent in 2004.

The big question that remains is where was everyone else, and why is U.S.-voter participation among the lowest in the Western world? Only

131 million of 206 million eligible voters actually voted that day. What will it take to convince Americans across the country and from all walks of life to participate in the American governmental system? After all, the nation was losing jobs and mired in what would be the most severe economic recession since the Great Depression. The United States was engaged in a two-front war in Iraq and Afghanistan. Ninety percent of those surveyed stated that their country was headed in the wrong direction.[103] The incumbent, George W. Bush, received the highest disapproval rating, 71 percent, since the Gallup Poll began its surveys in the 1930s.[104] Members of Congress received their lowest approval rating since Gallup began asking that question in 1974.[105] In spite of their unhappiness and distress, voters returned over 90 percent of all incumbents who sought reelection to Congress on 4 November. These incumbents then carried on business as usual with their familiar lobbyists and special interests that were standing in line to get their share of the largest budget ever enacted by any government anywhere in the world.

Americans generally treat politics as a spectator sport, one in which few have much of an interest, sort of like bowling, and not recognizing that their own futures are at stake. As Les Gelb laments: "The United States is declining as a nation and a world power with mostly sighs and shrugs to mark this seismic event. Astonishingly, some people do not appear to realize that the situation is all that serious."[106] More than seven in ten U.S. adults flunk a basic test in civics. For example, only 49 percent can name the three branches of government.[107] The genesis of the problem begins in U.S. public schools, where offerings in American history and civics are generally abysmal, and universities are not much better. In the most recent National Assessment of Education Progress tests on civics, 24 percent of fourth graders, 22 percent of eighth graders, and 27 percent of twelfth graders were deemed as being proficient.[108] Two-thirds of high school seniors did not comprehend the meaning of a photo showing a theater whose portal read: "Colored Entrance." Forty-five percent could not understand the basic instructions on a sample ballot, and only 5 percent could explain checks on presidential power. Only one in seven could identify a reason why the United States fought in the Korean War.[109] Colleges and universities do little to improve the understanding of American history and institutions, with seniors recording just 1.5 percent higher on administered tests than incoming freshmen. At elite universities, the improvement is only 1 percent over the four years of classroom work.[110]

Clichés are rampant concerning the possible consequences of an apathetic citizenry. On a very somber note, Edmund Burke warned: "All that is necessary for the triumph of evil is that good men do nothing."[111] At the dawn of the twentieth century, Mark Twain extolled the virtues of voting: "But in this country we have one great privilege which they don't have in other countries. When a thing gets to be absolutely unbearable the people can rise up and throw it off. That's the finest asset we've got—the ballot box."[112] But Twain warned that voting was not enough: "Every citizen of the republic ought to consider himself an unofficial policeman, and keep unsalaried watch and ward over the laws and their execution."[113] Will Rogers would have seconded Twain's admonition, as he often noted that "I don't make jokes. I just watch the government and report the facts."[114] Louis D. Brandeis shared this admonition with his fellow Americans: "The most important political office is that of the private citizen."[115]

At the close of the historic Constitutional Convention of 1787, Benjamin Franklin was asked: "Well, Doctor, what have we got—a Republic or a Monarchy?" Franklin replied: "A Republic, if you can keep it."[116] The future greatness of the United States largely will be determined by the quality of its citizens and their active participation in the governance of the nation. They now have a superpower, but can they keep it?

Chapter 5

An Unsustainable U.S. Foreign Policy

Introduction

U.S. foreign policy represents America's thirteenth major fault line, and if foreign policy is conducted in the same way as it has been over the past decade, it will definitely hasten the demise of the U.S. superpower. As Leslie Gelb has warned in a hard-hitting essay, the United States is suffering from "diminished economic strength, a less vital democracy, and a mediocrity of spirit," adding that the U.S. has used its international power "ineffectively."[1]

In his book *The Rise and Fall of the Great Powers,* published in 1987, Paul Kennedy predicted that the United States would follow the direction of previous superpowers and overextend itself abroad, resulting in its decline as the preeminent world actor[2]; this is now occurring.[3] In a variety of ways to be discussed later, Washington's response to the horrific events of 9/11 was abysmal. The war in Iraq has been an ill-fated venture and has not only cost thousands of American lives but will drain trillions from the Treasury in prosecuting the war, assisting Iraq financially, helping injured soldiers over their lifetimes, and revamping and replacing very expensive military equipment used in the conflict. Even more astonishingly, the world's sole superpower became bogged down in one of its longest wars ever, occupying and trying to pacify a small developing country with almost ideal terrain for fighting traditional conventional warfare (unlike Vietnam), with a population base far smaller than California's, and with a GDP half that of America's smallest state economy, Vermont.[4] Tragically, President Obama has now made a blunder of the first order by escalating U.S. involvement in Afghanistan's unwinnable conflict. The open-ended and ill-defined War on Terror will also cost countless dollars and needlessly place American military personnel in harm's way in various parts of the world.

America Overburdened at Home and Abroad

As President Dwight D. Eisenhower prepared to turn over command of the Oval Office to President-elect John F. Kennedy in 1961, he strongly emphasized that America was bearing too much of the burden in trying to defend so much of the world.[5] Earlier, Ike, the great general who had commanded all allied forces in Europe during World War II, had also warned that too much defense spending would do harm to America's economic foundations:

Let us not forget that the armed services are to defend a way of life, not merely land, property or lives. What is needed is a balance between the minimum requirements in costly implements of war and the health of our economy.[6]

Those words could be repeated today, and they characterize the entire period since World War II. In 2008, the United States spent $607 billion or 41.5 percent of the world's combined $1.46 trillion in annual defense spending, even though it represents less than 5 percent of the global population and about one-fifth of its GDP (see Figure V:1).[7] In fiscal year 2009, U.S. defense spending jumped to $654 billion, and in 2010, the defense allocation increased once again to $680 billion: $550 billion for the basic Pentagon budget and an additional $130 billion to finance the ongoing conflicts in Iraq and Afghanistan.

In the entire history of the country, the Bush doctrine enunciated in September 2002 stands out as having made the boldest foreign policy assumptions and advancing the most ambitious claims.[8] The doctrine called

FIGURE V: 1
Ten Largest Military Budgets, 2008

RANK	COUNTRY	SPENDING ($ b.)	WORLD SHARE (%)
1	USA	607	41.5
2	China	84.9	5.8
3	France	65.7	4.5
4	UK	65.3	4.5
5	Russia	58.6	4.0
6	Germany	46.8	3.2
7	Japan	46.3	3.2
8	Italy	40.6	2.8
9	Saudi Arabia	38.2	2.6
10	India	30.0	2.1

World total **1464** **100.0**

Source: SIPRI, *Military Spending and Armaments*, 2008, 11.

for "an American protectorate of the interstate system for an indefinite period of time," a protectorate premised on American primacy and the right of the U.S. to engage in preemptive warfare against those perceived as major threats to this system.[9] Even in the post-Bush era, the United States has pledged to defend Europe, North America, parts of Asia, the Pacific, and the Middle East, and has agreed to consider any attack on these areas as tantamount to an attack on the United States itself. The United States has a network of an estimated one thousand military bases and other installations in more than 130 countries.[10] These bases are home to more than a half million American military and civilian personnel and their dependents.[11] When one includes the deployment of U.S. naval vessels as part of the nation's eleven aircraft carrier task forces, an American military presence is found in or near most of the world's two hundred or so nations, and plans are under way to increase the number of U.S. ground forces and continue to produce the most modern and expensive weapon systems known to humankind. America's unilateral propensity in carrying out its international commitments simply adds to the great burden borne by American taxpayers.[12] The Iraq War quagmire has been a coalition effort in name only, with Americans incurring over 90 percent of all expenses and almost 90 percent of all fatalities. Quite bluntly, U.S. global military commitments are unsustainable over a long period of time when placed within the context of debilitating U.S. domestic problems, growing competition from abroad, and the changing dynamics of globalization.

Madeleine Albright referred to the United States as the "world's indispensable nation."[13] Unfortunately, as the U.S. goes deeper in debt at home and begins to fall behind other nations in a number of competitive arenas, it is still spending more than ever before in its efforts to remain indispensable, in a unilateral fashion, on the global stage. War, of course, is a horrific experience in terms of the loss of lives and injuries to military personnel. It is also an extremely expensive proposition. In assessing what they believe will be the $3 trillion in long-term costs of the war in Iraq, Joseph Stiglitz and Linda Bilmes reach this stark conclusion:

> Going to war is not to be undertaken lightly. It is an act that should be undertaken with greater sobriety, greater solemnity, greater care, and greater reserve than any other. Stripped of the relentless media and government fanfare, the nationalist flag-waving, the reckless bravado, war is about men and women brutally killing and maiming other men and women. The costs live on long after the last shot has been fired.[14]

The United States has intervened militarily in foreign countries more than one hundred times since the beginning of Ronald Reagan's presidency.[15] The costs and complexities of U.S. international involvement are multiplied because of America's forward-deterrence policy and its commitment to treat the invasion of over thirty countries around the world as equivalent to an invasion of the U.S. mainland. Rather implicitly or explicitly, America's collective security commitment now includes all NATO countries, Japan, Israel, Australia, New Zealand, South Korea, Iraq, Afghanistan, Saudi Arabia, and Taiwan. If the Bush administration had convinced the other NATO signatories to follow its advice, the security blanket would have been extended to Ukraine and Georgia. Some might also argue that, under certain circumstances, U.S. forces might intervene to protect India, Pakistan, Singapore, Thailand, Mexico, and several European countries not affiliated with NATO. U.S. global commitments, especially in the military sector, have become inordinately expensive, and Uncle Sam is treated as Uncle Sucker by most of the allies when it is a matter of equitable burden-sharing.

Post–9/11 "Homeland Security" a Big Mess

America's downward trajectory has been accelerated by policies implemented in response to the terrible attacks on New York City and the Washington, D.C., area on 11 September 2001. On that day, almost three thousand people from ninety countries were killed by the nineteen al-Qaeda terrorists who had hijacked four commercial aircraft. Much of the rest of the world rallied to America's cause, and the left-wing *Le Monde* newspaper in Paris proclaimed in a front-page article that "we are all Americans."[16] NATO invoked for the first time in its history Article 5 of its charter that required all members to come to the assistance of another member under siege, namely the United States of America. The world was ready to support the United States in its afflictions and its campaign to track down Osama bin Laden and his terrorist band.

The Bush administration, working with a compliant Congress, then proceeded to alienate many of America's allies, engage in a needless war, fall prey to an inane neoconservative perspective of the Middle East and Islam, openly flaunt several international agreements such as the Geneva Conventions, and brush aside basic tenets in the U.S. Bill of Rights.

As will be discussed later, Washington was totally justified in its efforts to track down al-Qaeda in Afghanistan. The U.S. mainland had been attacked for the first time since 1814 and U.S. territory for the first time since

Hawaii, the Philippines, and Guam in 1941. The United States had every right to defend itself and to retaliate. However, Iraq was altogether different and had nothing to do with 9/11. This was a war of choice against a nation that was not a direct threat to the United States.

At home, the creation of the Department of Homeland Security (DHS) turned out to be a major policy miscalculation. DHS was intended to bring about greater cooperation among agencies and avoid the interagency squabbles that were rampant between such organizations as the FBI and CIA prior to the attacks on 9/11. Instead, DHS became the largest reorganization of government since 1947, and many more layers of bureaucracy have been added to what was already an unwieldy decision-making process. Today, DHS is composed of twenty-two agencies with more than 200,000 employees. Its first great test of homeland security was Hurricane Katrina in 2005, and DHS failed miserably.

When Tom Ridge became the first secretary of DHS in 2002, he attempted to enhance security but was always mindful that life needed to be as normal as possible for U.S. businesses and the American public. For example, he helped to negotiate a reasonable Smart Borders Agreement with Canada, America's largest trading partner and leading source of foreign tourists. Unfortunately, once Ridge left and was succeeded by Michael Chertoff, DHS's philosophy was radicalized and security became the number-one concern even if the U.S. economy had to suffer and Americans were inconvenienced. DHS swung toward worst-case scenarios instead of prudent, policy-balancing security concerns, with the need to keep the U.S. economy thriving. Airport security was beefed up substantially, but more for appearance's sake than for sound policy reasons. The lessons to be learned from 9/11 were actually quite simple: fortify airplane cockpit doors, ensure that box cutters and the like could not get through screening, add air marshals on selected flights, and involve U.S. passengers who should never again take for granted that a hijacking would wind up in Havana. This last lesson was already applied by the heroic passengers on United Flight 93 on 9/11. Their plane was hijacked by four terrorists, and through cell phones, the passengers knew what had happened to the World Trade Center in New York City and the Pentagon in Arlington, Virginia. The thirty-three passengers and seven crew members surmised that the same fate was in store for them, and they acted to take back control of their plane. While on that flight, Tom Burnett phoned his wife, Deena, and told her "We're all going to die, but three of us are going to do something. I love you, honey."[17] Tragically, the plane did indeed crash in a field in rural Pennsylvania, but the hijackers had been thwarted from hitting their target, presumably the White House or Congress.

Collectively, passengers now spend millions of hours annually standing in long lines at airports and going through a laborious screening process.[18] Yet, the screening of what is placed in the plane's cargo hold under the passengers is much less thorough, as is the monitoring of employees and vendors who work at the airports and have direct access to the planes.[19] Fortunately, the cockpit doors have been fortified, more armed marshals are flying, and some passengers remain vigilant after they take their seats. The initial screening process could be streamlined significantly, but DHS is in no hurry to accommodate passengers or common sense in general. These time-consuming and at times humiliating procedures have also helped to decimate a once-vibrant U.S. airline industry. Potential passengers now take into consideration traveling to airports that are almost invariably located in the suburbs, arriving two hours in advance of the flight, enduring the screening process, landing at the destination airport in the suburbs, and then traveling downtown. If they can make the same trip from home to their destination within four hours by car, train, or bus, they often nix the flight option. Moreover, in comparison to the cumbersome screening procedures for passengers at airports, only cursory examinations are made of trains, buses, or containerized cargo on big ships. Damage that could be caused by terrorists using these modes of transportation would be almost as destructive as using airplanes as a form of guided missiles.[20]

DHS has also overestimated the capacity of al-Qaeda or related groups to inflict damage on the United States. The events of 9/11 were horrible, just as the previous attack on the World Trade Center in 1993 was terrible. Nevertheless, al-Qaeda is a ragtag group hiding in the mountainous areas of Afghanistan and Pakistan[21]; it is not the Empire of Japan that attacked Pearl Harbor on 7 December 1941. A sense of proportionality has evaded DHS and American leaders in general. Good intelligence, enhanced cooperation with allies, and periodic special operations or predator attacks will all be needed to quell the threat from al-Qaeda and its imitators. Tragically, the fixation with Islamic terrorism in general has resulted in Washington doing more harm than necessary to the U.S. economy, curtailing some of the freedoms of the American people, and not doing enough to combat a threat that has killed far more Americans than al-Qaeda, namely international organized crime.

The post–9/11 costs of U.S. government policies are staggering. Global tourism took a hit following 9/11 but recovered quickly. The same cannot be said for the United States that essentially removed the welcome mat for foreign visitors by imposing onerous visa and passport restrictions for business representatives, tourists, and students alike. In Brazil, for example, people wanting to visit the United States may have to travel over sixteen hundred kilometers (one thousand miles) within their own country for a personal visa interview. Business groups in Latin America and elsewhere that used to make regular trips to the United States were suddenly denied visas.[22] Las Vegas hotels that would charter planes for well-heeled gamblers in South Korea were suddenly told that the U.S. government would no longer offer them an expedited visa process.[23] Some local authorities ruefully complained that the War on Terror had morphed into the war on tourism. In 2000, 689 million people around the world crossed national borders for tourism purposes and they spent $476 billion, according to the UN-affiliated World Tourism Organization. In 2008, international tourism was up to 922 million people, about a one-third increase, and tourism spending almost doubled to $944 billion.[24] The United States was riding high in the year 2000, attracting 51.2 million foreign visitors who spent $103 billion for transportation and tourist-related activities in the U.S. In 2003, well after 9/11, the number of foreign visitors had plummeted by ten million from the 2000 level, and those who came spent $23 billion less than visitors in 2000.[25] The U.S. Travel Industry Association asserts that Washington's disdain toward foreign visitors, and the ponderous visa requirements, resulted in the U.S. losing 58.6 million international tourists between 2001 and 2005, costing $94 billion in tourism-related revenues and 194,000 American jobs.[26] By 2008, international visitors were returning again to the United States, but the fifty-eight million visitors were up by less than seven million from 2000, and expenditures were up by only 40 percent in nominal terms to $142 billion.[27] These post–9/11 losses attributable to short-sighted policies are even more glaring when one takes into account that travel and tourism represent 8 percent of total U.S. exports and 26 percent of all U.S. services exports.[28] Furthermore, these losses do not take into account the number of very bright foreign students who did not matriculate in the U.S. because of visa and other regulatory barriers or the number of scientists and others among the best and brightest in the world who found the new U.S. barriers to entry too burdensome or too humiliating.

What the Bush administration did after 9/11 was totally antithetical to Franklin D. Roosevelt's proclamation during the Great Depression that "the only thing we have to fear is fear itself." Americans were made to be fearful and distrustful of anything foreign, and a new "cottage industry of scaremongering" was permitted to flourish.[29] Americans were warned about terrorist sleeper cells that might be lurking in the neighborhood or around the corner.[30] They were told that their fellow citizens might be in league with the terrorists, and, thus, there was a need for domestic wiretapping and other intrusive surveillance techniques that called into question the preservation of liberty and privacy under the Bill of Rights.[31] They were informed that torture and secret prisons were acceptable, because the means justified the end of fending off any future terrorist attacks on U.S. soil.[32] Vice President Cheney tried to quash domestic opposition to the War on Terror by claiming that the critics were "validating the strategy of the terrorists."[33] As Zakaria correctly surmises, "Too many Americans have been taken in by a rhetoric of fear."[34] He further laments:

America has become a nation consumed by anxiety, worried about terrorists and rogue nations, Muslims and Mexicans, foreign companies and free trade, immigrants and international organizations. The strongest nation in the history of the world now sees itself as besieged by forces beyond its control.[35]

Americans have always been very fortunate in geopolitical terms because they have been sheltered from many of the intrigues of history. A former French ambassador to the U.S. spoke of this advantage: "On the north, she has a weak neighbor; on the south, another weak neighbor; on the east, fish; and on the west, fish."[36] How Belgium or the Netherlands would have liked some of this geographical isolation during the two great wars of the twentieth century. Reportedly, an ambassador from the Middle East region, on pondering the implications of America's geopolitical advantages, lamented that his own country has a weak neighbor to the north but sharks everywhere else.

Unfortunately, the siege mentality cultivated by Washington and some in the media after 9/11 has carried over to America's own borders, resulting in a serious disruption in the effort to rationalize the North American economy so that it would become more competitive vis-à-vis economic rivals across the Atlantic and the Pacific. The borders to the south and north were "thinning" prior to 9/11 because of the North American Free Trade Agreement (NAFTA) that went into effect in 1994 and was fully implemented over a fifteen-year period. After 9/11, that process reversed and resulted in a noticeable thickening of the two borders. Canada has been the leading trading partner of the United States for each and every year since the end of World War II. The U.S. exports only slightly less to Canada with its thirty-four million people than to the twenty-seven-nation European Union with a half billion people. Mexico is the second-largest recipient of U.S. exports, receiving more U.S. products annually than China and Japan combined. Canada and Mexico are also the leading sources of foreign tourists for the United States.

Prior to 9/11, some of the remote Canada–U.S. border crossings put out orange cones in the middle of the road during the night signifying that the driver was about to leave one country and enter the other. Those days are now long gone. All North Americans must now have passports to enter the United States, and Americans must also have passports to reenter the U.S. from Canada or Mexico. The big tightening began first on the border with Mexico, as thousands of new agents were hired to patrol the border and hundreds of kilometers of fence line are currently being constructed. Under plans first pursued by the Bush administration, and continued by the Obama presidency, the Border Patrol is being strengthened along the 49th parallel border with Canada. In addition, there are now drone surveillance flights, Blackhawk helicopter reconnaissance missions, and a plethora of other security measures in place. Washington may eventually spend the equivalent of two-thirds of Canada's entire defense budget on fortifying what was once known as the world's longest "undefended border."

To understand the Sisyphean task at hand, the United States shares a 3,220-kilometer (two thousand miles) border with Mexico and an 8,850-kilometer (fifty-five hundred miles) border with Canada along the 49th parallel, as well as in Alaska. The United States also has 19,920 kilometers (12,380 miles) in coastlines. Canada has the world's longest coastlines, covering 243,000 kilometers (151,000 miles), and Mexico has coastlines extending for 9,300 kilometers (5,800 miles). No matter how many Border Patrol or Coast Guard personnel are assigned, or drones or Blackhawks that observe from on high, or fences or barbed wire placed along land and water borders, the United States will never be totally secure. What is needed is a much more sensible policy to target potentially high infiltration areas for terrorists and organized crime figures. Any successful policy will also require continuous consultation with Canadian and Mexican officials and coordinated North American planning.

The strains at the two borders have also had an adverse effect on commerce, leading to the loss of hundreds of thousands of American jobs. Much of the trade in goods that occurs is intra-firm, meaning between subsidiaries of the same multinational corporation. NAFTA was intended to help General Motors, Ford, and Chrysler to rationalize their North American operations and become more competitive against overseas automakers. A typical Big Three car crosses the Canada–U.S. border a half dozen times before finally being assembled. However, with the thickening of the border leading to long lines of trucks and much more paperwork, the Big Three have been placed at a distinctive disadvantage, because their cars and trucks go through a half dozen border inspections whereas vehicles from Asia and Europe endure only one inspection. Although only one factor among many, U.S. border policy has helped put GM and Chrysler into bankruptcy and brought Ford to the brink of bankruptcy. The automakers and the Canadian government have offered reasonable solutions to part of the problem by establishing pre-clearance facilities for commercial shippers a few miles from the crowded border crossings and then having the truck doors sealed for the remaining few miles before crossing the border. DHS has stubbornly resisted the request because of its parochial mind-set. Its only concern is with keeping terrorists out of the United States no matter what the economic consequences. This same mind-set came into play when the historic Anchorage Inn was ablaze in Rouses Point, New York, a small community just across the border from Quebec. For decades, the two neighboring fire departments have rendered cross-border assistance to one another, and local officials in New York sent out the usual appeal for help. However, when this fire occurred in 2007, U.S. border agents held up the Quebec fire engines for about eight minutes, or just enough time for the inn to be totally destroyed.[37] From DHS' point of view, it had done its job; from the vantage point of most other people, this was ludicrous and self-destructive behavior. In a joint report issued in July 2009, the U.S. and Canadian Chambers of Commerce warned that in the world's largest bilateral economic relationship, the border was being transformed into a disaster area for the movement of goods and tourists.[38] Today, the bunker mentality of DHS and Washington in general stands in sharp contrast to what is transpiring in Europe. Recently, nine new members of the European Union, mostly from the former Soviet empire or the Soviet Union itself, have joined the Schengen Zone, allowing for passport-free movement through much of the European Union. Yet, Washington continues to tighten standards to an unprecedented degree for the movement of goods and people from Canada, a nation that has always been in close alliance with the United States during both the Cold War and post–Cold War periods, and with Mexico, a neighboring country desperately in need of closer economic ties with the U.S.[39] As Europe and America prepare for the special challenges of a globalized world, the European frame of mind seems to be more open and innovative than Washington's attitude toward its own North American neighbors. If America's backward-looking approach is to be changed, DHS should be dismantled as an unfortunate by-product of the post–9/11 period of paranoia and coordinating authority transferred directly to the White House.

Iraq

The painful lessons from Iraq and Afghanistan must also help guide future U.S. foreign policy. John Quincy Adams warned in 1821 that America should refrain from going abroad "in search of monsters to destroy."[40] Saddam Hussein was a brutal dictator in Iraq, but he was only one among at least a dozen megalomaniacs leading nations and exploiting their people at the time. Iraq represented no credible threat to the United States, in spite of outlandish comments from National Security Adviser Condoleezza Rice that she could see "mushroom clouds" forming on the horizon if Saddam remained in power.[41] Iraq's military capability had been decimated by the United States and its allies after Saddam's rash invasion of Kuwait in 1990. Once the Gulf War of 1991 was terminated, the United States, United Kingdom, and France set up two no-fly zones that prohibited Iraqi aircraft from penetrating airspace in the Shia-dominated south and Kurdish-dominated north. The Kurdish region was effectively free of control from Saddam's administration beginning in 1991. The unfortunate Shia uprising against Saddam in Basra in 1991 was put down ruthlessly, but with the implementation of the no-fly zone, Saddam and his mainly Sunni allies were not in full control of the southern region either. France would withdraw from participation in 1998, but the Americans and British maintained control of airspace until Bush ordered the invasion of Iraq in March 2003. The costs of maintaining the no-fly zones were modest and no manned U.S. or British aircraft was ever shot down during the period the zones were in effect. If Bush were unhappy with Saddam's policies, the zones that covered over half of Iraq's territory could have been expanded to all regions of the country except for Baghdad. Ground and logistical support could have been provided to the oppressed Shia majority in the south in an effort to weaken further Saddam's hold over what had already become a fractured Iraqi nation-state. Instead, Bush opted for a unilateral invasion, without UN approbation and in defiance of world opinion in general, and a very long period of occupation and nation-building.[42]

Bush was guided in part by the siren song of a few neoconservatives who were situated mostly in the Pentagon and Dick Cheney's office or served as special advisers to the administration. Some in this group included Paul Wolfowitz and Douglas Firth in the Pentagon, Cheney's chief of staff Lewis "Scooter" Libby, John Bolton in the State Department, and Richard Perle, an adviser to the Pentagon.[43] They fervently believed in the importance of the Middle East to global stability and considered that the United States, working informally in concert with Israel, could transform the oil-rich area into a pro-Western region. Failure to act in the Middle East, warned neoconservative academician Daniel Pipes, might eventually result in the creation of an Islamic caliphate stretching from Indonesia to Morocco and governed by Sharia law.[44] For the neoconservatives, democracy could finally be brought to Iraq through invasion and occupation, and what occurred in Japan and West Germany after World War II could be replicated in Iraq. Moreover, a pacified Iraq would then become America's beachhead for the entire Middle East. Air bases were constructed that were larger than many U.S. towns. The U.S. embassy in Baghdad is the largest and most expensive ever constructed by any country anywhere in the world. It consists of twenty-one buildings in an area the size of eighty football fields, larger than the Vatican.[45] It has enough space to accommodate over one thousand employees and is ten times larger than any other U.S. embassy.[46] This diplomatic fortress was initially intended to coordinate efforts not just in the small country of Iraq but for the Middle East as a whole. For the neoconservatives, victory in Iraq would be a major step toward bringing peace and stability to the region and ending any future Iraqi threat to Israel. Although not a neoconservative himself, Bush was persuaded by the arguments, because they coincided somewhat with his own Manichean vision of a world divided between the forces of good and evil, and he was certain that destiny had put him on the side of the guys wearing the white hats.[47] In spite of having their vision discredited because of what actually happened in Iraq, some neoconservatives are now clamoring for a U.S. invasion of Iran, using the same hackneyed arguments.[48]

The invasion of Iraq was definitely not in the U.S. national interest, and the initial error was compounded by inept political and military leadership once the occupation of Iraq had begun.[49] The occupation resulted in billions of dollars of incomplete projects and billions of dollars of missing

U.S. funds.[50] To date, more than forty-three hundred American soldiers and contractors have perished in Iraq and over thirty-one thousand have been wounded. Juan Cole, a Middle East expert at the University of Michigan, estimates that hundreds of thousands of Iraqis have died or been wounded since the U.S. invasion and more than four million have been displaced, out of a total population of twenty-eight million. He describes Iraq as "a burned-out hulk of a country, full of widows and orphans, of the unemployed and the marginalized, still infested with militias and suffering daily bombings and assassinations. The United States kicked off an ethno-religious-free-for-all that could still tear the country apart."[51]

Iraq was also the first significant war in modern times, where the American people in general were not asked to make one iota of sacrifice.[52] After 9/11, George W. Bush urged Americans to fly and visit places such as Disney World.[53] When the war effort was going badly, Bush encouraged the American people to go shopping.[54] He did not use his bully pulpit to request that citizens conserve energy and drive energy-efficient vehicles. He also instigated the greatest tax cut in modern history at the same time U.S. troops were fighting a two-front war in Iraq and Afghanistan. The only people the commander-in-chief asked to sacrifice were the full-time military, reserves, National Guard units, and their families. Instead of postponing tax cuts and funding major increases in Army and Marine personnel, Bush asked America's soldiers and Marines to deploy and then redeploy two, three, four, five, or six times to Iraq and Afghanistan. Casualties have mounted and post-traumatic stress disorder (PTSD), depression, and brain injuries may be affecting as many as one-third of all those who have fought in the Middle East.[55] Tragically, Bush asked so much, from so few, for far too long in pursuit of a vainglorious cause.

The Iraq War has brought misery to some Americans and many Iraqis. Instead of stemming terrorism, U.S. involvement in Iraq and the neoconservative vision that helped propel it have been used as major recruiting tools for Osama bin Laden and his ilk. Al-Qaeda was not present in Iraq before the invasion and the secularist Saddam Hussein looked down on al-Qaeda because of its extremist religious views. Once he was ousted, however, al-Qaeda began to make inroads in parts of Iraq. The average Iraqi, especially Shia and Kurds, had no use whatsoever for Saddam, but most abhorred the U.S. occupation. American troops are taught to kill and protect their own; they are not diplomats. Iraqis grew to resent American troops entering their homes unannounced or forcing them from the roads as convoys were passing by. They learned to despise the troops referring to Iraqis as *hajis* and wondered if the troops had any respect at all for Iraqi families, Iraqi women, and their Muslim religion. Most felt utter contempt for what happened at Abu Ghraib. From 1980 until 1988, Iraq under Saddam Hussein had fought a bloody war with Shia-dominated Iran, a war in which Iraq suffered at least 300,000 casualties. With the United States set to remove its troops from Iraq at the end of 2011, the only clear victor after the U.S. invasion and occupation that began in 2003 seems to be Iran—once Saddam's mortal enemy and still a bitter foe of the United States.

Afghanistan

In the case of Afghanistan, the initial invasion was totally justified and certainly in line with the U.S. national interest. Al-Qaeda was responsible for the terrible events of 9/11, and the Taliban government in Afghanistan was sheltering this terrorist organization. The Bush administration gave the Taliban leaders the option of expelling al-Qaeda from Afghanistan, but they adamantly refused. However, once the U.S. invasion occurred and the Taliban government was routed, Bush began to deviate from the mission of destroying al-Qaeda in order to pursue his questionable goals in Iraq. The Afghanistan mission was soon transformed into a very laborious nation-building endeavor, and the war effort has surpassed Vietnam as the longest in U.S. history—longer than U.S. involvement in World War I and World War II combined.[56]

Obama has wisely pledged to remove U.S. troops from Iraq, but he made a grave error in declaring U.S. involvement in Afghanistan "a war of necessity" and increasing the U.S. troop total in Afghanistan to 100,000. This occurred at a time when several NATO allies, which altogether had forty-two thousand troops in Afghanistan at the beginning of 2010, have warned that they will be pulling out their troops or not allowing them to be stationed in dangerous areas such as Kandahar Province or near Pakistan's Waziristan border region. In effect, Afghanistan is morphing into a unilateral U.S. occupation almost to the same extent as Iraq was. The escalation of the U.S. military presence in Afghanistan will likely become a greater policy blunder for Obama than the disastrous incursion into Iraq by Bush in view of (1) the corrupt nature of the national and provincial governments, (2) the entrenched power base of regional warlords and drug kings (with opium supplying the main source of income for much of the country), (3) the vast and mountainous Afghani terrain that is twice the size of

Iraq, (4) a destitute population that is over 70 percent illiterate but instinctively hates occupiers, and (5) the tense relations with neighboring Pakistan.

George Santayana warned that "those who do not learn from history are doomed to repeat it," and these words should be written on the door entering President Obama's Oval Office.[57] In his reflections on twentieth-century history, Tony Judt issues a similar warning to Americans who perceive that the past has nothing to teach them and adds that the U.S. "venerates its own past but pays the history of the rest of humankind insufficient attention."[58] One must be clear about the consequences of the United States remaining embroiled in the Afghan or Af-Pak (including Pakistan) conflict and occupation.[59] The Soviet Union invaded and occupied Afghanistan during the period December 1979 to February 1989. What resulted was not just utter defeat for the Soviet military but a cataclysmic event that hastened the end of the Soviet empire and later the disintegration of the Soviet Union itself. Afghanistan is pure and simple a death trap for foreign occupation forces, and the United States has shown no acumen whatsoever to avoid this lethal trap.

This does not mean the U.S. should abandon the Afghani government and people. In fiscal year 2010, the Obama administration earmarked $65 billion for the war effort in Afghanistan. To put this huge amount of money in perspective, the World Bank estimates Afghanistan had a total GDP in 2008 of $10.1 billion, smaller than the sum of goods and services produced that same year in Flint, Michigan. The cost to the United States of sending one American soldier to Afghanistan for a year is $1 million, compared with an annual cost of $12,000 for an Afghani soldier.[60] Washington can take a fraction of the $65 billion and still provide a tremendous boost to the economic well-being of the Afghanis. However, this would mean shifting the focus to providing humanitarian and development aid, placing much more emphasis on diplomatic and intelligence activity, and relying more extensively on high-tech weapons such as the unmanned predators. Afghanis, equipped with modern military equipment from the West, will have to bear the brunt of the struggle for whatever system of government they feel is worth fighting for, and American "boots on the ground" should be removed from Afghani soil in an expeditious fashion. To echo the words of General Omar Bradley when asked in May 1951 if the United States should extend the Korean War to the Chinese mainland, and applying these same words to Afghanistan today: "The wrong war, at the wrong place, at the wrong time, and with the wrong enemy."[61] Washington must abandon its occupation and nation-building strategies and instead focus single-mindedly on neutralizing

Osama bin Laden and destroying al-Qaeda, returning to the initial rationale for intervening in the region way back in October 2001.

A More Realistic Foreign Policy Agenda

The revisions needed in U.S. foreign policy should not be construed as a revival of George McGovern's plea during the Vietnam War: "Come home, America!" The United States must remain integrally involved in international affairs and play a leading role in helping to solve the problems associated with globalization and complex interdependence. In the early period of the Obama administration, public opinion toward the United States has strengthened dramatically in most parts of the world, in sharp contrast to the previous few years when America was less well regarded "than at any time in its history."[62] This renewed sense of goodwill toward the United States provides Obama with maneuvering room to shift policy away from many of the hubristic and self-destructive priorities of the previous Bush administration. It also provides an opening for the United States to revive its enviable "soft power" as a foreign policy tool, including culture, political values, personal contacts and exchanges, and active participation in institutions that help shape the global agenda.[63]

In addition, the use of military force must always remain a viable option when U.S. vital interests are in jeopardy, but diplomacy, better intelligence-gathering capabilities, and more reliance on soft-power capabilities should be moved up the foreign policy priority list.[64] The budget of the State Department has been constrained for many years, and it is ironic that there are more personnel playing instruments in military bands, and almost as many lawyers assigned to the Pentagon, as there are diplomats in the entire U.S. Foreign Service.[65] The State Department needs to move out of its shadow of being the weak sister of the Department of Defense. United States embassies and consulates abroad have been transformed into imposing walled fortresses because of the fear of terrorist attacks. While still keeping security in mind, these facilities need to be welcoming to the residents in the countries where they are located. U.S. diplomats need to be out in the local communities and making contacts and winning new friends. This new outreach effort abroad should be combined with a concerted campaign to put out the welcoming mat for foreign visitors to the United States. America's greatest strength is its people, and foreigners need to intermingle with them and see how they live, warts and all. Continued American strength abroad will simply be an extension of growing strength and vitality at home, if

Washington ever gets its act together and the American voters demand the changes needed to reverse deteriorating domestic conditions.

Although terrorism remains a clear threat, it must be placed in proper context. Following 9/11, the FBI diverted huge resources away from organized and white-collar crime to counter-terrorism. If those resources had remained intact, would organized crime have made such sweeping inroads into the United States? Would Wall Street's collapse have been mitigated somewhat by closer scrutiny of unscrupulous financiers such as Bernie Madoff or those who perpetrated the subprime crisis?[66]

Every year, illegal drugs kill an average of seventeen thousand Americans and ruin the lives of tens of thousands of other residents, a toll far beyond what the terrorists have inflicted on the United States.[67] Illicit drug activity also imposes about $160 billion in social and economic costs on the United States annually and $67 billion in direct costs.[68] Cocaine is considered to be the greatest drug threat to U.S. society, followed by meth and heroin.[69] Most of these illegal drugs are provided by organized crime cartels from Mexico, Colombia, the Dominican Republic, Cuba, parts of Asia, and Italy.[70] The U.S. Department of Justice estimates that in September 2008 there were one million gang members belonging to more than twenty thousand gangs located in all fifty states and the District of Columbia.[71] Many of these gangs have ties to international organized crime.[72] In Mexico, upwards of 450,000 residents are involved in the drug trade.[73] Denise Dresser, a Mexican political scientist, offered this grim assessment in 2009:

> Mexico is becoming a country where lawlessness prevails, where more people died in drug-related violence last year than those killed in Iraq, where the government has been infiltrated by the mafias and cartels it has vowed to combat.[74]

Just one Mexican crime family, la Familia Michoacana, is suspected of operating drug-running operations in two dozen or so American cities.[75] The U.S. Department of Justice estimates that Mexican cartels in general have expanded operations into at least 230 U.S. cities.[76] When the drug trade is combined with trafficking in persons, intellectual property violations, money laundering, and other sordid activities, the overall threat of international organized crime to the well-being of American citizens is substantially greater than the threat posed by al-Qaeda or other Middle Eastern-based groups.

Organized crime must also be viewed within the prism of what has become a very violent American society. The United States is an armed camp with 283 million privately owned firearms currently in circulation.[77] As one critic laments, the U.S. has spawned "a culture in which it is harder for me to purchase over-the-counter sinus medication than to buy a firearm at a gun show."[78] Since 9/11, 120,000 Americans have been killed by non-terror homicides, mostly committed with guns.[79] Annually, roughly sixteen thousand Americans are murdered and three thousand children shot to death.[80] The United States incarcerates 2.3 million of its residents, representing 24 percent of the world's total prisoners and more than any other country.[81] Fifty-two percent of federal prisoners are sentenced for drug offenses, and many others in all prisons or jails have either trafficked or used illegal drugs.[82] Both U.S. foreign policy and domestic crime prevention must be adjusted to reflect the nature, ferocity, and pervasiveness of this burgeoning danger.

Washington must revamp its statecraft—the art of conducting the affairs of state and how it allocates its political, economic, military, and other resources to pursue U.S. interests in a rapidly changing international environment.[83] It needs to rethink its international priorities, cast aside the three "demons" of "ideology, politics, and arrogance," jettison the illusory notion of "Pax Americana," and stop using military force as one of its first options in the conduct of foreign policy.[84] In a scathing critique, Zakaria condemns:

a Washington establishment that has gotten comfortable with the exercise of American hegemony and treats compromise as treason and negotiations as appeasement. Other countries have no legitimate interests of their own—Russian demands are by definition unacceptable. The only way to deal with countries is by issuing a series of maximalist demands. This is not foreign policy; it's imperial policy. And it isn't likely to work in today's world.[85]

Above all, policymakers must accept the fact that the world is in the midst of dramatic change, and the U.S. position on the global stage is also being transformed. For too long, Washington has been transfixed by the Middle East and its various conflicts and vast reserves of oil.[86] Within the panoply of challenges facing the U.S. specifically and the world in general, the Middle East should not be at the top of the list, nor should al-Qaeda and the Taliban, which are essentially rag-tag bankrupt organizations having absolutely no appeal in their doctrines or practices to 99 percent of all Muslims.[87] Economic and political power is gravitating from the Atlantic region to the

Pacific region, and the United States must adjust quickly to this tilt toward Asia.[88] Madeleine Albright suggests that "America's interest is to secure its place as a Pacific power in what may well become known as the Asian century."[89] U.S. ties to China must evolve in a mixed-sum fashion—meaning that both can win at the same time or both can lose, contrasted to the zero-sum adversarial game scenario—where if one wins, the other automatically loses. Europe and other parts of North America will remain critical allies for the United States politically, economically, and culturally. As for the Middle East, U.S. energy dependence on the region is actually relatively low and this should be reflected in the country's new foreign policy priorities. The United States must work with allies more dependent on Middle East oil to develop alternative sources of energy and implement sound conservation practices related to households, transportation, and businesses in general. Within two decades, new technological developments will, hopefully, result in a world less dependent on the use of fossil fuels, such as oil. If technology can eventually provide for the widespread use of coal without serious environmental consequences, the United States will be in the catbird seat because it possesses centuries of coal supplies.[90] If the same can be done with the extraction of oil and natural gas from shale deposits, the U.S. is once again in very good shape.[91] Until such time that new technology brings about watershed changes in the use of energy, the U.S. should continue to purchase oil from abroad, mostly from non-Middle Eastern sources, and not get hung up on the notion of total energy independence, a flawed mantra that has been voiced by every administration since the time of Richard Nixon.[92] Even more importantly, the perceived need for oil should not fixate U.S. foreign policy on the volatile but increasingly less-significant Middle Eastern region.

In general, multilateral cooperation should take precedence over unilateral actions, and the United States should expect more burden sharing, diplomatically, financially, and militarily, on the part of its allies.[93] This will result in a somewhat messier world, and U.S. influence is bound to diminish somewhat in various foreign capitals. Unless there is a clear external threat to U.S. vital interests, American defense spending should be gradually reduced to no more than 3 percent of the nation's more than $14 trillion in annual GDP, once withdrawal of troops from Iraq and Afghanistan has been completed. Many U.S. troops should be brought home from countries that were at risk during the height of the Cold War but are now relatively safe. Of all the troops in the world stationed outside their home countries, almost three in four are Americans.[94] Why at the beginning of 2008 were eighty-six thousand and thirty-three thousand U.S. troops respectively still stationed in Europe and Japan?[95] In addition, why does the United States need to maintain eleven carrier task forces, and build a twelfth, when no one else has more than two, and Russia has only one carrier and China an antiquated carrier purchased in an auction held in Ukraine? The North Atlantic Treaty Organization (NATO) was created in 1949 to dissuade the Soviet Union from attacking Western Europe. The Soviet Union no longer exists, and the extension of NATO's mandate to Afghanistan has been problematic at best, with many NATO allies either refusing to send troops in the first place or demanding that the troops be kept out of the most dangerous areas within Afghanistan. Should NATO be transformed into an alliance of democracies that includes several nations outside of the North Atlantic region?[96] If such a transformation occurs, the United States must demand equitable burden sharing and in return agree to collegial decision-making. The major U.S. contribution to such a revamped alliance would be its planes with heavy-lift capacity, rapid deployment and counter-insurgency special forces, expansive intelligence networks, spy satellites, unmanned drones, cyber-warfare capabilities, and vast air and naval superiority.

Even if these recommended changes are made, the United States will still exert a strong voice in the development of a rapidly changing global landscape. For example, the United States and other leading nations should work together to prepare for the day when the third of all humanity in China and India demand the same cars, air conditioning, and other modern conveniences enjoyed by Western countries. How can these requests be accommodated without severe repercussions related to energy use and climate change? The U.S. can lead the way in thwarting cyber attacks and other vexing security challenges to be found in cyberspace.[97] It can be a leading player in a strictly multilateral effort to engage in interplanetary voyages as well as mapping the vast depths in earth's own ocean kingdoms. With about four thousand operationally deployed strategic nuclear warheads in its arsenal, the United States will be the pivotal player with Russia in forging new nuclear non-proliferation agreements and a major reduction in nuclear armaments.[98] Most importantly, if it can begin to solve its own vexing problems at home, a stronger U.S. economic and political foundation will lend credibility and gravitas to Washington's stances on pressing international and regional issues. Strength at home will also reinvigorate some of John Winthrop's famous "City upon a Hill" appeal made in 1630 that has resonated through subsequent generations of Americans but has been allowed to become so tarnished in recent years.[99]

The First Major External Challenge to America's Superpower Status: The Rise of Competitor Nations

Introduction

In his very interesting and provocative book, the *Post-American World*, Fareed Zakaria argues that there have been three "tectonic power shifts" in the past five hundred years: (1) the rise of the Western world beginning in the fifteenth century; (2) the rise of the United States at the close of the nineteenth century; and (3) the "rise of the rest," which is currently taking place.[1] Zakaria insists the issue is not one of the U.S. declining but rather competitor nations being in the ascendancy. As documented in earlier chapters, the U.S. is declining in a number of important arenas, but there is no doubt that other nations or groups of nations have made remarkable progress in recent decades.[2]

Illustrations from the sports world indicate both the severity of global competition that lies ahead and American complacency about such future competition. For years, Americans thought their tennis stars would always rank near the top of global listings, and the U.S. would be a shoo-in to win the Davis Cup, the emblem of male team superiority, almost every year. Yet, since 1996, the United States has won the Davis Cup only once and has only captured the Fed Cup, the women's equivalent of the Davis Cup, four times during the same period. American men used to romp in men's basketball at the Summer Olympic Games, using mostly college athletes. In 1972 at Munich, the United States lost its first game ever in Olympic competition to the Soviet Union. In 1988, the U.S. lost again in Seoul, but Americans could still take comfort in thinking their best players in the National Basketball Association (NBA) could easily defeat any team in the world. NBA players were finally allowed to compete in 1992, and the "Dream Team" completely dominated all the global competition. However, in 2004 at Athens, a team of NBA all-stars could do no better than third, losing to Argentina in the semifinals. The final bastion of U.S. sports supremacy was supposed to be baseball, which is only played seriously in about a dozen nations around the world. However, baseball was part of the Summer Olympics from 1992 to 2008, and American teams won the gold medal only once and did not medal at all in two Olympics. Once again, these teams did not feature the best Major League Baseball (MLB) players, and Americans remained confident of their overall superiority in a game they invented. This sense of confidence proved to be delusional because two World Baseball Classics were played in 2006 and 2009 featuring the best professional baseball players in the world. In the final game of 2006 played in San Diego, Japan defeated Cuba, and the U.S. team was not among the top four finishers. In the final game played in Los Angeles in 2009, Japan defeated South Korea, and the United States this time managed to finish fourth. In effect, the rest of the world has caught up and now surpassed the United States in areas where most Americans perceived they would always have a clear edge. This same analogy may be applied to what is transpiring in the global business and economic sectors.

China's explosive growth will permit it to surpass the U.S. as the world's largest economy in roughly two decades. The European Union, with twenty-seven nations and a half billion people, is also becoming a more prominent international economic and political actor, and the euro may one day challenge the U.S. dollar as the world's major trade and reserve currency. India, Japan, Brazil, Russia, and the Association of Southeast Asian Nations (ASEAN) are among the other nations or groups of nations that might exert a larger voice in international decision making within the next twenty years. Even if the U.S. economy continues to grow, its portion of the global economic pie will undoubtedly shrink, and the United States will be perceived as a major nation among several major nations or blocs of nations but no longer as a superpower exerting the dominant authority of a "unipolar hegemon."[3]

America's Shrinking Economic Presence

The federal government's cumulative debt continues to mount and will likely deteriorate to levels far worse than any encountered since the end of World War II. U.S. GDP as a percentage of global production is decreasing significantly. In 2000, the World Bank estimated that the United States accounted for 31 percent of the world's nominal GDP of $31.5 trillion. In 2008, the U.S. was down to a 23.6 percent share of $60.1 trillion in global

GDP. When the purchasing power parity (PPP) formula is used to adjust exchange rate values to reflect more accurately actual purchasing power, the U.S. share of global GDP decreased further to 20.3 percent in 2008.[4] The United States continues to be the world's major international direct investor, but its portion of the stock of world inward direct investment has gone from 20.4 percent in 1990 to 21.8 percent in 2000 and then down precipitously to 13.8 percent in 2007.[5] Inward direct investment continues to increase, but foreign-owned companies' share of value added by private industry is only up to 6.1 percent in 2006 compared with 5.9 percent in 2000, and their share of total private industry employment actually fell from 5.0 percent in 2000 to 4.6 percent in 2006.[6] The United States also remains the world's largest trading nation, but Germany, with eighty million people, has surpassed the U.S. as the leading merchandise exporter, and China has also surpassed the United States and has recently moved in front of Germany.[7] As a group of nations, the European Union exports a third more than the United States.[8] In 1995, the United States was responsible for 11.3 percent of global merchandise exports, but this had dwindled to 8.5 percent by the end of 2008.[9] The United States also ranks sixtieth in the world in terms of total international trade as a percentage of GDP, demonstrating that its economy is still relatively insulated.[10] The United States is an export underachiever, and many U.S. businesses are not willing to venture out into the international trading arena at a time when globalization is more entrenched than ever before. Over the past four decades, nearly 60 percent of per-capita GDP growth in the United States has been dependent solely on increases in U.S. domestic consumption, consumption that is now in question because of huge consumer debts and losses incurred in the value of Americans' homes and stock portfolios.[11] In spite of relative insularity within the United States, global cross-border assets ownership is in the process of internationalizing economic decision-making with aggregate asset holdings already topping $60 trillion, or about 120 percent of the world's GDP.[12] Foreign-owned assets within the United States have recently exceeded U.S.-owned assets abroad, $23.4 trillion versus $19.9 trillion in 2008.[13] This trend is far different from a quarter of a century earlier when U.S.-owned assets abroad were almost twice as high as foreign-owned assets in the United States.[14]

U.S. corporate leadership in an increasingly interdependent world is also at risk. In 1980, 217 of the world's five-hundred-largest corporations were American. In 1990, the number was down to 164; a decade later it had rebounded to 185, only to fall back to a record post–World War II low of 140 in 2008—far less than the 164 in the European Union and slightly more than the 120 in East Asia.[15] In 2007, there were an estimated seventy-nine thousand multinational corporations (MNCs) with 790,000 foreign affiliates. The total FDI stock of these MNCs was $15 trillion and their total annual sales eclipsed $31 trillion.[16] The annual value added by the foreign affiliates accounted for about 11 percent of the world's total GDP in 2007, and they employed eighty-two million workers.[17] These are the giants in the fields of direct investment and trade, and the U.S. share of these giants is diminishing. In addition, a new breed of players called "state capitalists" has emerged in recent decades in the international trade and investment arena.[18] They are primarily controlled by governments and not by investors in the private sector. The four major actors in state capitalism are national oil corporations, state-owned enterprises, privately owned "national champions" that closely identify with their home governments, and sovereign wealth funds.[19] State-owned oil companies currently control over three-fourths of world production and reserves.[20] Sovereign wealth funds were hurt by the recent global economic downturn but still have a net value exceeding $3 trillion, more than the combined assets of all the hedge funds in the world.[21] U.S. companies may be the recipient of funds from state capitalists, but they do not make the investment decisions. Chief proponents of state capitalism are concentrated in East Asia (especially China), Russia, and the Middle East.[22]

With more than one-third of humanity in China and India now beginning to be integrated into the worldwide market system, and others in the developing world certain to follow over the next few decades, far fewer American corporations will be world leaders in the foreseeable future. Developments in the auto industry may be emblematic of what is in store for the American corporate sector in the decades ahead. Through much of the post–World War II period, the Big Three in Detroit and their overseas subsidiaries dominated global auto sales. Today, however, two of the three have entered bankruptcy proceedings. General Motors is now just a shadow of its former self, and Chrysler has been absorbed by the Italian automaker, Fiat. Toyota has assumed the position of the world's largest automaker, and foreign-owned companies account for over half the sales in America's own domestic marketplace. In contrast, the share of sales of U.S.-owned automakers within the American market is at the lowest point in United States' history.

America's diminished economic role internationally is also reflected in the dwindling importance of the U.S. dollar. Dollar reserves as a percentage of total global central bank reserves fell from 73 percent in 2001 to 64 percent at the end of 2008, and in mid-2006 the euro displaced the dollar as the world's preeminent currency in international bond markets, even though the euro was only formally adopted as a currency in January 1999.[23] The U.S. dollar is perhaps under greater stress than at any other time since the end of World War I. With China assuming the role of America's international banker and holding about $1.7 trillion in dollar-denominated instruments as part of its vast $2.1 trillion worth of total reserves, Beijing can tremendously influence the fate of the dollar. At the beginning of 2009, China possessed approximately $900 billion in U.S. Treasury bonds, $550 billion in U.S. agency bonds issued by Fannie Mae, Freddie Mac, and Ginnie Mae, $150 billion in U.S. corporate bonds, $40 billion in U.S. equities, and $40 billion in U.S. short-term deposits.[24] Several leading Chinese officials have formally called for a new reserve currency to replace the dollar.[25] If these same officials ever announced publicly that China's central bank would no longer buy U.S. dollars or would begin to liquidate its existing dollar reserves, the U.S. currency would plunge and its value as a trading and reserve currency would be greatly tarnished, perhaps irreparably. Furthermore, if Beijing were also to announce that it would begin to allow its own currency, the yuan, to trade freely on international markets without government interference, then both the euro and the yuan could potentially surpass the dollar as the world's leading international currencies. Staggering U.S. federal government deficits as far as the eye can see, combined with continuing huge imbalances in the U.S. current account, do not bode well for the future viability of the American dollar as a global currency. The fact that China is now capable of engineering the crash of the U.S. dollar is even more discomfiting.

The Competitor Nations

A recent Goldman Sachs report predicts that China will pass the United States as the world largest economy in dollar-based GDP by 2041, and the so-called BRICs (Brazil, Russia, India, and China) will by 2039 produce more than the United States, the United Kingdom, France, Germany, Japan, and Italy combined.[26] Another major study by the Carnegie Endowment for International Peace contends that China will match U.S. GDP by as early as 2035 and double it by 2050.[27] America's own National Intelligence Council considers the chances are very good that the twenty-first century will be known as the "Asian century."[28]

China

China looms as America's chief rival for global influence. Kegley and Raymond assert, "China's growing economic strength is expected to transform the twenty-first-century geopolitical landscape as dramatically as did America's rise at the end of the nineteenth century."[29] Some observers are already predicting Chinese supremacy, which may have grave consequences for the Western world. Martin Jacque hypothesizes that the world has entered one of its rare historical periods characterized by a shift in global hegemony from one great power to another, similar to the period from 1931 to 1945 when the United States finally replaced the United Kingdom as the ascendant global power.[30] In the short term, China will spread its influence around the world and establish significant commercial linkages with Africa, Latin America, and other parts of Asia in particular, helping to solidify its access to vital natural resources and energy. It may also discredit the U.S. dollar and eventually make the yuan internationally convertible, providing the world with a viable alternative to the dollar. As the dollar's preeminent position erodes, so will New York City's status as the world's predominant financial center.[31] China's influence will grow substantially and U.S. influence will wane, setting the stage for a world that is far less permeated by traditional Western values.[32]

Niall Ferguson is increasingly disturbed by the consequences of China's sudden rise on the global stage. For a time he promoted the idea of "Chimerica," an informal partnership between China and the United States with China providing the cheap goods for U.S. consumers, cheap labor for U.S. multinationals, and financing for the U.S. government, which helped keep interest rates historically low and inflation firmly under control. In return, the United States provided China an insatiable consumer-driven paradise to sell its goods. Ferguson now contends that a divorce is in process and within five or ten years China will remove its capital controls and allow the yuan to develop as an international currency. What may eventually result are two competing nations much more equal in many dimensions than the United States and the Soviet Union ever were during the Cold War. This could set the stage for a new Cold War, with India and the Western group of countries moving closer to the United States, and Russia and various parts of the developing world moving closer to China.[33] The opening for China to challenge the United States is largely predicated on America's inability to tackle its own wide range of domestic problems.

What has occurred in China since 1978 qualifies as one of the greatest economic success stories in history. Prior to his death in 1976, Chairman Mao Zedong, through the Great Leap Forward (1958–1961) and the Great Proletarian Cultural Revolution (1966–1976), had driven a very backward country further back into the Stone Age, and in the process caused the deaths of millions of his fellow citizens. Deng Xiaoping consolidated his control over the Communist Party of China beginning in 1978 and decided that a "socialist market economy" would be a much better option for his country, even though the political system would remain strictly authoritarian.[34] The most populous nation in the world had the tenth-largest economy at the time but ranked only 175th on the basis of its per capita income of $190. Today, with 1.34 billion people, China has the third-largest national economy with a $4 trillion GDP and has moved up to 130th in the world with a per capita income of about $2,770 (in 2008).[35] During this period, China has also become the third-largest trading nation and the number-one holder of foreign reserves that were valued at $2.1 trillion in 2009—more than twice the value of reserves held by second-ranked Japan.[36] Remarkably, China has grown faster economically over the past three decades than any other major nation in history and has successfully moved 400 million people out of poverty.[37] Its economy has been doubling in size about every eight years over the past three decades, and GDP grew a remarkable thirteen times between 1978 and 2006.[38] In 2009, it also surpassed the United States as the world's largest automobile market and is gradually shifting from export-driven economic growth to consumption-driven growth.[39]

China has achieved a high literacy rate of 93 percent and has been willing to send its best and brightest off for training at the most prestigious universities in the world. Although known for its very cheap and abundant unskilled labor, China is also developing a huge cadre of highly skilled and highly educated young people, who will serve the nation well in the twenty-first-century brainpower marathon.[40] It is currently investing billions of dollars in developing one hundred world-class universities and scores of university science parks specializing in leading-edge research and development. Women have also been given the opportunity to move forward in most of the major professions, which will determine China's competitiveness in the future. In general, people do enjoy more significant individual freedom, at least within the Chinese context.[41] China is also spending hundreds of billions of dollars on infrastructure modernization and clearly impressed the world with the transformation of Beijing during the 2008 Summer

Olympics. Shanghai is now its most modern metropolis and has become the Manhattan of Asia.[42] The city spent $45 billion, more than was expended on the Beijing Olympics, in preparation for the 2010 World Expo.[43] If China achieves its goal of world preeminence, Shanghai may become much more important to world finance than Manhattan, whose Wall Street district is currently struggling with Washington, D.C., to determine who will ultimately be in charge of the U.S. financial sector.

China's military budget has grown at an annual double-digit rate for most of the past two decades, and it maintains the world's second-largest national budget for defense after the United States, spending $85 billion in 2008.[44] It has by far the largest number of active-duty military personnel—2.3 million versus America's 1.5 million—and has developed a potent nuclear weapons' arsenal. It is modernizing all aspects of its military and has purchased at auction a partially completed aircraft carrier from Ukraine and is considering building its own aircraft carrier in the foreseeable future.[45] China is only the third nation after the United States and Russia to put a human in space orbit and is spending billions of dollars developing a program to construct its own space station, send astronauts to the moon, and land sophisticated equipment on Mars.[46]

China's ability to work peacefully and constructively with neighboring countries will help to determine if the twenty-first century will be known as the Asian century or the Chinese century. If China, Japan, South Korea, Taiwan, the ASEAN nations, and, perhaps, India could join together to form a common market using the Chinese or some regional currency similar to the euro, an economic juggernaut would be formed without parallel in the rest of the world.[47] This common market would encompass half of humanity and close to half of global GDP. It would assume the role of the world's leading exporter and probably attract more direct investment than anywhere else. Conceivably, it would also be the major center for technology development and enjoy the largest concentration of sophisticated brainpower on the planet.

Such a degree of regional cooperation would also call into question the continued viability of parts of the liberal Western model first embraced by the British hegemon and later its American successor.[48] Many in Asia are sympathetic with Kishore Mahbubani's argument that Western notions of democracy and individual freedom are fine up to a certain point. However, if a widow living in her home in Newark, New Jersey, behind reinforced doors and barred windows, is afraid to go out night or day, then the model has deep flaws. Mahbubani argues that an Asian model, which might have a tinge of authoritarianism but also places a premium on community rights over individual freedom, may be superior in the long run to the Western model. In effect, the same widow could safely walk the streets of most East Asian cities night or day, even though she could be punished for chewing gum in public or protesting too vehemently about inefficient government services.[49] T.R. Reid agrees that Mahbubani makes a good point in emphasizing that any measurement of a society's overall standard of living should take into account safety, decency, and security. Reid adds:

> Judging from some standard social indicators—crime rates, family stability, educational achievement—East Asians have done a better job than most of the Western democracies in recent decades of building stable and civil communities.[50]

On the other hand, China still faces some very severe challenges. Hundreds of millions of its residents are impoverished peasants, and China's per capita income will remain comparatively low even after its GDP surpasses that of the United States. In 2006, medical insurance and pensions were available to only half of workers in urban areas and one-tenth of workers in the countryside.[51] Areas of the country are environmental cesspools, and China has already supplanted the United States as the leading emitter of carbon dioxide and other harmful greenhouse gases. As more Chinese consumers clamor for cars, the results will be greater air pollution, far more consumption of imported oil, and horrendous traffic congestion.[52] As television viewers from around the world can attest after watching the 2008 Summer Olympics in Beijing, residents of China's capital only occasionally see sunshine through the thick and pervasive layers of smog as four million vehicles slowly make their way through the crowded streets—a seven-fold increase in cars and trucks over the past fifteen years.[53]

The government in Beijing is strictly authoritarian, and leadership succession and the future role of the military in the political sector remain open questions. Can an authoritarian political system actually maintain over the long term a flexible and progressive market economy and an active commercial and political presence in various parts of the world? As Rob Gifford observes, "What we have in China is a mobile twenty-first century society shackled to a sclerotic 1950s Leninist-style political system."[54] Many state-owned industries should be closed because of their inefficiencies, but the loss of jobs might lead to serious worker unrest. Corruption is also rampant at all levels of government and within the ruling communist party. Most leaders turn a blind eye to the nation's blatant piracy of goods and intellectual property, with Hollywood movies available on DVD for a dollar or less within days of the films' initial opening in theaters.[55] Moreover, will much of the rest of the world actually embrace a Chinese government guilty of perpetrating the Tiananmen Square massacre in 1989 and openly persecuting some of its own ethnic and religious groups, including Tibetans, Uighurs, and the Falun Gong? Beijing has exhibited no tolerance whatsoever for efforts to form labor unions and improve the lot of the average worker. Civil society is completely stunted.[56] Many wonder whether Beijing can ever reach a workable compromise concerning the future status of Taiwan and its twenty-two million people without resorting to warfare. The impoverished western portion of the country is growing impatient as it observes the great economic bonanza over the past three decades being concentrated in the east, adding to the nation's vast income and regional inequality.[57] The one-child policy in place for so many years has also led to a gender imbalance of men over women and a rapidly aging population, with almost a quarter of the Chinese turning sixty-five or older in the year 2020.

The European Union

The second great economic and political miracle over the past half century has been the development of the European Union, which currently has twenty-seven member states. During the period 1870 to 1945, Europeans fought one another three times, with the final two conflicts escalating to include much of humanity in World War I and World War II. During these latter two conflicts, upwards of 100 million people perished and generations of young men were decimated. Niall Ferguson has referred to the twentieth century as the "bloodiest century in modern history," and much of this violence was precipitated by events in Europe.[58]

Through the Marshall Plan announced in 1947, the United States urged the devastated countries to work together on a pan-European basis in order to qualify for desperately needed American aid. The rationale for this demand was to diminish the intense nationalism that had provoked so many conflicts and to develop a regional economy based on capitalism that would be strong enough to resist the temptations of communism from within and the external threat posed by the Soviet Union. The North Atlantic Treaty Organization (NATO) was formed in 1949 and joined together many western European countries with the United States and Canada. The intent of NATO was to provide military protection so that Europe could continue to develop economically and politically while not worrying too much about what was transpiring in the Soviet empire behind the Iron Curtain. Cynically, many considered NATO's real purpose was to keep the Soviets out, the Americans in, and the Germans down, reflecting the pariah status of Germany following the Second World War.

The European Economic Community was formed by the Treaty of Rome of 1957 and originally consisted of six member-states: France, Italy, West Germany, the Netherlands, Belgium, and Luxembourg. The membership expanded through the years, and the ambitious Maastricht Treaty was signed in 1992, creating the European Union and committing the member states to a broad range of political, economic, and social integration.[59] Pro-European integrationist forces hope that one day regional cooperation will be so extensive that national boundaries will have little significance and the EU will morph into the United States of Europe, perhaps comprising as many as fifty nation-states, including Russia and Turkey.[60] The EU also maintains special relations with 109 countries sometimes referred to as the "Eurosphere," mainly former colonies of a handful of European countries.[61] Europe has fully recovered economically from the nearly complete devastation of World War II, and the EU has a GDP larger than that of the United States. Moreover, it is a much more active player than the United States in international trade, with Germany alone exporting more than the United States. London has also been revived as a global financial center and is currently the major rival of New York City. The euro, in existence for only a decade, has also enjoyed a mercurial rise as an international currency and ranks second to the dollar in central bank reserves and international trade transactions.

In challenging the U.S. for global leadership, the EU must overcome some very significant obstacles. Above all, it is still composed of individual nation-states that often place their own interests before the European Union's interests, as illustrated by the failure to ratify the proposed European Union constitution in 2005. The EU is nowhere close to evolving into a United States of Europe with a federalist structure, even though the Lisbon Treaty ratified after the failure of the EU constitution will promote greater cooperation in certain domains and creates the high-profile positions of EU president and EU foreign minister. Centuries-old animosities and prejudices toward other nations or peoples remain an impediment to integration, although notable progress has certainly been made. The United States operates with one official language whereas the EU has twenty-three official languages and sixty indigenous regional or minority language communities.[62] The EU also faces a demographic time bomb as a result of a very low birthrate and very limited immigration. The current twenty-seven member states are projected to have twenty million fewer people in 2050, and the percentage of retirees will be higher than in the United States. The EU is also much more dependent than the United States on external energy sources, although its conservation and alternative-energy programs are more advanced than those in the U.S., and Europeans use mass transit in far greater numbers than do Americans. Two nuclear powers, France and the United Kingdom, are among the members of the European Union, but in general, EU countries spend very little on defense and remain dependent on the U.S. to do the heavy lifting in various conflict areas, including the former Yugoslavia since the early 1990s. There is no such thing as an EU-wide defense force, and national governments continue to have the final say on how their military forces will be used. Critics argue that with so many members having to reach a consensus before decisive action can be taken, the EU will be plagued by sclerotic foreign and defense policies, resulting in a community of nations that one critic refers to as "an economic giant, a political dwarf, and a military worm."[63] This is a harsh commentary, and EU policy toward the Middle East and much of the developing world may actually be more innovative than comparable U.S. policy.[64] Nonetheless, the EU is relatively weak militarily and for decades has shunned its fair share of defense obligations in the trans-Atlantic region.

India

When the Soviet Union disappeared in 1991, China and India were not on the radar screen of major international economic players. As the second decade of the twenty-first century commences, India has now moved up to be a significant global player.

India has the second-largest population with 1.15 billion people and is the youngest among the major countries, with half its population under twenty-five.[65] Its economy has been growing far more rapidly than any nation in the West, and it currently ranks as the twelfth-largest economy in the world. The area around Bangalore has also emerged as one of the leading high-tech regions on the planet. Along with China, India has been the major source of immigrant entrepreneurs for America's Silicon Valley, and this home-grown talent is now creating high-tech miracles in India. Indian universities and technical institutes continue to produce some of the very best global talent to fuel this massive growth in internationally competitive industries. Unlike China, India is moving forward economically within a democratic political structure. The federal government, in conjunction with many state governments, is spending billions of dollars to upgrade and expand the nation's infrastructure, especially in sectors linked to transport, communications, and trade. India sent an unmanned mission to the moon in 2008 and has been launching satellites into space since 1976.[66] Closer to home, the Tata Group in India is now selling the Nano car to middle-class Indians for $2,000, and Indian scientists have developed the prototype for a $20 computer.[67] Bollywood has also eclipsed Hollywood in terms of movies made and tickets sold.[68] In the military sector, India also possesses an arsenal of nuclear weapons.

On the down side, hundreds of millions of Indians scattered among the nation's 600,000 villages live in abject poverty as population growth continues at a robust pace, and 40 percent of urban dwellers are considered to be poor.[69] The World Bank estimates that 40 percent of Indians live in extreme poverty with an income below $1.25 per day, compared with 16 percent in China.[70] Seventy-five percent of Indians survive on less than $2 a day versus 36 percent in China.[71] Forty percent of India's children are considered malnourished in comparison to 7 percent in China.[72] Mumbai, formerly known as Bombay, is on course to have almost twenty-nine million residents by 2020, making it the largest city on the planet. Unfortunately, it also has the largest slum area in all of Asia.[73] By 2030, India will probably be more populous than China. Women are widely mistreated and discriminated against, and female literacy is 54 percent versus 76 percent for males.[74] Many who go to school receive no more than four years of formal education.[75] The health-care system is often abysmal, with little more than 1 percent of the government budget dedicated to this vital sector.[76]

India also exists in a very dangerous neighborhood. There are various regional tensions, with the most explosive being the ongoing dispute between India and Pakistan over Kashmir. India's relationship with neighboring China has also been frosty for most of the past several decades. In addition, terrorism strikes the country from time to time as illustrated by the bloody attacks in Mumbai carried out in November 2008. Hindu and Muslim nationalists within India also clash periodically.

On a number of fronts, India has made tremendous strides and is emerging as a powerful regional actor. Globally, however, it is still a major second-tier player. For example, between 2000 and 2007, China's merchandise exports almost quintupled in value to capture nearly 9 percent of world exports. India's exports also went up significantly, but its share of global exports only increased from 0.7 percent to 1.0 percent.[77] Much more progress must be made domestically before India may ascend to the ranks of the small coterie of world powers.

Russia

Russia must be included on the list of potential rivals to the United States, because its nuclear arsenal is second only to the U.S. and far beyond what any other nation has developed. In effect, Russia is the most dangerous potential adversary of the United States if a cataclysmic nuclear confrontation were ever to occur. In the economic realm, if oil can go for a long period of sustained pricing above $100 per barrel, Russia will do well financially with its vast petroleum and natural gas reserves. The Russian people are also well educated and many can contribute to the advancement of various world-class economic sectors, including its vaunted space industry.

On the opposite side of the coin, Russia in many respects resembles a developing nation. Even during the Cold War, the Soviet Union could match the U.S. nuclear arsenal and some of America's overall military capability, but its underlying economic foundation was in a shambles and its GDP was only a fraction of America's. This wide disparity helped convince Gorbachev to halt the arms race with the United States, and economic turmoil, combined with the disastrous war effort in Afghanistan, helped precipitate the unraveling of the Soviet Union. Russia today has a semi-authoritarian system of government and an inefficient and poorly diversified economy. Everything is propped up by commodity prices, and when commodities lose their value, Russia loses GDP. The overall political and economic systems are riddled with corruption, and organized crime has a foothold in many economic sectors. There is also regional unrest linked to radical Islamists and some secular separatist groups, especially in the North Caucasus region including Chechnya, Dagestan, and Ingushetia.[78] Health care is shoddy, and the average Russian man has a life expectancy of sixty years compared with seventy-seven years for a German male.[79] A Russian man, who often consumes large quantities of alcohol and tobacco and lives in the midst of heavy pollution, has less than a 50 percent chance of living until retirement age.[80] Russia's population, which stood at 142 million in 2010, is expected to dwindle to 111 million or less by mid-century, a combination of premature deaths, a low birthrate, and very limited immigration.

To optimize its economic potential and spur much-needed modernization, Russia would do well to turn westward and eventually join the European Union. The most worrisome scenario would be a new military-economic alliance with China, predicated on authoritarian governance and the intent to put Humpty Dumpty together again—in other words, restore as much as possible the old Soviet Union. This ominous turn of events could make the Cold War period look rather tame and provoke a return to very tense East–West relations.

Japan

At the end of the 1980s, many Americans perceived that Japan had surpassed the United States as the world's premier economic and technological power.[81] In actuality, Japan was on the verge of one of the greatest economic collapses in modern history. Its Nikkei stock market average would plummet from a high of 38,915 at the end of 1989 to below 7,000 in October 2008, before recovering to about 10,500 by the end of 2009. Just before the stock market crashed, the real estate in Japan was four times more valuable than all the real estate in the much larger United States.[82] At the time, a $1,000 bill would not pay for the surface area it would cover if placed on the pavement in Tokyo's Ginza district.[83] Real estate values started to fall in 1990, and Japan has never fully recovered from the bubbles bursting in stocks and real estate.

Nonetheless, Japan still ranks as the world's second-largest national economy, although it will soon be surpassed by China. However, its per capita income of $38,210 is still thirteen times higher than China's.[84] Japan remains a premier industrial power with major strengths in the automobile and electronics sectors. Its citizens are highly educated and, in spite of the turmoil in the stock market and real estate sectors, enjoy a high standard of living. Although it has denounced the development of nuclear weapons, it has the capability to fabricate them at any time and may do so in consideration of the potential threats from North Korea and perhaps China. Its overall annual defense spending of $46 billion is the seventh highest in the world.[85]

On the down side, the island chain of Japan is home to 127 million people in an area the size of Montana (whose population is 960,000). The islands are devoid of most precious resources, leaving Japan almost totally dependent on imports of energy and other raw materials. Japan's birthrate is very low, and the central government has permitted very few immigrants to settle. As a result, Japan is already the world's "oldest" big nation and the elderly over sixty-five will comprise a quarter of the total population by 2020.[86] By 2050, Japan's population may shrink to below 100 million.[87] The government's debt also makes the U.S. debt look puny, with Japan's indebtedness as a percentage of GDP spiraling up to 200 percent.[88]

In the future, Japan will need to decide who its best friends will be. Since the end of World War II and the subsequent occupation by U.S. troops under the command of General Douglas McArthur, Japan has been a stalwart ally of the United States and is home to more than thirty thousand U.S. troops. Will Tokyo continue to choose the trans-Pacific option and feel assured that the United States will protect it from potential threats coming from the neighboring countries of North Korea, China, and Russia? Or, with all the economic growth occurring around it, will it de-emphasize the U.S. alliance, develop its own nuclear capacity, and join with its East Asian neighbors in forming the most powerful economic bloc in world history? How Japan swings will go a long way toward determining the future strength of Asia in general and the overall influence of the United States in the vast Asian-Pacific region.

Other Potential Rivals

Brazil is the dominant player in Latin America and almost single-handedly scuttled the proposed Free Trade Area of the Americas (FTAA) because it did not want to see growing U.S. influence in the region.[89] Brazil has a population base of 192 million, the fifth largest in the world, and is the fifth-largest nation territorially. Its GDP of $1.6 trillion in 2008 was the eighth largest among national economies. Oil was recently discovered off its coast, and if this new resource is developed properly, Brazil's economic influence could expand significantly.[90] Its weaknesses include widespread poverty, corruption and crime, and major disparities in economic development among its vast regions. An old adage described Brazil as "the country of the future, and always will be." It has yet to live up to its tremendous potential but has certainly made significant strides in recent years.

Finally, Indonesia is the fourth-largest nation population-wise with 231 million people. Its GDP of $514 billion ranked as the nineteenth largest in 2008. It is a member of OPEC but has now become a net importer of oil. Indonesia is a noteworthy leader in ASEAN and will probably be content to play a regional role in the future. It is beset with numerous domestic problems, including widespread poverty, corruption, terrorism, and major regional and ethnic conflicts.

In the future, several of the countries highlighted in this chapter will likely become permanent members of the UN Security Council, if they are not already. The G8, composed of the United States, Canada, United Kingdom, France, Germany, Italy, Japan, and Russia, will also morph into G20, an organization also including China, India, Brazil, Indonesia, Argentina, Australia, Mexico, Saudi Arabia, South Africa, South Korea, Turkey, and the European Union. This much larger group of countries, plus the EU, is much less Westernized, and U.S. influence within the forum will gradually erode.

As individual nation-states, only a few are major rivals to the United States today or in the foreseeable future. However, the creation of an East Asian Common Market, the enlargement of the European Union to include up to fifty members, the expansion of Mercosur in South America to encompass most of the continent's countries south of the equator, and other such regional alliances could dramatically shift the overall power equation in the world.[91] The formation of formal or informal military alliances could also have severe repercussions, especially if Russia were to turn eastward toward China or Japan westward toward China. Most plausible scenarios would suggest that the United States will be relatively weaker and some of its major rivals relatively stronger within the next few decades.

An Emerging External Threat to America's Superpower Status: The Combination of Globalization, Technology Change, and Creative Destruction

Introduction

In addition to rival nations or groups of nations that may diminish America's international influence over the next few decades, another potent combination of factors may also weaken the position of the United States as the world's only superpower. These factors include expanding globalization, unprecedented technology change, and "creative destruction" at home and abroad.

Globalization

For the first time since World War II, international trade did not expand in 2009. Over the quarter of a century up to the Great Recession, the global economy doubled in size every decade, growing from $31 trillion in 1999 to $62 trillion in 2008.¹ In spite of the recent economic downturn, the world is definitely becoming more globalized, with a growing interconnectedness and interdependence among nations, societies, businesses, and peoples. All nations are vulnerable to decisions rendered or events that transpire outside their borders, and this vulnerability reaches down to the neighborhood and household levels of every nation-state. For example, the U.S. must import over 60 percent of its petroleum requirements. Eighty percent of computer components used in the U.S. are also fabricated abroad. Most military weapons could not be assembled without major parts supplied by overseas sources. To be blunt, the U.S. standard of living would not be nearly as high without America's active economic interaction with the rest of the world. Figure VII: 1 illustrates that, whether Americans like it or not, they are very much an integral part of a globalized economy. In addition to what is listed on the chart, approximately six million American workers are employed by foreign-owned businesses in the United States, including 12 percent of all jobs in manufacturing, and these businesses also account for 19 percent of U.S. merchandise exports and 26 percent of all imports.[2]

FIGURE VII: 1
The United States and Economic Globalization

World's leading importer of goods
($2.10 trillion 2008)

World's third leading exporter of goods
($1.29 trillion 2008)

World's leading foreign direct investor
($3.70 trillion 2008—current cost basis)

World's leading host nation for foreign direct investment
($2.65 trillion 2008—current cost basis)

World's leading holder of foreign assets
($19.9 trillion 2008)

World's leading host nation for foreign-owned assets
($23.4 trillion 2008)

World's leading source of international tourists
(63.6 million 2008)

World's number-two recipient of international tourists
(58.0 million 2008)

World's leading host nation for spending by international tourists
($110.5 billion 2008—including transportation costs)

World's leading recipient of immigrants
(1.11 million became legal permanent residents 2008—excludes undocumented immigrants)

49 percent of U.S. government's publicly held debt owned by foreign investors

At first glance, many Americans would reject out of hand the notion that the planet is in the process of evolving into "spaceship earth." Jeffrey Sachs asserts:

The defining challenge of the twenty-first century will be to face the reality that humanity shares a common fate on a crowded planet. That common fate will require new forms of global cooperation, a fundamental point of blinding simplicity that many world leaders have yet to understand or embrace.[3]

Globalization will require progressively more cross-border cooperation to solve international problems, and this trend runs contrary to the ambitions of any one nation to exert disproportionate unilateral influence on the international stage.

Never before has it been so easy for Washington, as well as state and local government leaders and representatives of the private sector, to be engaged internationally, due primarily to the tremendous advancements in information technology, communications, and transportation. It is now quite simple and relatively inexpensive for them to be in touch with counterparts and business contacts around the world via telephone, fax, the Internet, and other modes of communication. Distance has been conquered in the age of wondrous communication advancements, with a telephone call from the U.S. to many parts of the world costing a few pennies per minute. To put these costs in historical perspective, a three-minute phone call from New York City to London in 1930 cost the equivalent of three hundred current dollars and still cost several dollars just a decade ago. The World Wide Web on the Internet was not invented until 1990, but it is now having a revolutionary effect on communication among households, governments, and businesses in many countries. Currently, there are over a billion people connected to the Internet, and the number of users is expanding rapidly.[4] With messages traveling from one part of the world to another in less than a second, communicating three thousand miles away is often no more difficult than being in contact with someone in the same city. International transportation is more cumbersome, but costs of traveling and shipping goods abroad have dropped precipitously over the past few decades, and international airline connections have proliferated dramatically.

The Internet has also become a useful tool to spur on U.S. economic development. Many large local governments have created web sites highlighting the strong points of their cities and encouraging people from abroad to visit or foreign companies to invest either locally or enter into joint ventures with local companies. Some, such as the Greater Seattle Alliance, have web sites in multiple languages. This is prudent, because too many Americans perceive that a web site exclusively in English works as a result of the proliferation of the use of English around the world, especially in the business community. A superior strategy is to embrace the notion that the most important language in the world is the language of existing or potential customers. Following this philosophy would lead to core information on web sites being listed in at least four or five major languages.

In spite of major advances, the world is only somewhat globalized and is not yet "flat."[5] McKinsey and Associates estimated several years ago that only one-fifth of annual world output was open to global competition in products, services, and ownership, but that within thirty years four-fifths would be "globally contestable."[6] In other words, globalization may only be in its early stages in terms of the cross-border movement of goods, services, capital, know-how, and people.[7] If this is indeed the case, then governments and businesses must prepare for much further intensification of the globalization phenomenon and adjust their domestic and international pursuits accordingly. This will obviously be a formidable task and will go a long way toward determining how competitive the United States will be as a nation over the next few decades.[8]

With over 95 percent of all potential customers and more than 80 percent of all economic activity located beyond the borders of the United States, and with globalization gradually increasing, one is hard pressed to comprehend why governments in the U.S. federal system and the business community in general have taken so long to develop their international economic strategies. Moreover, there are certainly downside risks associated with globalization.[9] In particular, the U.S. federal system is facing the challenge of coping with the growing influence of "intermestic" politics,[10] referring to the growing overlap of domestic and international policies in an era of globalization. As illustrated in Figure VII: 2, many challenges facing the American people in their everyday lives may have their origins in events or decisions occurring outside the United States. These phenomena are making governance at all levels much more complicated, at a time when citizens are clamoring for more effective government policies to shield them from influences that originate beyond America's borders. Whether in domestic or foreign affairs, the U.S. federal system will be evolving substantially over the next few decades, and the slogan "think globally and act locally" will be more germane than ever before.

FIGURE VII: 2
Connecting the International to the Local

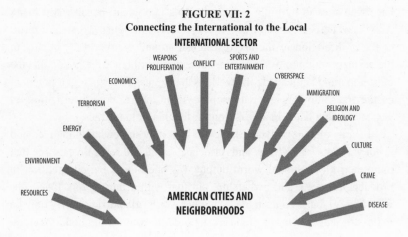

A number of examples linked to Figure VII: 2 illustrate why all nations, even a superpower, are affected by decisions made or events that transpire outside their national borders. Nuclear weapons proliferation, a slew of environmental issues such as climate change and ozone deterioration, terrorism and international crime, the spread of endemic diseases, energy shortages, and myriad other issues will necessitate unprecedented domestic and cross-border cooperation in order to solve many international problems that threaten the day-to-day quality of life on Main Street, U.S.A.[11]

Widespread warfare is the most ominous potential problem, especially if nuclear weapons are ever employed. Ferguson writes:

> on the eve of the twentieth century, H.G. Wells had imagined a "War of the Worlds"—a Martian invasion that devastated the earth. In the hundred years that followed, men proved that it was quite possible to wreak comparable havoc without the need for alien intervention. All they had to do was to identify this or that group of their fellow men as the aliens, and then kill them.[12]

If the twentieth century was the "bloodiest century in modern history," what is to keep the twenty-first from being even worse, especially with the proliferation of nuclear weapons and other sophisticated weapons of mass destruction?[13] Even a superpower cannot solve this vexing problem single-handedly. For example, what if India and Pakistan eventually go to war against one another and employ their nuclear arsenals? The widespread devastation and spreading radiation would injure people thousands of miles from the South Asian battlefields. What if Iran were to procure nuclear weapons and use them on Israel, provoking immediate nuclear retaliation from the Israelis? Once again, the lethal consequences of such an action would reverberate far beyond the Middle East. Without any doubt, nations must come together in an effort to defuse problems before they escalate into unspeakable consequences for the planet as a whole.

In the environmental arena, how will the anticipated improvement in the standard of living of billions of people in developing countries not result in growing pressure on the earth's capacity to sustain such economic prosperity?[14] For example, in the auto sector, only 12 percent of the earth's inhabitants owned vehicles in 2007.[15] How will climate change be affected when that percentage increases to 50 percent or more? The United States has eliminated the use of chlorofluorocarbons (CFCs), which cause damage to the fragile ozone layer high in the earth's atmosphere. Yet, if other nations do not join in this ban, the ozone layer will continue to deteriorate and Americans will still suffer the consequences.

Some of the important diseases facing humankind today have been discovered in just the past few decades, including HIV/AIDS, hepatitis C, Ebola, and the H1N1 (swine flu) virus. It is doubtful that any of these originated in the United States, yet millions of Americans have suffered from their effects. All Americans want to avoid a repeat of the Spanish flu outbreak of 1918–1920. During a period of less than two and a half years, one-third of all humans were infected by this flu and 50 to 100 million perished, more than the total dead caused by World War I.[16] Among those who succumbed to this pandemic disease, 675,000 were Americans. Today, more people are crossing national borders than at any other time in history for tourism, business, and immigration purposes. With advances in transportation, people may travel from one part of the planet to most other parts within a day or two. In 2001, a Congolese woman suspected of having Ebola traveled from Ethiopia to Hamilton, Ontario, stopping along the way at the Newark and Toronto airports.[17] Thousands of people could have been exposed to this illness during her sojourn halfway around the world. Fortunately, she was later diagnosed with a less virulent disease, but this type of travel pattern is repeated tens of thousands of times each day.

Invasive species also travel internationally by planes and boats and may be responsible for up to $137 billion in economic damage in the United States every year.[18] Asian carp, which may grow to be more than one meter in length and weigh forty-five kilograms (about one hundred pounds), now infest waterways from the Mississippi Delta to the Great Lakes.[19] Chinese mitten crabs are prominent in San Francisco Bay, and veined rapa whelks native to the Sea of Japan are prominent in Chesapeake Bay. As Taras George explains, "Supertankers and cargo ships suck up millions of gallons of ballast water in distant estuaries and ferry jellyfish, cholera bacteria, seaweed, diatoms, clams, water fleas, shrimp and even good-sized fish halfway around the globe."[20] In his provocative book on what would happen to the planet if humankind suddenly disappeared, Alan Weisman suggests that kudzu, a climbing, deciduous vine brought originally to Philadelphia from Japan in 1876 as a centennial gift to the American people, would spread rapidly and infest a large part of U.S. territory.[21] Kudzu already infests seven million acres in the southeastern region of the United States.[22]

The good news for many in the world is that life expectancy is improving as a result of better medical treatment and nutrition. According to the World Health Organization, the life expectancy of people around the world should increase from forty-eight years for those born in 1955 to seventy-three years for those born in 2025.[23] With birthrates continuing to outpace mortality rates in many parts of the planet, and life spans expanding, almost three billion people should be added to the current population rolls by 2050.[24] Unfortunately, almost all of the population increase will occur in developing countries and many of these people will still live in poverty (see Figure VII: 3). Two percent of the planet's richest people now control half of the world's wealth, while the poorest 50 percent control 1 percent.[25] The income of the 225 richest people is about equal to the combined income of the poorest 2.7 billion people.[26] By 2025, 1.8 billion are expected to live in water-scarce regions and many more in areas of severe environmental degradation.[27] When these negative living conditions are combined with the lack of job opportunities, unprecedented immigration will occur from the south to the north. Already, seventy-five million residents who live in OECD nations were not born in those countries.[28] The

FIGURE VII: 3
The World's Youth Population, Ages 15 to 24

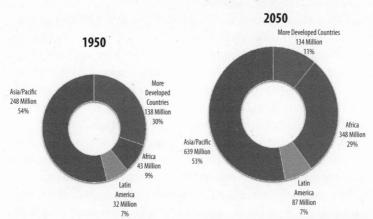

Source: UN Population Division, *World Population Prospects: The 2008 Revision*, medium variant (2009) and Population Reference Bureau.

United States, of course, has been the leading host nation for immigrants in the entire world, although immigrants as a share of the overall population are now significantly higher in Canada, Australia, and Switzerland than in the United States. Unless the U.S. can work together with other nations in the north and south to solve problems associated with poverty in developing countries, no superpower status will keep desperate immigrants from flocking to America's shores.

Americans will need to adapt to the notion that their country is one major player among many, and with the increasing overlap of domestic and international issues in an age of globalization, cross-border cooperation will be requisite to safeguard and enhance their own well-being. Historically, the United States has had a rather unique geophysical advantage over other major players, because it has been isolated and insulated from various traumatic events due to the two mammoth oceans to its east and west and friendly and much weaker nations to its north and south. This geophysical advantage at times evoked envy on the part of other leaders around the world, as manifested by Otto von Bismarck's famous utterance: "There is a Providence that protects idiots, drunkards, and the United States of America."[29] However, this propitious circumstance has eroded substantially in the new era of interconnectedness, interdependence, and, quite frankly, vulnerability to events that transpire or decisions taken outside the confines of one's own nation-state.[30]

Unprecedented Technology Change

In the mid-twentieth century, the president of the U.S. Chamber of Commerce expressed his astonishment that the global information base was doubling every decade.[31] Recently, the American Society of Training and Documentation estimated that information would soon be doubling every eighteen months, and an IBM research group asserts that within a few years the information base would double every eleven hours.[32] Part of this massive addition of information is attributable to ultra-fast computers. Moore's Law is named after Gordon Moore, the co-founder of Intel, who predicted in 1965 that the number of transistors that could be placed on a chip would double every two years. This law has been fairly accurate, and computers are now much smaller but also far more powerful than ever before, especially when they are networked together. The information explosion is also attributable to the rapid expansion of the Internet and the ability of people around the world to contribute to the information base. Furthermore, the combination of digitization and satellite technology, which "allows messages, pictures, data, or any other form of information to be transmitted almost instantly to any part of the world that can receive the electronic signals at ground stations," is making it virtually impossible for dictators to maintain closed societies, even though some continue to try.[33] Even within democratic societies, the communications revolution has prompted government officials to be less rigid and more transparent in their decision-making processes, although much more progress remains to be achieved.[34]

Newt Gingrich predicts there will be more growth in scientific knowledge over the next twenty-five years than occurred during the past century, and the rate of change will be four to seven times greater than during the past quarter century.[35] Others contend that scientific knowledge accumulation will be more rapid than Gingrich is predicting. Marvin J. Cetron and Owen Davies believe that "all the technical knowledge we work with today will represent only 1 percent of the knowledge that will be available in 2050."[36] They argue that technological obsolescence is gaining momentum as technology change accelerates with each new generation of discoveries and applications.[37] They add that the half-life of an engineer's knowledge is only five years and that in electronics half of what a student learns as a freshman in college is obsolete by the time he or she is a senior.[38] These new tidal waves of information will require many U.S. workers to be engaged in lifelong learning and retraining. Unfortunately, even during the Great Recession when so many people were looking for employment, three million jobs in the United States were going begging because applicants did not have the requisite educational backgrounds or skills.[39]

In light of the challenges facing the United States that have been chronicled in this volume, can America keep pace with the rest of the world in this critical area of technology innovation? A RAND Corporation study frames the question quite well:

> Two developments drive much of the concern that U.S. leadership in science and technology is slipping. First, globalization and the rapid growth in science and technology of other nations, such as China and India, may make it increasingly difficult for the United States to retain its comparative economic advantage. Second, some fear that the building blocks of science and technology within the United States—science and engineering (S&E) infrastructure, education, and workforce—are not being sustained.[40]

Nevertheless, RAND researchers contend that the United States maintains a clear lead in critical scientific and technological fields. For example, the U.S. accounts for 40 percent of the world's scientific R&D, employs 70 percent of all Nobel Prize winners, and has three-quarters of the top forty universities worldwide.[41] EU researchers now have a larger share of scientific publications than Americans, 37 percent to 35 percent, but U.S. researchers account for almost two-thirds of the articles in the world's most highly cited publications.[42] Among the patents issued by the U.S., EU, and Japan in 2002, Americans were still in the lead—38 percent to 31 percent to 26 percent respectively.[43] Even with this solid research foundation, the RAND report warns that there is too much complacency in the United States and insufficient scientific collaboration with the rest of the world.[44] Cetron and Davies are deeply distressed about the prospects for America's future leadership role, claiming the U.S. is ceding its scientific and technical leadership to other countries and has done little to prepare for the imminent retirement of nearly half of all U.S. scientists and engineers.[45] Moreover, almost three-fifths of government-sponsored research is devoted to the military, with up to 40 percent of these military R&D contracts being wasted on congressionally mandated earmark projects.[46] They predict that by 2015, artificial intelligence, data mining, and virtual reality will be used extensively in the global business community, and the average product cycle will be measured in little more than a few months.[47] The Information Technology and Innovation Foundation ranks the United States sixth out of forty countries in innovation competitiveness but dead last among the forty in terms of the rate of change in innovation over the last decade, using such key metrics as human capital, entrepreneurship, economic policy, and information technology infrastructure.[48] Nanotechnology, a new kind of molecular-scale technology, also has the capacity to transform the way people do many things in everyday life, offering unprecedented opportunities but also some dangers if used by unscrupulous leaders for nefarious purposes.[49] Can the United States continue to compete, as well as protect and enhance the lives of its citizens, in this rapidly changing technological environment?

Creative Destruction

The economist Joseph Schumpeter wrote during World War II of an age of "creative destruction" characterized by constant business creation and failures.[50] One can only marvel at the massive economic and social changes that occurred in the United States during the twentieth century—the century beginning with 41 percent of its workforce employed in agriculture but ending with only 1.9 percent in the agricultural arena.[51] For the world in general, there were also major transformations. As Paul Kennedy suggests:

> Of all the ways in which the twentieth century makes its claim to a special place in history, few can equal in importance the enormous

transformation of economic life. Were a farmer in Illinois or a peasant in Bangalore, both struggling to make ends meets around 1900, brought back to our planet today, he would be astounded at its transformation. The massive increases in productivity and wealth, the mind-boggling new technologies, and the improvement in material comforts would have made him speechless. Astonished though he would be, he would not of course have guessed at the many convulsions and setbacks that had occurred to the world economy in the hundred-year interval.[52]

The twentieth century was transformational in so many ways, but its changes will pale in comparison to the nature and rapidity of change in the current century. The phrase "creative destruction" has never been more applicable for the United States than in the current era characterized by globalization and unprecedented technological innovations. In 2006, a total of 627,000 employer firms were created in the United States, but 596,000 also ceased to exist.[53] In the twelve months ending in June 2008, 29.4 million jobs were created but 30.2 million were lost.[54] By mid-2009, almost fifteen million Americans were officially unemployed, another nine million were underemployed, and more than two million more were too discouraged to even look for work.[55] Silicon Valley can persevere in the era of creative destruction, but Detroit, Newark, St. Louis, and many other communities have struggled to keep up. Detroit, for example, was the fourth-largest city in the United States in 1950. In 2007, it ranked eleventh and had lost half of its population since 1950, in part because of people moving to the suburbs and in part due to very difficult economic and social challenges, especially related to the downturn in the auto sector.

Titans of America's industrial and financial world have also collapsed. In 1917, *Forbes* issued its first list of the hundred-largest U.S. companies measured by assets. By 1987, sixty-one of the businesses on the inaugural list had disappeared or been absorbed by other companies and only eighteen remained in the top hundred.[56] The first S&P 500 list of the largest U.S. companies was released in 1957. By 1997, only seventy-four of the original five hundred were still on the list.[57] In 1990, General Motors was the largest corporation in the United States, Ford was the second largest, and Chrysler ranked eighth. General Motors, founded in 1908, was the global sales leader for motor vehicles for seventy-seven consecutive years until 2008. For most of the second half of the twentieth century, it was the largest company in the world measured by revenues. In June 2009, it fell into bankruptcy, was essentially taken over by the U.S. government, and then reorganized as a mere shadow of the former global giant. Chrysler fell into bankruptcy a month before GM, and its assets were taken over by Fiat. Citigroup used to be the world's largest financial institution but has essentially been nationalized and traded at one time as a penny stock, below a dollar per share. American International Group (AIG) was once the world's predominant insurance company, but it, too, has traded at times as a penny stock and has been nationalized. Over $170 billion of taxpayer money has already been pumped into AIG, which lost over $60 billion during the fourth quarter of 2008, the highest short-term loss of any company in history. Enron, Lehman Brothers, Bear Stearns, Merrill Lynch, Countrywide Financial, Washington Mutual, Thornburg Mortgage, Conseco, Pacific Gas and Electric Company, Texaco, United Airlines, WorldCom, Circuit City, and Woolworths are among well-known companies that entered bankruptcy in recent years, were in deep distress and absorbed by other companies, or simply disappeared.

With change occurring so quickly, how many more "giants" of industry will survive? Facing billions of dollars in annual losses and unable to turn a profit in the face of competition from the Internet, cell phones, and specialized private carriers, will the 234-year-old U.S. Postal Service remain in business beyond the next decade?[58] Will it have to revert to delivering mail only four or five days a week, or will it be broken up into smaller units and sold off to the private sector? Will a similar fate face the newspaper and magazine industries that now compete with new forms of communication to transmit information to American households?

Will creative destruction be a net plus or minus for the United States as a country? Will the largest U.S. corporations and banking institutions continue to lose ground as *Fortune* releases its annual Global 500 list? Will manufacturing jobs continue to decrease in the U.S. because of overseas competition and the introduction of new technology in industrial plants? How will the emergence of state capitalism, in which the United States is a peripheral player, affect global investment decisions in the future?[59] Can the United States move forward and continue to lead the pack in the face of the potent combination of globalization, rapid technology change, and "the gales of creative destruction?"[60]

Chapter 8

America's Strengths and a Plan for Renewal

America the Powerful

When asked the question whether the twenty-first century will also be known as the "American century," many in the United States would answer in the affirmative, and there are some good reasons to support this outlook. After all, the U.S. has been in deeper craters linked to its revolutionary period, the destructive Civil War, the "Long Depression" period of 1873–1897, the Great Depression, World War II, and the Cold War.[1] In every case, the United States has recovered and then experienced long periods of prosperity. Richard Florida observes that during the course of the nineteenth-century's "Long Depression," America transformed itself from an agrarian to an industrial power.[2] After the Great Depression, Florida asserts that the United States "discovered a new way of living, working, and producing, which contributed to an unprecedented period of mass prosperity."[3] He concludes that "at critical moments, Americans have always looked forward, not back, and surprised the world with our resilience."[4]

Fareed Zakaria echoes some of the same sentiments when he points out that the United States has faced three serious challenges in the post–World War II period and has emerged on top each time: (1) the late 1950s when the Soviets were the first into space after launching Sputnik, (2) the early 1970s when OPEC suddenly quadrupled oil prices and U.S. economic growth slowed to a crawl, and (3) the mid-1980s when some experts were predicting that Japan would emerge as the technological and economic superpower of the future.[5] Josef Joffe dismisses any banter about America's decline, insisting the United States "remains first on any scale of power that matters—economic, military, diplomatic or cultural." He emphasizes that, unlike Europe, the United States maintains a "warrior culture" and is the "default power," because nobody else in the world possesses the requisite power and purpose. Finally, he adds that as the twenty-first century progresses, the U.S. will enjoy additional advantages because it will be "younger and more dynamic than its competitors."[6]

The nineteenth century was dominated by the United Kingdom, and at one time, the "sun never set on the British empire." In political, military, cultural, and economic terms, the UK qualified as that century's superpower. By the end of the second decade of the twentieth century, Great Britain had been surpassed by the United States, which emerged from World War I with its territory unscathed and producing more in goods and services than any other nation in the world.[7] With both Great Britain and the European continent devastated by what was then called the Great War, the United States would emerge as the world's largest creditor nation and many countries would make the pilgrimage to America's shores to seek public and private financing in order to rebuild their own war-ravaged infrastructures.

Indisputably, the twentieth century was the "American century," with three high points of American ascendancy. Arguably, at the end of World War II in 1945, the United States emerged as the most powerful nation to have existed. Once again, the U.S. mainland was unscathed, although some overseas territories in the Pacific had suffered considerable damage. The conflict also resulted in many more American casualties than in World War I, which the U.S. had entered in April 1917 and the hostilities were terminated in November 1918. Nevertheless, the United States in 1945 accounted for roughly one-half of total world production and its economy was in a full production mode—in sharp contrast to the utter devastation of key infrastructure in parts of Europe and Asia. The U.S. military was also by far the most powerful in the world, and the United States would end the war with a total monopoly on atomic weapons, two of which were exploded with cataclysmic consequences over Hiroshima and, later, Nagasaki.

World War II was eventually replaced by the Cold War, pitting the Western world led by the United States against the communist world led by the Soviet Union. In 1989, the Berlin Wall came down, and the Soviet empire disintegrated. Two years later, the Soviet Union itself fragmented into its fifteen constituent republics. This represented the second high-water mark of U.S. superpower. Russia was the largest unit of the former Soviet Union, but at one time during the 1990s, its economy was no larger than that of the state of Illinois. The Cold War was over, Russia was still militarily strong but an economic basket case, and the United States had moved into its "unipolar" phase.

The third pinnacle of U.S. dominance occurred at the end of the twentieth century. Not only was the United States the world's major military and political power, but its economy grew dramatically during the 1990s and early in the new century. For example, from 1994 through 2001, the growth in the U.S. economy during that period was larger than the entire gross domestic product of any other nation in the world, including second-ranked Japan.

The fifty U.S. states combined comprise the fourth-largest territory in the world. However, when one includes U.S. commonwealths and territories, the United States stretches more than ninety-four hundred miles from the U.S. Virgin Islands in the east to Guam in the west, passing through nine time zones, second only to the eleven zones in Russia. For example, when it is 11:00 A.M. in New York City on a Friday, it is already 1:00 A.M. on Saturday in Agana, the capital of Guam.

The U.S. recently surpassed 300 million inhabitants and ranks as the world's third-most-populous nation. It will continue to grow for many decades and is the only major nation in the developed world over the past several years to be close to the 2.1 children-per-woman replacement level needed to maintain a stable population, exclusive of immigration. It took one hundred years from 1776 for the United States to reach 100 million people, fifty-two years thereafter to reach 200 million, and only thirty-nine years later to achieve the 300 million milestone in 2006. If birthrates and immigration flows remain at current levels, the population could surpass 400 million within little more than three decades.[8] The U.S. will face its share of demographic challenges in the near future, but not to the same degree as Russia, Japan, or Germany, which are already losing population, or Canada or most nations in Europe, which will soon reach their population plateaus. Rather astonishingly, Japan, Europe, and Russia could conceivably have total populations below half of their current levels by 2100.[9]

In addition, the United States has a huge and vibrant economy and is blessed with an expansive and diverse natural-resource base that is rivaled today only by Russia and Canada. According to World Bank statistics estimating the GDPs of 186 nations and territories in 2008, and similar U.S. Department of Commerce statistics for the fifty U.S. states, one U.S. state, California, would have ranked that year among the ten largest "national" economies in the world, eleven states among the top twenty-five, twenty-six among the top fifty, forty-five among the top seventy-five, and all fifty states among the top eighty-six (see Figure VIII: 1 and Figure VIII: 2, with

FIGURE VIII: 1
If Each State Were a Nation, 2008

© 2009 Earl H. Fry

the former, instead of listing states, showing countries that produce about the same as the individual states on an annual GDP basis).

No major Western nation has matched America's job-creation performance, with forty-four million net new jobs created in the United States from 1980 through 2008.[10] Inflation has remained relatively low for many years in spite of a significant spike in energy and health-care prices, and, until recently, housing prices. America's entrepreneurship and corporate prowess are legendary.[11] Most Americans continue to be homeowners and a third have paid off their mortgages altogether.[12] In addition, housing on average is much more spacious and luxurious than ever before.

In the military sector, the United States spends far more than any other nation on defending itself and its allies. Its weapons systems are widely considered as far superior to those of any other country or groups of countries, and it is one of a handful of nations possessing the lift capacity to move significant numbers of weapons and personnel to any part of the world within a few days.

Whether in the development of weaponry or decisions rendered in corporate boardrooms, America remains innovative and its R&D capacity is unsurpassed—accounting for 40 percent of global R&D spending in recent years.[13] Its universities are ranked at the top echelons of the world's institu-

FIGURE VIII: 2
U.S. States and Nation-States:
Comparable Gross Products (Billions of Dollars, 2008 Data)

STATE	GSP	NATION-STATE	GDP	WORLD RANKING
ALABAMA	170	Chile	169	46
ALASKA	48	Lithuania	47	72
ARIZONA	249	Portugal	243	35
ARKANSAS	98	Libya	100	56
CALIFORNIA	1847	Brazil	1613	8
COLORADO	249	Portugal	243	35
CONNECTICUT	216	Czech Republic	216	37
DELAWARE	62	Belarus	60	63
DISTRICT OF COLUMBIA	97	Libya	100	56
FLORIDA	744	Turkey	794	17
GEORGIA	398	Austria	416	25
HAWAII	64	Croatia	69	62
IDAHO	53	Luxembourg	54	67
ILLINOIS	634	Turkey	794	17
INDIANA	255	Thailand	261	34
IOWA	136	Kazakhstan	132	52
KANSAS	123	Peru	127	54
KENTUCKY	156	Hungary	155	51
LOUISIANA	222	Czech Republic	216	37
MAINE	50	Serbia	50	70
MARYLAND	273	South Africa	244	32
MASSACHUSETTS	365	Greece	357	27
MICHIGAN	383	Iran	385	26
MINNESOTA	263	Finland	271	33
MISSISSIPPI	92	Slovak Republic	95	57
MISSOURI	238	Colombia	242	36
MONTANA	36	Oman	36	78
NEBRASKA	83	Angola	83	60
NEVADA	131	New Zealand	131	53
NEW HAMPSHIRE	60	Belarus	60	63
NEW JERSEY	475	Sweden	480	22
NEW MEXICO	80	Bangladesh	79	61
NEW YORK	1144	India	1217	12
NORTH CAROLINA	400	Austria	416	25
NORTH DAKOTA	31	Uruguay	32	81
OHIO	472	Sweden	480	22
OKLAHOMA	146	Hungary	455	51
OREGON	162	Egypt	463	50
PENNSYLVANIA	553	Poland	527	18
RHODE ISLAND	47	Lithuania	47	72
SOUTH CAROLINA	156	Hungary	155	51
SOUTH DAKOTA	37	Guatemala	39	77
TENNESSEE	252	Thailand	261	34
TEXAS	1224	India	1217	12
UTAH	110	Kuwait	112	55
VERMONT	25	Ethiopia	26	86
VIRGINIA	397	Austria	416	25
WASHINGTON	323	Argentina	328	29
WEST VIRGINIA	62	Belarus	60	63
WISCONSIN	240	Colombia	242	36
WYOMING	35	Oman	36	78

GSP= Gross State Product   GDP= Gross Domestic Product
Sources: U.S. Department of Commerce, Bureau of Economic Analysis, and World Bank.

tions of higher learning, and students from around the globe continue to flock to America's undergraduate and post-graduate programs. Until the recent recession, almost forty million Americans moved to new residences each year.[14] This reflects in part the mobility of Americans and their willingness to take risks and seek opportunities away from the familiar settings where they grew up.[15] Figure VIII: 3 illustrates many of the overall strengths of the United States as it enters the second decade of the twenty-first century.

FIGURE VIII: 3
AMERICA'S STRENGTHS

World's largest national economy with strong economic union
World's only military superpower
World's largest trading nation
World's largest foreign direct investor
World's third most populous nation
World's fourth largest nation territorially
World's most dynamic and diversified economy
World's most attractive nation for foreign direct investors
World's foremost university system
World's leader in spending on research and development
World's leader in technological innovation
Among top three nations in natural resources and energy reserves
Very stable political system
Very stable market-oriented economic system
World's leader in entrepreneurialism
Western world's leader in job creation
Disciplined workforce with minimal work stoppages
Strong sense of nationalism and unity
Dominance of one language in political and economic sectors
World's foremost currency
Pervasive log cabin syndrome facilitating success based on merit
(Lincoln, Clinton, Obama)
Enviable geographic location
Most desirable country for potential immigrants, including the best and brightest
Federalist system facilitates laboratories of democracy and
promotion of "best practices"

Most Americans may also learn from their personal mistakes and make course corrections in their individual lives. For example, tobacco addiction peaked at 42 percent of adults in 1964, compared with a record low of 20 percent today.[16] Drunk-driving deaths are down by 50 percent in the past generation, and the death rate from heart attacks is down 72 percent since 1960.[17] The vast majority of Americans are also more enlightened, opposing any discrimination based on race, ethnicity, or gender. Perhaps the ultimate statement of gender equality is the stationing of female soldiers on the front lines, even in combat situations.[18]

The U.S. federal system of governance may also be innovative and resilient, and when voters consider that their nation is moving in the wrong direction, they may vote decisively for change in political leadership, much as they did with the White House in November 2008. In a backhanded way, Winston Churchill understood the ability of Americans to correct mistakes and then move forward: "The American people always do the right thing after they tried every other alternative."[19] When all of the economic, political, diplomatic, and military dimensions of what constitutes a superpower are added up, the United States would seem to be in good shape to maintain its dominant status internationally for many decades to come. Indeed, this is exactly the argument put forward by David Levey and Stuart Brown in a *Foreign Affairs* article.[20] They are confident that the "hegemon" has been built on a solid foundation because of the massive size, resiliency, and technological dynamism of the U.S. economy; the misreading of the true U.S. savings rate due to official calculations, which exclude home equity values and 401(k) pension funds; the overwhelming international status of the U.S. dollar; and the failure to appreciate that international direct investment is actually a positive feature of America's perennial current-account deficits. Walter Russell Mead also chimes in when he emphasizes that many of America's major rivals have their share of problems. Russia has a one-dimensional economy and is badly damaged whenever oil prices fall. China has suffered major employment losses during the recent recession and is dependent on the United States to buy its exports in order to maintain manufacturing jobs. India faces an uncertain future with mass poverty, hunger, and significant domestic strife.[21] Much of Europe also suffered more economic damage during the Great Recession than did America, even though the recession began in the United States.

A Plan for Renewal

The following policy recommendations will require Americans to become more active players in the political process and be willing to endure a great deal of transitional pain. Some will argue that the current system is too entrenched and the average citizen's input is peripheral at best. Admittedly, changes will not be easy, but they are within the realm of possibility. George Bernard Shaw once said that "some people see things as they are and say why. I dream things that never were and say why not."[22] Both the Republicans and Democrats are equally at fault for many of the problems the United States now confronts. After the 2002 mid-term elections, Republicans controlled the White House and both chambers of Congress and had very high public approval ratings. They then proceeded to govern in an absolutely dismal fashion. Democrats have been in a similar situation in the past and governed poorly. After the 2008 elections, they enjoyed the same advantages as the Republicans in 2002, and the jury is still out in terms of their overall effectiveness. The policies listed below may be embraced by Republicans, Democrats, segments of each party, or perhaps a new political movement if incumbents on Capitol Hill stubbornly persist in maintaining the status quo.

To be blunt, some of the most powerful interest groups in the nation will have to be confronted and then defeated if these reforms are going to work. A few decades ago, no one thought the tobacco industry could ever be tamed. For years, King Tobacco held off any reform movements requiring the labeling of cigarettes as dangerous or measures that would protect nonsmokers. In 1964, the U.S. Surgeon General issued a report labeling smoking as harmful and a major cause of increased mortality. Yet it was not until 2000 that smoking was banned on all airplane flights to and from the United States. Progress was terribly slow with the Civil Aeronautics Board not ordering separate smoking and non-smoking sections on planes until 1973, and the Federal Aviation Administration not mandating a prohibition on smoking on domestic flights of two hours or less until 1988. Nevertheless, positive results have now been achieved, and King Tobacco has forfeited its crown.

Congress

The physical setting of Capitol Hill in Washington, D.C., is one of the most majestic sights in the entire world. However, what is transpiring within the chambers and congressional offices is responsible for much of America's decline. It has often been said that there are two things Americans do not want to witness firsthand in their lifetimes: how sausage is made at a packing plant and how a law is made in Congress. Peter G. Peterson provides a despondent perspective that would fit in quite well with the Book of Lamentations in the Old Testament:

> For the first time in my memory, the majority of the American people join me in believing that, on our current course, our children will not do as well as we have.

> Underlying these challenges is our broken political system. Our representatives, unlike our Founding Fathers, see politics as a career. As

a result, they are focused not on the next generation, but on the next election. When the long-term problems are large and real, they anesthetize us, mislead us, divert us—anything to keep us from giving up something or having to pay for it. Too often, our political leaders are just enablers, co-conspirators in a disingenuous and greedy silence. Our children are unrepresented. The future is unrepresented.[23]

CAMPAIGN FINANCING

The epicenter of America's current travails is situated in Congress. The most pressing reform is to break the chain linking many members of Congress to special interests with deep financial pockets used to finance congressional campaigns and provide lucrative benefits to the members, their staff, and their families. Public financing of congressional elections would be the easiest and most effective solution. Even though it might cost a few billion dollars of taxpayer money every election cycle, it would save hundreds of billions of dollars in earmarks, tax favors and exemptions, and unjustified government contracts. Any public financing scheme should also include free television and radio time for debates and town hall meetings as quid pro quo for stations using public airwaves for their programming. Under this system, House and Senate members would not have to be engaged in a perpetual campaign to raise more money for the next election. They could actually focus on major issues facing the country and work closely with constituents at home, without invoking the "pay-to-play" mantra that is pervasive on Capitol Hill today. Average Americans would be less cynical about who actually controls elections, and some might have an opportunity to run for Congress, in sharp contrast to so many who now run who are either millionaires or supported by well-heeled special interests.[24] The cycle of reelecting on average 95 percent of incumbents in Congress and, by the way, in state legislatures (during the period 1980–2006) might finally be broken.[25]

A mixture of public and private financing schemes is the more likely outcome, at least in the short term. Already, eleven states and twelve local jurisdictions provide partial public financing or matching funds, so workable models are available that can be easily implemented at the national level.[26] Common Cause has also submitted a "Fair Elections" model that would provide qualified congressional candidates, who voluntarily take no individual contributions larger than $100, with some public funding.[27] Obama's 2008 campaign provides some inspiration for what might be accomplished in the Internet age. During his twenty-one-month campaign, three million donors made 6.5 million financial contributions, mostly via the Internet, with six million of those contributions being for $100 or less.[28]

Incumbency on Capitol Hill is reinforced by name recognition and amassing huge "war chests" for reelection, with most of the money coming from sources outside the state or district where the incumbent is seeking reelection.[29] This would end or be mitigated by public financing or partial public financing. Gerrymandering could also be terminated by establishing impartial commissions to redraw each state's congressional districts every ten years after the census has been completed. Neither governors nor state legislatures nor political parties should be given the upper hand in determining these districts.[30] The selection of impartial commission members would be fully scrutinized by the media and the members' resumes posted on the Internet and the public allowed to comment on each member's qualifications. Each commission would write an exhaustive report justifying its decision-making process and appeals could be made to the federal courts if wrongdoing were suspected.

Moving toward at least partial public funding of congressional elections could also bring an end to the Leadership PACs that are little more than slush funds for individual members of Congress. In general, the United States would be much better off without career politicians who at the end of their public service in Washington, D.C., will retire as multimillionaires. Their congressional pay tops $170,000 per year, but if they also spend a half dozen years as lobbyists after retiring from Congress, they will easily obtain seven-figure bank accounts. Americans should be willing to pay senators and representatives $250,000 per year, if in return they pledge to take public money for their campaigns, reject any individual private donations over a few hundred dollars per year, end all PACs, and refrain from lobbying Congress in any way for a three-year period after leaving their elected positions.

Finally, partial public funding of campaigns would also mitigate the stranglehold lobbyists and well-funded special interest groups have on Capitol Hill. If members of Congress have to raise little or no money for re-election, they will not be beholden to these special interests. Americans should rightfully be disturbed that Washington, D.C., and the close suburbs of northern Virginia and southern Maryland are near the top of the wealthiest enclaves in the entire country. This wealth has not been achieved by the growth in high-tech companies or other industrial sectors. Rather, most of the wealth is linked to feeding off a government trough that is getting larger and larger as the years go by. Lobbying companies, law firms, campaign consultancies, public relations organizations, think tanks, and a vast array of private contractors and service industries feed out of this expanding trough. Many individuals get immensely rich from this trough that is funded by average taxpayers scattered across the vast American landscape. If the politician-lobbyist-special interest group money chain can be disrupted, and the revolving door from public service to lucrative Beltway lobbying slowed dramatically, then the nation will be much better off.[31] Many companies would welcome the change, because they will no longer have to hire expensive lobbyists and spend so much money within the Beltway.[32] As Robert Reich has suggested, many corporate executives resent being "extorted" for money by members of Congress or lobbyists, who insist they must "pay to play" in order to get their opinions heard on Capitol Hill.[33] Lobbying will still be perfectly legal and everyone will maintain the right to petition their government representatives, but the eight-hundred-pound money gorilla will have exited through the side door.[34]

EARMARKING

The number of earmarks tripled between 1994 and 2006.[35] This number should be curtailed sharply, and Norman Ornstein has offered the best solution to ensure the remaining earmarks actually serve the public interest. Projects at the local level should be considered by Congress for limited funding, but these projects would be selected in advance and rank ordered by panels of local experts in each congressional district, including some local elected officials, plus business, labor, civic group, and academic representatives. Each panel would publicize its preliminary selections and then react to public comments. Any member of Congress who ignored the recommendations of these panels in order to fund projects proposed by political friends or campaign contributors could face stiff opposition at the next election.

APPROPRIATIONS AND BALANCING BUDGETS

The U.S. government's budget is in a shambles, and America's triple A bond rating, which has never been downgraded since 1917, is understandably in jeopardy.[36] In fiscal year 2009 alone, each American household was saddled with an additional $16,000 in debt obligations.[37] Members of Congress have a mind-set that it is their money, and they will spend it any way they please—forgetting that all the revenue is generated from the American populace, and their spending should result in the betterment of the American people in general. Moreover, the United States has experienced many years of robust economic growth in the past, but Congress has managed to balance the budget only five times in the past half century. In order to make the deficits look less imposing, Congress also allows itself to use accounting gimmicks that would be considered as fraudulent in the corporate world. The U.S. Department of the Treasury calculates the total U.S. government debt is currently $12 trillion, but when one takes into account liabilities already assumed by Congress, which will span the next few decades, the debt actually exceeds $56 trillion, or $184,000 per capita, according to the Peter G. Peterson Foundation.[38] Joseph J. DioGuardi, a practicing certified public accountant and former member of Congress from New York, insists:

> that the financial management failures of U.S. corporations cannot come close to rivaling the budget and bookkeeping shambles of the U.S. government. At the federal level, there are myriad off-budget gimmicks, unrecorded liabilities, and financial manipulations on a scale that would put many executives of publicly traded companies in prison for securities fraud.[39]

The White House has also contributed to this evasion, as in the case of the Bush administration taking the costs of fighting the wars in Iraq and Afghanistan, Medicare reimbursements to physicians, and disaster relief "off budget."[40] The "unified budget" also takes annual surpluses in trust fund accounts such as Social Security and uses them to lower the government's annual deficits, even though these trust funds are pledged for retirees and other targeted groups.[41] Congress must jettison its flawed, current-cash basis accounting system in favor of the generally accepted accounting principles (GAAP) required by the Securities and Exchange Commission of all public corporations and used by all fifty state governments and tens of thousands of local governments.[42] Unfortunately, if the GAAP system is adopted, the American people will soon realize the government's debt is much worse than has been publicized and is tantamount to a "fiscal cancer."[43]

Much more public scrutiny, transparency, and accountability are required in terms of how Capitol Hill allocates money and provides favors to special interests.[44] As will be discussed later, tens of billions of dollars in annual revenues are lost because of the thousands of new insertions into the tax code since the last major revisions were made in 1986. Many of these insertions exempt or cut the tax burdens of well-heeled individuals or groups.

Agriculture is another can of worms. Franklin D. Roosevelt pushed for the Agricultural Adjustment Act of 1933 in an effort to provide temporary relief to farmers during the Great Depression. At the time, a quarter of Americans lived on farms and 44 percent lived in rural areas. Today, fewer than 2 percent live on farms and less than 17 percent are rural-based.[45] Yet today, over $20 billion in taxpayer funds are dispensed annually in the form of price supports for a couple of dozen commodities, drought aid, crop insurance, and other questionable programs. In 2006, the *Washington Post* published a series of articles documenting huge waste in government agricultural expenditures, including large sums given to people who do not farm, compensation to agribusinesses even when market prices are high, drought aid in the absence of droughts, and crop insurance abuses.[46] Under the current arcane rules, Congress protects a handful of sugar cane and sugar beet businesses, forcing Americans to pay twice the world price for sugar.[47] More than four hundred commodities are grown in the United States, but only a few receive subsidies or protection from imports, with sugar, dairy products, rice, cotton, wheat, and soybeans receiving the lion's share of the money. Why are the vast majority of crops grown without a cent of government assistance, while a few still require huge financial outlays by the government? Why is so much money going from Washington to corn farmers for the ill-conceived and environmentally damaging production of ethanol? The answer is politics pure and simple, with members of Congress dispensing special favors to local constituents or campaign contributors, all cloaked in the mythical image of helping "small farmers." In 2007, 43 percent of agricultural aid went to congressional districts whose members served on the House Agriculture Committee.[48] A year later, two-thirds of the subsidies were funneled to 10 percent of big farms and corporate agribusinesses.[49] The government took a favorable step in 2008 by limiting most subsidies to those with a farm income below $750,000 per year. President Obama has asked that the threshold be reduced to $250,000, but Congress has thus far refused to act on his proposal.[50] Without any doubt, more stringent reform measures are required. Almost all subsidies and import protection must be phased out quickly, saving taxpayers and consumers tens of billions of dollars per year and helping end the huge distortions in international agricultural trade that favor a few U.S. agribusinesses at the expense of farmers located predominantly in the developing world.

A cleaver must also be taken to contracts awarded by Congress to the private sector, especially in the military arena. In 2008, the government issued 3.7 million contracts, up 76 percent since 2000, worth $368 billion.[51] Far too many of these contracts are issued to "friends" of members of Congress or in an effort to save or create jobs in local districts, without any benefit to U.S. national security. Many are also in the form of suspicious no-bid contracts. Defense spending should never be viewed as a way to create or preserve jobs within congressional districts, but tens of billions of dollars have been allocated over the objections of the Defense Department, which does not even want these weapon systems. For example, the Obama administration submitted a huge $636 billion budget request for the Pentagon to cover fiscal year 2010. The House of Representatives tacked on a thousand spending projects to the proposed defense bill that the Obama administration had not requested, including the purchase of several additional government aircraft that could be used by members of Congress.[52]

Most importantly, a balanced budget amendment needs to be added to the U.S. Constitution. The amendment would stipulate that Congress by law must balance the budget each year, with exceptions for wars and recessions. It would also require Congress to limit yearly budget increases to the rate of population growth and inflation, excluding interest payments on the national debt.[53] This would represent a "pay-as-you-go" formula mandating that every budget increase be offset by decreases in other parts of the budget. Once the private sector begins to grow and revenues increase from expanded economic activity, any surplus would be used to pay down the mammoth federal debt, which would first decrease as a percentage of GDP and later in nominal dollars. Forty-nine U.S. states have a statutory or constitutional requirement to balance their budgets, and the federal government can do the same. Even with an amendment in place, voters and the media must remain constantly vigilant to potential gimmickry used by Congress to skirt around the intent of the amendment.[54]

PROCEDURES AND THE LINE-ITEM VETO

Law-making is already an excruciating labyrinth, but it can be improved by adding much more transparency to the entire process and ensuring that all proposed legislation is placed on the Internet at least seventy-two hours before the final vote, except in cases of dire emergency. Omnibus bills should be banned. These are bills passed at the end of congressional sessions that cover hundreds of pages and usually expend hundreds of billions of dollars. No one can read all of the material in time, which opens the way for the insertion of last-minute earmarks, new tax code revisions providing favors to individuals or groups, and other practices that work against the best interests of the citizens in general. In the Senate, cutting off the filibuster should require fifty-five votes instead of the present sixty, and senatorial courtesy allowing a single member to hold up proposed legislation or nominations, often anonymously, should be banned altogether. The president should be extended a line-item veto so he may veto parts of a proposed bill but allow the other parts to become law. Forty-six governors have access to line-item vetoes, but the chief executive of the United States does not. Consequently, Congress often sends along legislation to the White House with parts the president desperately wants but other parts he despises. The tactic is meant to force the president to hold his nose and sign the whole bill. The line-item veto would end this tactic and, in the process, save the country billions of dollars in unnecessary expenditures. Federal courts have thus far argued that such a veto would shift the balance of power toward the executive branch and away from the legislative branch. This shift is completely warranted, even if it requires a constitutional amendment to override the opinion of the federal judiciary.

Congressional sessions should also be revised from the current Tuesday afternoon–Thursday afternoon routine to five days a week for two weeks, and then a week off to return to the members' states or districts.[55] This revision would allow members to work together and get to know one another in a collegial fashion. It might spur on more cooperation across party lines and build a spirit of problem solving instead of partisan wrangling. Freed from the necessity to raise campaign funds on a regular basis, the members could easily adjust to a job routine that mirrors what most Americans do in their own workweek.

Voter Turnout

Much more can be done to facilitate voter registration that would assist the U.S. to improve what is one of the worst voter turnout records among the Western democracies. The National Registration Act of 1993 mandates motor-voter provisions permitting people to register to vote when they are receiving or renewing their driver's licenses.[56] States are also required to provide voter registration opportunities for applicants for public assistance such as food stamps, Medicaid, or temporary assistance for needy families. Nine states permit voter registration on election day, and their turnout was seven percentage points higher in 2008 than states that did not permit same-day registration.[57] Hours that polls are open on election day should be lengthened in some of the states to encourage greater participation. Casting pre-election day ballots, absentee ballots, or voting by mail should be made easier.[58] Whenever feasible, naturalized Americans should be registered to vote immediately after they have been administered the oath of citizenship.[59] Optimally, elections should be scheduled on weekends so people could vote either on a Saturday or Sunday, but this might require a cumbersome constitutional revision process. Above all, higher voter participation should engender greater interest in the political and governmental processes and increase public scrutiny of what transpires in governments at the federal, state, and local levels.

Constitutional Amendments

The U.S. Constitution is a "living" document and will always remain a work in progress. Just before his return from France in 1789, Thomas Jefferson sent a letter to James Madison and emphasized that "no society can make a perpetual constitution of perpetual laws. The earth belongs always to the living generation. They may manage it then, and what proceeds from it, as they please."[60] Madison felt constitutional change should be more gradual, viewing the document as a "timeless constitution" but still subject to some revisions.[61]

The Constitution does need to be amended periodically to reinvigorate America's democratic system and its future global competitiveness. Almost all previous amendments have followed this route: passed by the two chambers of Congress with at least a two-thirds vote, followed by ratification by at least three-quarters of the state legislatures. One amendment, the twenty-first repealing prohibition, was passed by Congress and ratified by at least three-quarters of state-sponsored conventions. Two other routes have never been used successfully: amendments proposed by at least two-thirds of the delegates assembled in a convention of the states and then ratified by at least three-quarters of individual state conventions; and amendments proposed by at least two-thirds of the delegates assembled at a convention of the states and then ratified by at least three-quarters of the state legislatures. One will notice the president of the United States has no direct role in any of these amendment paths, and the latter two would remove Capitol Hill entirely from the process. This is a function of federalism and could theoretically provide the states with an influential voice over future constitutional change.

At least three-fifths of Americans believe that a constitutional amendment should be ratified that would elect as president the candidate who receives the most popular votes.[62] The Electoral College could be legally or functionally disbanded and voters allowed to select the president and vice president directly through two methods. The most arduous would be a formal constitutional amendment process as outlined above. This may be difficult because sparsely populated states feel empowered by the Electoral College process. The second route is now in process. As of April 2009, Maryland, New Jersey, Hawaii, Illinois, and Washington have passed laws to participate in a "national interstate popular vote" compact that would allocate all of their electoral votes to the presidential candidate who wins the most votes nationwide.[63] The pledge would be activated when states representing at least the 270 electoral votes needed to win the presidency have formally joined the compact. So far, these five states with a combined sixty-one electoral votes have signed on.

Larry Sabato has suggested twenty-three specific ways to revitalize the Constitution.[64] Among the most worthwhile amendments would be the following:

(1) require nonpartisan redistricting for elections to the House of Representatives;

(2) pass a balanced budget amendment with appropriate safeguards and escape clauses;

(3) extend a line-item veto to the president over all appropriations bills;

(4) eliminate the "born in the U.S." requirement for the president and vice president and replace it with having been a U.S. citizen for at least twenty years;

(5) do away with lifetime tenure for Supreme Court justices in favor of a single, nonrenewable term of fifteen years;

(6) grant Congress the power to set a mandatory retirement age for federal judges;

(7) establish regional primaries that would all take place within four months prior to the August party nominating conventions for the president and vice president;

(8) reform campaign financing by permitting Congress to place reasonable limits on campaign spending by the wealthy and mandate partial public financing for House and Senate election campaigns;

(9) adopt an automatic voter registration system for all qualified American citizens eighteen and older; and

(10) stipulate that all able-bodied young Americans devote at least two years to some form of national service.

The American political system is currently deeply flawed and changes are desperately needed. If Capitol Hill is not willing to make the necessary revisions, the states, either through the legislatures or citizen groups demanding the creation of state conventions, should get the reform process rolling.

The Tax Code

The U.S. tax code is byzantine and cleaning it up will add tens of billions of dollars in revenues each year and help to balance the budget.[65] Since the Tax Reform Act of 1986 was enacted during the Reagan administration, more than fifteen thousand changes have been made by Congress to the tax code.[66] The code should be updated to include three or four categories, with the top marginal tax rate set at about 39 percent. Almost all exemptions or special favors found in the more than fifteen thousand revisions would be eliminated. The only possible exceptions would be exemptions for children or the infirm being cared for at home and for clearly identified charitable contributions. The tax deduction on interest payments for home ownership would also be phased out because most of the benefit has gone to those buying homes above $750,000. The tax deduction for medical insurance would also be phased out because it, too, tends to benefit disproportionately those with very expensive plans.

The Internal Revenue Service (IRS) must vigorously pursue individuals and corporations openly evading taxes through overseas tax havens. The IRS has alleged that as many as fifty-two thousand U.S. residents invested in United Bank of Switzerland (UBS) accounts that were openly marketed for the purpose of evading U.S. income taxes.[67] The Swiss government has ordered UBS to release the names of a few thousand individuals who might have been engaged in gross felonious actions, arguing that in Switzerland people who evade taxes in countries other than Switzerland have not broken any Swiss laws. Some experts have estimated that up to $100 billion is lost in U.S. tax revenues each year from tax cheats taking advantage of offshore tax havens.[68] Washington should threaten onerous economic sanctions and a suspension of diplomatic relations with any tax haven unless the entire list of American depositors is divulged to the U.S. Department of Justice. This is the optimal opportunity to break the back of tax havens, and the European Union is in lockstep with the United States in ending secret offshore accounts that are opened for tax evasion purposes. A tentative agreement has been reached between the IRS and UBS to release the names of some account holders, but this should be only the first step in a much more comprehensive process.

The much simpler tax code will also save Americans tens of billions of dollars in preparation costs every year.[69] Ending the tax favors given to certain individuals and corporations, combined with vigorous pursuit of tax cheats, will also add many billions of dollars to government coffers without raising the tax burden on most Americans.[70]

Entitlements

Hopefully, if the other reforms mentioned in this chapter are implemented, the challenges linked to entitlements will mostly dissipate. The Social Security system will require gradually raising the retirement age to seventy and means testing some of the benefits so that the wealthy receive smaller benefits. The Social Security tax on employment may also require another 1 percent contribution from both workers and employers, and the amount of earnings subject to the FICA tax, which was $106,800 in 2009, must also increase. More constructive ways for investing the Social Security funds should also be explored, because the real rate of return of between 1 and 1.5 percent on the Social Security savings of most workers is woefully inadequate.[71]

Medicare and Medicaid are much more serious problems and will require wholesale changes in America's health-care system as recommended below. Extensive fraud in both programs must be eliminated and eligibility standards for Medicaid recipients scrutinized more closely. The Medicare tax on earnings, which is currently 1.45 percent, should go up modestly. Medicare eligibility must gradually increase to age seventy and require means testing to determine post-retirement premiums and benefits.

Health Care

America's health-care problem is immense but also solvable.[72] Over $2.5 trillion a year is funneled into health care, and the annual augmentation in spending is far above increases in the overall consumer price index. In 2009, the average annual health-insurance premium for a family was $13,375, more than double the average premium of a decade earlier and only slightly more than the yearly earnings of a full-time, minimum-wage worker.[73] On average, Americans spend twice as much per capita on health care as those in other major Western countries, and per capita U.S. administrative costs are about six times more expensive.[74] If health-care reform is successful, most Americans will receive good coverage at a more affordable price, and no longer will 20 percent of adults under sixty-five have no insurance coverage and at least another twenty-five million inadequate coverage.[75] The United States will also become more competitive internationally. U.S. companies will not be tempted to offshore their production because of the high cost of medical insurance within the United States. Workers will also have more flexibility to change jobs because their health insurance would be portable and no one could deny them or family members coverage because of pre-existing medical conditions. The average family's disposable income would also increase because it would no longer be spending $1 of every $6 of earnings on doctors, hospitals, pharmaceuticals, and related expenses.[76] Washington's budgetary problems would also be improved immensely by less spending proportionally on Medicare, Medicaid, Veterans', and civil service health programs.

Currently, the United States has a hodgepodge of health insurance plans. It has one of the most centralized government-run programs in the world in its Veterans Affairs, which maintains twelve hundred hospitals and other medical facilities to care for America's twenty-four million honored military veterans. Medicare is a single-payer, social insurance program administered by the U.S. government and covers forty-five million older people who receive treatment in the private sector. Medicaid is jointly paid for by Washington and the state governments, administered by the states, and provides direct payments to health providers furnishing services to fifty-eight million people who are considered to have low incomes. In 2007, Massachusetts began to implement its own health-care plan intended to provide insurance for almost all of its residents. More people than ever before are now receiving coverage in Massachusetts, but health-care costs are also up significantly.[77]

In his comparative view of health care in Western countries, Atul Gawande has illustrated that a variety of options are available to the United States. His research also indicates that residents of other Western nations are generally satisfied or very satisfied with their systems, they pay far less than Americans for treatment, and the overall treatment results are as good as or even better than comparable results in the United States.[78] The United Kingdom has the most socialized system in the industrialized world. France has a mixed system and has more physicians per capita than the United States.[79] Switzerland made the switch to universal coverage in 1994 and requires residents to purchase private health insurance, while providing subsidies to limit overall costs to no more than 10 percent of an individual's income.[80]

Gawande has also shown that health-care expenses and treatment outcomes vary dramatically within the United States. McAllen, Texas, ranks second to Miami in the amount of money spent per person on health care. In 2006, Medicare spent $15,000 per enrollee in McAllen, almost twice the national average. El Paso, also located in Texas, cost only half as much per Medicare enrollee, and its treatment outcomes were almost universally better than McAllen's.[81] Indeed, the states with the highest levels of health-care spending, Louisiana, Texas, California, and Florida, "were near the bottom of the national rankings on the quality of patient care."[82] When Secretary of Health and Human Services Mike Leavitt needed a colonoscopy, two doctors in the Beltway region quoted him prices of $5,750 and $6,750. Leavitt decided to return to his home state of Utah where Intermountain Healthcare, a network of hospitals and clinics in Utah and Idaho, quoted a price of $3,200. Moreover, the Utah facility's treatment record was at least as good as its counterparts within the Beltway.[83] Gawande also provides specific examples of organizations that offer excellent care at relatively low costs, such as the Mayo Clinic facilities in Minnesota, Florida, and Arizona, and the Kaiser Permanente network in northern California.[84] Medical facilities in Grand Junction, Colorado, also stand out because of high-quality treatment for Medicare patients at lower prices than almost anywhere else in the U.S.[85]

Based on "best practices" and "comparative pricing" in other countries, as well as within the United States itself, America can build a much more efficient health-care system at significantly lower prices.[86] The big challenge is defeating a group of powerful interest groups even more imposing than the once-legendary King Tobacco. Insurance companies must be confronted, because their administrative costs are far higher than anywhere else in the Western world. Insurance companies are also guided by the profit motive that prompts them to turn down requests for the optimal treatment for patients based strictly on costs. Hospitals must be run more efficiently and held accountable for every expense incurred by patients. Doctors must consider their livelihood as a profession and not a business—one of the glaring problems discovered in the McAllen case study.[87] Most doctors must transition to being salaried and the ultra-expensive fee-for-service system must give way to a "fee-for-health system" that will be much more efficient, patient-friendly, and affordable.[88] The health-care system of the future will need more general practitioners (GPs) and fewer specialists, and the pay scale differences between GPs and the specialists must be reduced substantially. Governments at all levels will need to provide more funding to pay for the advanced education of doctors so they do not leave medical school with enormous debts. Pharmaceutical companies stick Americans with most of the costs for drugs, while providing cut-rate deals for health-care systems in other countries. This practice must be ended, and groups of companies and groups of states must be permitted to negotiate their own drug deals within the United States and from overseas suppliers, including much wider dissemination of generic drugs.[89]

The power base of trial lawyers must also be reduced and tort law reformed. States and the federal government should work out new compensation limits on malpractice suits that have resulted in skyrocketing insurance premiums for doctors and a tendency for them to order an array of unneeded tests and examinations to protect themselves against potential lawsuits.[90]

The health-care package considered by Congress in 2009 should be viewed as only a starting point for more extensive revisions in the future. In order to mitigate the massive lobbying influence of special interest groups, the White House and Congress should jointly establish a commission of eminent experts to recommend wholesale changes in America's health-care system, including specific ways to reduce medical-related costs. The base-closing model used in past years would be replicated, meaning Congress would consider the recommendations and then vote on the entire package, with no amendments permitted. If approved on Capitol Hill, the president would then sign or veto the entire set of recommendations.

America will be much better prepared to face the challenges of the future if comprehensive health-care reform is implemented over the next decade. However, Americans must also do their part. Much of the medicine practiced in the United States today is "disease care" that responds to the sedentary daily lives of many Americans after they become ill. The nation will be in much better shape if the average American will pursue healthier lifestyles and the medical establishment will focus more intently on disease prevention.[91] Americans lead the Western world in the rate of obesity, with one-third of adults being obese and another third overweight.[92] One third of children and teens are also overweight or on the verge of being so, and one in seven pre-school kids is overweight.[93] Type 2 diabetes, often linked to obesity, is spreading rapidly. Overweight people are also much more susceptible to heart disease, liver failure, and a variety of other life-threatening diseases. Governments, schools, and families must all place greater emphasis on good health practices, and success in this area will lead to major dividends in terms of lower "disease-care" costs in the future.[94]

The Institute of Medicine, part of the National Academy of Sciences, proposes that a successful health-care system will include the following: (1) universal coverage; (2) coverage not tied to jobs; (3) affordable coverage for individuals and families; (4) an affordable system for society as a whole; and (5) access to quality care for everyone in society.[95] The changes recommended in this section will meet some of these criteria but not all. Some plans may still be linked to businesses or groups of businesses. Some expensive medical procedures may have to be rationed. For example, a seventy-five-year-old may not be covered by Medicare insurance for a liver transplant, but all women would be entitled to pre-natal care.[96] The rate of discovery of new pharmaceuticals may slow as R&D moves away from some pharmaceutical companies and toward government and university laboratories. The pace of introducing new technologies used in a doctor's office or in hospitals may also slow for cost-containment reasons. Waiting periods to see the doctor or enter a hospital may also lengthen a bit. On the whole, however, the U.S. system will be vastly improved and health-care costs as a percentage of GDP will decline significantly.

Education

The K–12 public education system must be fixed. Obama's Secretary of Education Arne Duncan has been blunt about primary and secondary education in the United States: "We've seen a race to the bottom. States are lying to children. They are lying to parents. They're ignoring failure, and that's unacceptable. We have to be fierce."[97]

No longer should it be necessary to maintain a school-year calendar based on a nineteenth-century agrarian society. School should be year-round with generous breaks to allow students to rest a bit and vacation with their families. The school day should be eight hours in length, and each state must put forward rigorous and transparent proficiency standards. Basic and advanced reading, writing, and math must be supplemented with knowledge germane to the twenty-first century, including computer literacy, foreign-language training, geography, history, cultural awareness, and civics. Astonishingly, the United States is only one of the three nations in the world not to have adopted the metric system, along with Liberia and Burma.[98] This should be rectified immediately, and all students should become familiar with the metric system. Concerned and aware citizenship should also be fostered in schools as students learn about American history and American government. Students should also learn about the world around them and be part of what John Zogby has referred to as "the First Globals."[99] Exercise must be a part of the daily routine and junk food and junk drinks banned from school grounds. Proper nutritional and exercise habits should be taught from the earliest grades. The most up-to-date technology should be employed to enhance teaching efficiency and personalize the learning experience for every child.

Teachers are the key to future success. A Los Angeles study indicates that a good teacher ranked within the top 25 percent of all teachers would erase the gap in testing between white and black students if given four consecutive years to work with the young black students.[100] Teachers in general should be paid more, but their qualifications should improve and performance expectations heightened. For example, half the math teachers had no formal training in mathematics before entering the classroom.[101] The National Center on Education and the Economy declares that a disproportionate share of U.S. teachers is among the "less able" of high school students who go to college.[102] School unions should not be permitted to protect the jobs of grossly underperforming teachers. Wage increases should be based primarily on merit and not time served in the profession.

Half of the dropout problem is concentrated in about 12 percent of schools.[103] These schools must be revamped and competition enhanced through the creation of charter schools that are publicly funded and generally free from local school board and teacher union controls. Parents and other family members must also play a critical role in emphasizing the importance of a quality education for all children and assist in making sure that homework assignments are completed. President Obama's mother is certainly a model for what can be done, as she would often awaken at 5:00 A.M. to tutor her son.[104] Obama himself is also a model for being willing to get up at 5:00 A.M. to complete his homework.

Universities offer a world-class learning experience, but they are becoming too expensive. Greater attention should be given to the classroom performance of professors and more of the research pursued by professors should be directed at solving real-world problems related to the everyday lives of people in the United States and other countries.

Federalism

If America is to maintain its federal system of governance, the system must be revitalized. Once campaign-finance reform is implemented, state governments will, by default, be given a greater voice within the Beltway, because they will no longer be competing for attention against so many well-heeled special interest groups and their lobbyists. The president and the leaders of Congress should hold two-day summits with governors and state legislative leaders every year, focusing on intergovernmental relations and the special concerns of the states.

Many states must also clean up their own systems of government. Most states have suffered huge losses during the Great Recession and must now work to revive their economic bases and enact reasonable budgets. Two of the three largest states, California and New York, have become disaster areas in terms of effective governance.[105] Far too much corruption and cronyism exists at the state level, and the retention rate of incumbents in most state legislatures, about 95 percent, rivals that of incumbents on Capitol Hill. The states should move toward total or partial public financing of campaigns for governors, legislators, and elected judges. States should also focus on providing world-class infrastructures and reasonable tax and regulatory regimes and move away from handing out to specific corporations about $50 billion a year in dubious incentives.

Urban areas must also be given more attention by both Washington and the state capitals. Richard Florida estimates the world's forty largest urbanized mega-regions have only 18 percent of the global population but account for almost two-thirds of the global GDP and nearly 90 percent of patented innovations.[106] All levels of government must cooperate in making urban areas more competitive in the U.S., and their progress will help determine how well the United States as a country will fare in the global economy over the next several decades. Specific steps to be taken would include facilitating greater cooperation and planning on a municipal-wide basis, strengthening K–12 and post-secondary education, modernizing all facets of the urban infrastructure, and promoting the development of "clusters of excellence" in the mode of Silicon Valley.

Foreign and Defense Policy

This may be hard to swallow for many Americans, but the United States should heed the words of candidate George W. Bush in his second debate with Al Gore in October 2000. In that debate, Bush urged the United States to "be humble in how we treat nations." He added that the U.S. should "be judicious as to how to use the military. It needs to be in our vital interest, the mission needs to be clear, and the exit strategy obvious." Finally, he warned against being bogged down in nation-building.[107] Of course, he violated all of his recommendations when he ordered the invasion and occupation of Iraq, and Obama is doing the same in his open-ended military build-up and occupation of Afghanistan. Almost all U.S. troops are expected to exit Iraq by the end of 2011, and the same exit date should be used for most U.S. troops in Afghanistan. As emphasized in Chapter 5, the long-term costs to the United States of the Iraqi escapade may top $3 trillion, and Afghanistan in the short term has cost over $230 billion with casualties and expenses mounting rapidly.[108] The Brookings Institution ranks Afghanistan as the second-"weakest" state in the developing world after Somalia.[109] Its GDP is smaller than that of any U.S. state, and $3 billion of the GDP comes from opium production.[110] The United States can help the Afghani people in a number of ways, especially in economic development and to prepare them to fight against the Taliban and al-Qaeda, but U.S. troops are mired in a quagmire and their heroic efforts are being wasted.[111] A long-term U.S. military occupation of Afghanistan does not remotely serve U.S. vital interests and diverts attention from the dramatic reforms that must be pursued back home in the United States.[112]

American presidents in the future must be continuously reminded of the hard lessons from the Vietnam debacle. John F. Kennedy told his close adviser Kenneth O'Donnell in 1963 that he would start exiting from Vietnam after his reelection in 1964. Kennedy said that he could not do so earlier, because he would be labeled as soft on communism and this might ruin his reelection chances.[113] JFK also told Charles Bartlett, a close friend in the press corps, that "[W]e don't have a prayer of staying in Vietnam. Those people hate us. They are going to throw our asses out of there at almost any point. But I can't give up a piece of territory like that to the Communists and then get the people to reelect me."[114] In the above sentence, substitute Obama for JFK, Afghanistan for Vietnam, and al-Qaeda and the Taliban for the Communists: *Plus ça change, plus c'est la même chose.* As Gordon M. Goldstein emphasizes in his insightful book, *Lessons in Disaster*, foreign intervention is a presidential choice, not an inevitability; politics is the enemy of sound foreign policy strategy; conviction without rigor is a formula for disaster; and the long-term deployment of troops abroad in pursuit of indeterminate ends often results in catastrophic consequences.[115]

The U.S. military budget may be trimmed by at least $200 billion once the military campaigns in Iraq and Afghanistan cease. The U.S. Navy and Air Force are light-years ahead of any other competitor in the world. As J. Peter Scoblic emphasizes:

> Our fleet of stealth fighters and bombers can establish air dominance in virtually any scenario, allowing us to obliterate an adversary's military infrastructure at will. At sea, the U.S. fleet is larger than the next seventeen navies combined and includes eleven carrier battle groups that can project power around the globe. (By contrast, few of our potential adversaries field even a single carrier).[116]

The Navy and Air Force will continue to be far ahead of any other country even if the number of aircraft carrier task forces is reduced from eleven to nine, and the Zumwalt class destroyer, the Virginia class submarine, the Marine Corp's V-22 Osprey aircraft, and the Air Force's F-22 Raptor aircraft cease production.[117] Moreover, any military item not wanted by the Pentagon that continues to be produced for pork-barrel reasons by members of Congress should be immediately axed from the budget. A sharp knife should also be used to pare many defense contracts issued to private companies, whose paramilitaries and support staff in the fall of 2009 added up to a staggering 120,000 personnel in Iraq and 74,000 in Afghanistan—all being paid for by U.S. tax dollars.[118] Some resources should be shifted to the Army and Marines, which have borne the brunt of fighting in recent years and are likely to be front and center in any future conflict area. America must always be prepared to strike back when its vital interests are jeopardized, but hard-headed lessons should be learned from Vietnam, Iraq, and the continued occupation of Afghanistan even after the Taliban government had been overthrown.

Washington must also send a clear message to its allies that it is willing to cooperate in bringing an end to hostilities and other dangerous situations around the world, but equitable burden-sharing is the new name of the game. President Obama reinforced this change in policy in his September 2009 address at the United Nations:

> Those who used to chastise America for acting alone in the world cannot now stand by and wait for America to solve the world's problems alone. We have sought—in word and deed—a new era of engagement with the world. Now is the time for all of us to share the responsibility for a global response to global problems.[119]

Diplomacy, intelligence gathering, selective deployment of Special Forces, and the use of sophisticated equipment such as satellites and unmanned aircraft and naval vessels will constitute America's first response to international crises.[120] Ideally, America will lead by example as it regenerates its economy and revitalizes its flagging political system. In tandem with growing strength at home, the United States will project its influence abroad in a more collaborative, less belligerent and unilateralist, "humble" way.[121]

Immigration

The United States is the world's foremost immigrant nation. Between 1970 and 2005, an estimated forty million people came to America's shores legally or illegally.[122] Although most came with exuberance and energy, about a third lacked a high school diploma.[123] Future policy must ensure that at least 90 percent of the million or so who migrate legally to the United States each year have strong educational backgrounds and possess skills needed to strengthen the U.S. economy. Foreign students who attend American universities and graduate with distinction in science, engineering, computer science, and related fields should be offered green cards with their diplomas.[124]

As for those who enter the country illegally, they are lawbreakers pure and simple. The Immigration Reform and Control Act of 1986 offered amnesty to many illegals in the U.S. prior to 1986, but stipulated that amnesty would not be offered in the future and new illegal immigrants would be prosecuted. Of course, these threats were never carried out and roughly twelve million illegals currently reside in the United States. The best way to handle the situation is to require employers to use the E-Verify system for all prospective employees, and federal authorities should begin to punish employers who knowingly hire illegals. When the jobs dry up, many will return with their families to their homelands, and generous assistance should be made available to those who relocate voluntarily. In addition, a new program should be created that would allow for the temporary entry of seasonal workers into the United States and safeguards put in place to make sure they receive a decent wage and benefits and are not exploited by unscrupulous employers. Children born in the United States to illegals should be allowed to stay with their parents. However, a new amendment to the Constitution should be enacted to end the automatic citizen designation for anyone born in the United States to illegal residents. Illegals should not be covered by the expansion of health-care benefits, although emergency treatment should never be denied. America has been the most generous country in the world in welcoming legal immigrants to its shores, and it has nothing to apologize for by clamping down on the entry of those from abroad who knowingly violate U.S. laws.

The Private Sector

The wisdom of the writers of the Constitution to establish a national economic union, combined with the resourcefulness and dynamism of the private sector, goes a long way toward explaining why the United States achieved a superpower status. After the recent gross failures on Wall Street, the private sector has been under siege. The federal government has moved in to broaden regulation and assume a direct ownership position in General Motors (sometimes referred to as Government Motors), Chrysler, Citigroup, AIG, Fannie Mae, and Freddie Mac. It also assumed an interest in a large number of banks through the Troubled Asset Relief Program (TARP). Some have argued that Wall Street has ceded its position, both as the largest financial center in the world and as the largest in the United States, because so much financial decision-making has been transferred to Washington, D.C.—a very unfortunate trend.

Global business competition is also becoming much more intense. As John Kao emphasizes, Silicon Valley replicas are springing up around the world.[125] Talent, capital, and government investment in a variety of sectors have also spread around the world.[126] All of this can be positive for global society as a whole, because as Kao insists:

> Talent is not confined to any culture or geography. No one has a monopoly on ideas. And that will make the world a more thrilling place to inhabit, one in which the catalytic nature of diversity and the power of innovation on a planetary basis may well unleash the full potential of human beings to better themselves and to create a world well worth living in. All of which is a very good thing, because there are still many El Capitans left to climb.[127]

The big question is whether the U.S. private sector will remain the leader in this innovation or be shuffled back to the middle of the pack.

As quickly as possible, the Beltway must remove itself from the day-to-day business of governing the private sector in general. Washington faces tremendous challenges trying to achieve effective governance, let alone meddling in the intricacies of business affairs. With the notable exception of implementing a workable regulatory system to avoid a repeat of the recent Wall Street carnage, including the possible breakup of huge financial institutions once considered as too big to fail, Capitol Hill should tread lightly and allow the private business sector to innovate and expand.

American Workers

Many American workers are facing dire challenges, if they even have jobs. At the beginning of 2010, twenty-seven million were jobless when one counts the officially unemployed, part-time workers seeking full-time employment, and those marginally attached to the labor force.[128] Unemployment among sixteen to twenty-four year-olds not enrolled in school exploded to a post–World War II high of 53 percent in September 2009.[129] There were more private-sector jobs in the year 2000 than at the end of 2009 even though twelve million people had been added to the labor force during the decade.[130] For those with jobs, special stress is felt by those who earn $20,000–40,000 per year, wages above the minimum but below a secure standard of living. They tend to have no savings, no income beyond the next pay check, and little chance of paying to send their kids to university.[131]

More than one in ten Americans is receiving food stamps. Over 40 percent of mortgages could be under water by 2011 unless economic conditions improve dramatically.[132] America is the only major Western nation that does not mandate some form of paid leave to care for newborn children.[133] Vacation days for workers are also the lowest among the major Western countries. Defined benefit pension plans for workers are being jettisoned by corporations in favor of 401(k)-style plans that put the onus on the workers to invest their own money and frequently lack any form of corporate match. Companies are also dropping health insurance plans at a precipitous rate or requiring their employees to pay higher premiums and co-pays.[134] The days of graduating from high school, working for a single company throughout one's career and receiving a decent wage, and then retiring with solid pension and health-care benefits are relics of history. For a growing number of working-age Americans, the job environment is much less hospitable and tinged with greater uncertainty. On the other hand, the ticket to the "middle class" is almost guaranteed if a young person is disciplined and fortunate enough to finish high school, work full-time, and marry before having children.[135] Only 2 percent of those who master this rather simple three-step formula will end up in poverty, whereas three-quarters of those who have failed to complete any of these three steps will be mired in poverty "in any given year."[136]

One tangible solution includes a more solid K–12 learning foundation and easier and less expensive entry into community colleges and universities. Another includes examining the compensation policies of all executives and making sure the average worker in each company is not shorted in terms of wages and fringe benefits. Profit sharing should also be expanded. The cult of executive leadership accompanied by extravagant pay and privileges needs to end. Entrepreneurs will continue to do very well as their innovation and know-how push their companies to higher profits and share prices. Managers, on the other hand, will continue to be amply rewarded for competent service but not at a rate several hundred times higher than workers in their own companies. Their skills are important, but not in the same league as the truly entrepreneurial types such as a Bill Gates or Steve Jobs.[137] Conditions should also be put in place to facilitate higher rates of unionization in the private sector. In 2008, only one of every fourteen workers in this sector was unionized, close to a historic low.[138] Management holds all the trump cards, and the workers are at their mercy—explaining in part why compensation for CEOs went from twenty-five to thirty times the average worker's wages in the 1945–1975 period to several hundred times higher in 2001.[139] This imbalance needs to change in favor of more management-worker consultation and cooperation, and the "cult" of the celebrity CEO should fade into oblivion.[140]

Workers also need to be better aware of what is affecting their employment prospects and what can be done to strengthen America's economic base. They need expanded civic literacy and to learn how to organize not only in the office or on the shop floor but in their communities as well.[141] American adults now spend an average of eight hours per day in front of screens—televisions, computer monitors, cell phones, and other devices.[142] Some of this time is productive, but much is devoted to infotainment. A portion of this time should be shifted to civic concerns and improving American society in general. "Social capital" should expand, developing networks that weave individuals into groups and communities.[143] "Civil society" should be solidified and made more robust, as people learn to trust one another and work together for common purposes in groups and organizations.[144] In this way, the average American will be in better shape to stand up to the influence of those who attempt to buy their way in Washington, D.C., and in most state capitals. As Bill Moyers insists, "the only answer to organized money is organized people."[145]

The Environment, Energy, and Stewardship

One can argue about the timetable when environmental and energy challenges will begin to cause major damage to Americans, but there can be little disagreement that these challenges are serious. The National Intelligence Council argues that climate change alone will cause significant geopolitical problems in various parts of the world, including poverty, environmental degradation, and the weakening of national governments.[146] The world's "rising temperatures, surging seas, and melting glaciers" are viewed as a direct threat to the U.S. national interest and must be factored into future foreign policy decisions.[147] America's reliance on foreign oil for over 60 percent of its energy needs is also a source of consternation for many policymakers.

Greater collaboration will be needed with nations around the world to solve these environmental and energy challenges. Hopefully, new technological discoveries will greatly mitigate some of these onerous problems. Americans, however, can do more to ease the problems by exercising plain and simple stewardship, which may be defined as leaving a place in at least as good a shape as when one first arrived. The size of the average American family has been decreasing, but the size of U.S. homes and U.S. motor vehicles is far larger than in any other Western nation. If families have an average of two children in an increasingly urbanized environment, why have gas-guzzling

SUVs, big recreational trucks, and, worst of all, Schwarzenegger-style Hummers been in such high demand? Why are freeways in large urban conglomerates clogged with driver-only cars during rush hours, when most cities offer convenient and affordable mass-transit alternatives? Why do so many need mini-castles, often dubbed "McMansions," replete with every energy-consuming convenience under the sun, when only four people are living in them? Historian James Truslow Adams coined the term "the American dream" that he defined as "a better, richer, and happier life for all our citizens of every rank." However, during the Great Depression, he clarified his definition by emphasizing "that dream has always meant more than the accumulation of material goods."[148]

So many relatively small and pragmatic steps could be taken to encourage conservation by individuals and families that would pay absolutely huge dividends for them and the nation as a whole. Commercial and residential building codes could emphasize energy efficiency, and existing homes could be weatherized and the four billion standard-sized light sockets could use compact fluorescent and other low-energy bulbs instead of the inefficient incandescent variety.[149] People could use vehicles that achieve European-like fuel efficiency. The four-fifths who live in urban areas could consider mass transit and telecommuting as viable options to car-dominated traditional commuting. They could landscape their yards in a fashion that demands very little if any water use. A culture of energy conservation and environmental sensitivity, when combined with a deep-rooted commitment to the principle of stewardship, would bring a sea change to America's energy and environmental outlook. U.S. companies could also lead the world in providing products and services to American consumers that are both green and energy efficient.[150]

Chapter 9

The United States in 2050

A Major Shift in the Global Balance of Power

The world of 2010 has 6.8 billion people and one somewhat "enfeebled" superpower, the United States.[1] In contrast, the world of 2050 will have about 9.4 billion people, with India being the most populous country at 1.75 billion, China second at 1.4 billion, and the United States third at 439 million.[2] The more developed countries, which accounted for 30 percent of the global population in 1950, will be down to 11 percent in 2050.[3] Several key global actors will be present in 2050, including China, Japan, India, Russia, Brazil, the European Union, ASEAN, and the United States. At best, the U.S. will be *primus inter pares* among this "pivotal" group.[4] It will not be a dominant superpower by any stretch of the imagination.[5] Although the U.S. will continue to be the leading military power with the most lethal collection of nuclear weapons and delivery systems, it will be unable to utilize this arsenal as a bargaining chip to force compliance on important issues from other countries. Instead, a marked proliferation in satellite systems with dual-use applications, the continuing development of weapons of mass destruction, the capacity to engage in cyber warfare, and counter-insurgency capabilities will all become much more prominent dimensions of defense strategies by 2050.[6] In a world where any widespread use of nuclear weapons would obliterate modern civilization, such weapons will count only modestly in determining the global influence of individual nation-states. The U.S. nuclear arsenal will dissuade other nations from attacking the American homeland directly, but even here there is a remote chance that terrorist groups might detonate a small nuclear device or "dirty bomb" on U.S. soil.[7]

China will have the largest national economy at mid-century, surpassing the United States within the next few decades and possibly doubling the size of U.S. GDP by 2050.[8] An expanded EU will also have a larger economy, India could possibly match U.S. GDP by mid-century, and the combination of Japan, Korea, and the ASEAN countries would be only slightly behind the United States.[9] The total American share of global production will fall from the low 20 percent range in 2010 to the low teens by 2050. America's per capita GDP will still be much higher than China's and India's as both nations struggle to bring hundreds of millions of their own residents out of poverty.

How far will the United States fall and how long will it take the average American to catch on to this downward trajectory? The United Kingdom's decline as a global power was manifested very clearly when its government devalued the pound in 1967 and formally abolished its "East of Suez" policy in January 1968. At the time, British leaders faced up to their country's relative decline, which had begun in World War I, and accepted that the UK would be relegated to the status of a regional "middle power" whose future prosperity would be largely linked to the European continent.

Americans have thus far been hard pressed to view their own country through the same prism of relative decline. One bleak set of developments could see Americans stunned by the gradual demise of the U.S. dollar as the primary currency for international trade and central bank reserves. Perhaps they will notice a marked shift in international decision making away from G8 to a non-Western-dominated G20. A jolt would definitely strike the American heartland if there were an overwhelming UN General Assembly vote within the next couple of decades in favor of moving UN headquarters from New York City to Hong Kong, to the country that may replace the U.S. as the largest financial contributor to this international organization. John F. Kennedy's words early in his presidency are even more appropriate today than almost a half century ago:

> We must face the fact that the United States is neither omnipotent or omniscient—that we are only 6 percent of the world's population; that we cannot impose our will upon the other 94 percent of mankind; that we cannot right every wrong or reverse each adversity; and therefore there cannot be an American solution to every world problem.[10]

Already the United States has a much smaller percentage of the global population and GDP than it did back when Kennedy uttered this warning, and its proportion of the global economy will be smaller yet by mid-century.[11]

The new era of 2050, which will reflect the shifting power equations now in progress, will be devoid of superpowers, and a premium will be placed on multilateral over unilateral solutions to pressing regional and international problems.[12] Perhaps this new epoch will be called the post-superpower or post-hegemonic era, much as previous periods in international relations were called the post–World War II or the post–Cold War eras. Americans will be forced to adjust to the diminishing influence and prestige of their nation, but the rest of the world will also have to adjust to the loss of some security and stability that the mainly benign U.S. superpower provided internationally for several decades.[13] Charles Kupchan warns:

> the end of the American era is not just about the end of American primacy and a return of a world of multiple centers of power. It is also about the end of the era that America has played such a large role in shaping—the era of industrial capitalism, republican democracy, and the nation-state.[14]

Michael Mandelbaum echoes this sentiment when he depicts the U.S. in the post–Cold War era as having been like Goliath of old, acting more like the monitor of world governance than an empire builder.[15]

Without any doubt, more of the burden for global security will have to be assumed by other major nations, and China and Japan and several other countries will no longer be able to rely on export sales to the United States as the primary means to boost their own economic fortunes. The year 2050 will bring its own set of new challenges and uncertainties, but governments, businesses, and civil societies will be intertwined more closely and interdependently than at any other time in human history.[16] Globalization will be much more entrenched in 2050 than in 2010.

Americans and others around the globe will become more focused on the "planet earth" concept and what the carrying capacity of the planet will be in view of rising populations and GDP growth and the burgeoning demand for energy as a few billion more people come within reach of Western middle-class lifestyle emblems such as cars and larger homes.[17] Ominously, the National Intelligence Council estimates that twenty-one countries with a combined population of 600 million are already considered to be cropland or freshwater scarce.[18] With continuing population growth, this number should increase to thirty-six countries and 1.4 billion people by 2025.[19] By 2050, the number of countries having cropland or water shortages could easily top fifty with a combined population exceeding two billion people. The World Bank estimates the demand for food will rise by 50 percent by 2030, due primarily to population growth, rising affluence, and shifts to Western dietary preferences by a growing middle class.[20] By mid-century, twice as much food will be needed to feed the world's growing population. Potable water is becoming a scarce commodity in various parts of the world, along with clean air and non-renewable petroleum resources.[21] Roughly 86 percent of the world's inhabitants will live in developing countries, and even with growing affluence in some of these areas, many people will suffer from endemic poverty, dead-end job prospects, and the potentially dire impact of climate change and rising oceans.[22] Military and intelligence analysts in the U.S. are already predicting that climate change could present "profound strategic challenges" to the United States in forthcoming decades, perhaps requiring military intervention to confront the effects of "violent storms, drought, mass migration, and pandemics" in various parts of the world.[23]

On the other hand, unprecedented technological innovation and international collaboration to solve global and regional problems have the potential to mitigate many potential challenges and improve the quality of life for most inhabitants of the earth.[24] The United States does not need its own go-it-alone space program and should be an integral part of an international space consortium involving both the public and private sectors. The same international cooperation will be needed to conquer diseases, improve the production of food, discover pragmatic "green" energy substitutes for fossil fuels, bring quality education into schools, homes, and villages around the world, stem the proliferation of nuclear weapons, and engage in constructive problem-solving before major regional disagreements escalate into cataclysmic conflict.[25] Pertinent best practices will be replicated around the world and "glocalization" will be in vogue—embracing various dimensions of globalization but adapting them to local circumstances and customs. The process at times will fall far short of perfection, but the world in general could experience a quantum leap forward by 2050 in terms of international collaboration, communication, educational opportunities, blockbuster scientific and technological discoveries, and personal empowerment.

Americans Still Largely Responsible for Their Own Destinies

The worst of the Great Recession has passed and many Americans have breathed a sigh of relief and expect their country is on the road to full recovery. However, as troubles mounted during the Great Recession, about two-thirds of Americans believed their nation's future would not be as good as its past,[26] four-fifths perceived their government no longer cared about them or their views, and three-quarters were not convinced their government leaders would do the right thing.[27] In the post-recessionary period, there are now some glimmers of sunshine, and quite a few Americans are convinced that some tinkering here and there will solve the problems of the immediate past, thereby permitting the United States to continue on its path as the world's one and only superpower. Unfortunately, this type of complacent thinking will actually hasten the relative demise of the United States among the world's community of nations.

America is in desperate need of bold, reform-minded leaders. The first ten years of the twenty-first century comprised the lost decade for many Americans, with fewer private-sector jobs at the end of the decade than at the beginning, with median household income being below the income of 1999 in real terms, and with record levels of government spending still leaving most American households worse off than ten years earlier.[28] The U.S. reputation for fair and efficient "democratic capitalism" also took a big hit during the past decade.[29] In his book *Presidential Courage: Brave Leaders and How They Changed America 1789–1989*, Michael Beschloss shows "how American presidents have, at crucial moments, made courageous decisions for the national interest although they knew they might be jeopardizing their careers."[30] His examples include George Washington's peace treaty with Britain, John Adams refusing to fight against the French, Andrew Jackson's battles against the Bank of the United States, Abraham Lincoln freeing the slaves, Teddy Roosevelt taking on J.P. Morgan and the Wall Street tycoons who dominated his party, FDR defying the isolationists to thwart Hitler, Harry Truman recognizing the new state of Israel, John Kennedy standing up for civil rights, and Ronald Reagan seeking an end to the Cold War. Beschloss worries, however, that "the political culture of our time—the instant communications, polls and oceans of money—may inhibit future American leaders from performing such well-considered acts of bravery."[31] It will be absolutely devastating for the future of America if the current political culture thwarts the courageous efforts of key statesmen and stateswomen to remake the Beltway and state and local governments around the country. Enlightened and reform-minded leadership will be needed in the White House, on Capitol Hill, in governors' mansions, and in city halls for America to dig itself out of its current rut. Sometimes such leadership comes from unlikely sources. For example, Franklin D. Roosevelt came from a wealthy family and never depended on a paycheck in his life. However, this "Hudson River aristocrat" would gain a worldwide reputation for being "the champion of the common man."[32] Nor is it imperative that leadership come from the liberal side of politics, à la FDR. Conservatives have much to contribute in terms of restricting government spending, balancing budgets, relying on the private sector for economic advancement, and insuring that U.S. forays abroad are limited to enhancing and preserving U.S. vital interests.[33] Above all, the United States must find stalwart leaders who want to solve problems and improve the prospects for young people and future generations of Americans not yet born. America will also be very reliant on positive contributions made by new immigrants and their children and grandchildren, because they will likely account for over four-fifths of U.S. population growth between now and 2050.[34]

America and the world around it are changing rapidly. At home, a third of U.S. manufacturing jobs have disappeared—a combination of new technology and stiffer competition abroad.[35] China may soon surpass the U.S. in areas identified with American leadership, such as information technology and telecommunications.[36] The U.S. government is mired in debt and unless current trends are changed drastically, the GAO estimates that by 2040 interest payments on the debt will consume 30 percent of all revenues and entitlement spending will absorb most of the rest.[37] Globalization, major demographic shifts, technology change, and creative destruction are potent ingredients that have been stirred in a cauldron, and no one is quite sure what the ultimate concoction will mean for the average American.[38] Hopefully, citizens of the United States in 2050 will still enjoy a reasonably high quality of life and sense of personal fulfillment in an era of unprecedented change at home and abroad, although their nation will still be adjusting to the end of the American century and the demise of America's superpower status. All aspects of American society will have to make major adjustments to what will transpire over the next generation and a half. As Peter Drucker emphasizes, "all institutions have to make global competitiveness a strategic goal. No institution, whether a business, a university or a hospital, can hope to survive, let alone to succeed, unless it measures up to the standards set by the leaders in its field, any place in the world."[39]

The Positive Scenario—A Blueprint for Relative Decline but a Better Quality of Life

It is difficult to imagine the United States would see the dismal performance of the first decade of the twenty-first century continue until 2050, resulting in an ignominious absolute decline in Americans' quality of life and their country's standing in the world. The big question is whether relative decline between now and 2050 will be steep or modest. The challenges ahead are daunting but not in the same league as the devastating one-two punch Americans suffered during the Great Depression and then World War II. If the policy recommendations made in this volume are implemented, the relative decline of the United States in the global system will be modest and Americans' quality of life will be much better in 2050 than in 2010. In addition, America's Human Development Index, which goes beyond raw GDP calculations and considers such measures as life expectancy, good health, literacy, educational attainment, and other factors linked to a decent standard of living, would also be much higher forty years from now.[40] In 2008, the United States ranked only fifteenth among nations in the HDI annual report prepared by the United Nations.[41]

The fate of the United States will largely be determined by what Americans do at home. Although there are rival nations and groups of nations on the immediate horizon, all of these competitors face their own significant challenges. Can China actually move ahead as dramatically as it has over the past three decades with an authoritarian political structure that lacks transparency and grants its own citizens very limited political freedom, especially the hundreds of millions of poor peasants who inhabit the countryside?[42] Can Russia ever diversify its unidimensional economy under authoritarian leadership, or will it suffer through volatile boom-or-bust cycles predicated on the price of oil? Will India feed its vast legions of poor people as its population continues to expand rapidly? How will all three of these nations handle the rampant graft, corruption, inefficiencies, environmental degradation, and ethnic and religious tensions that plague their societies? The European Union continues to struggle to bring about internal harmonization and a working consensus on external issues. When major problems arise, many of its members fall back to the default option, namely retreating back to the nation-state and adopting national solutions to regional and international challenges. Japan will continue to lose population and must face the rigors of a rapidly aging society. It must also confront a potentially very dangerous neighborhood with North Korea, China, and Russia within close proximity.[43] Japan will continue to be a significant economic power but will trail far behind the United States. Brazil certainly has the potential to move from an emerging market economy to a developed economy, but this transition may not be accomplished for at least a couple of decades, if not longer.

America's private sector is legendary for its innovation, dynamism, and resiliency, all of which should permit the United States to lead the world in confronting the triad of challenges represented by globalization, unprecedented technology change, and creative destruction. Instead of cringing at this triple threat, Americans should push ahead and adapt to these evolving trends, because mastery of these challenges will undoubtedly lead to a much better way of life for most Americans.

The blueprint for future success is linked to the following:

(1) Meaningful campaign finance reform will greatly dilute what has been the distorting policy influence of money, wealth, and special interests. It will also revitalize America's system of representative government and the notion of government of, by, and for the people.[44]

(2) Congressional reforms will result in more timely and efficient policymaking on Capitol Hill focused on problem solving and enhancing the general interests of the American people.

(3) Health-care and tort reforms will enhance competition both for services and pharmaceuticals, expand coverage to all legal residents, and significantly diminish health-care spending as a percentage of GDP, even in the face of an aging population.

(4) In the entitlement arena, Medicare and Medicaid expenses will be controlled as the overall health-care reform is implemented. The retirement age will increase to reflect the longer life span of Americans. Modest increases will be needed in FICA and Medicare taxes, and some means testing will be enacted for Social Security and Medicare recipients.

(5) The tax code will be thoroughly revamped and tax compliance strengthened. These actions should add at least $100 billion annually to the U.S. Treasury without increasing taxes, except for a small augmentation in the top marginal tax rate to 39 percent.

(6) The federal government will be forced through a constitutional amendment to begin balancing budgets within the next three years and then for every year thereafter, except for periods of recession or war. Increases in expenditures will be limited to no higher than the percentage of growth in the population and the annual rate of inflation.

(7) The United States will revamp K–12 education with the same spirit and determination that it tackled the space challenge after the Soviets launched Sputnik in October 1957. The new challenge will be couched in terms of leading the twenty-first century in "brainpower." Curricula and the organization of schools and school years will finally

be brought into the twenty-first century. Education will become compulsory through age seventeen and those desiring to drop out will be funneled into special second-chance programs. Teachers will be better prepared coming out of college and paid higher salaries. New technology will be introduced to enhance teachers' efforts and also personalize education for individual students. Community colleges, four-year colleges, and universities will be made more affordable though expanded grants and loans for students and strict cost containment at public institutions of higher learning.

(8) American citizenship will be "reborn." In Japan, twenty-year-olds take part in the "Coming of Age" day when they gather at the local city hall and are given lectures about their responsibilities as adult citizens.[45] Legal immigrants who become U.S. citizens must first pass a citizenship exam outlining their responsibilities as productive Americans, and they often know more about civics than native-born U.S. residents. American history and civics training will become mandatory in K–12 schools and will be strongly encouraged at the college level. Young adults will be asked to spend one or two years in service to their country, helping to improve the competitiveness of the United States and the general well-being of their fellow citizens. All people will be encouraged to vote and be active in the civic affairs at the local, state, and national levels. A well-educated and energetic citizenry will have few qualms about tossing out incumbents on Capitol Hill or in their state legislatures who stubbornly attempt to maintain the status quo and their own privileged positions within governmental circles. Voters will be sophisticated enough to read beyond headlines or lead stories on the evening TV news, recognizing that "TV devotes its resources to sizzle, not steak."[46] They will actually take time to learn about important issues in depth and understand the range of policy alternatives available to overcome America's deep-seated problems. They will be more sensitive to environmental and energy challenges and become more knowledgeable about the world around them and cognizant of the fact that the United States can learn a great deal from other societies. They will also embrace the concept of stewardship, personal responsibility, and the wisdom of pursuing a healthy lifestyle.

(9) A revitalized private sector, unencumbered from strict controls put in place by politicians in Washington, D.C., will return to the robust growth experienced during most of the period since the end of World War II. The

federal government will prudently divest itself of its ownership interest in corporations such as General Motors, Citigroup, and AIG. This unwinding will be painful, because in the autumn of 2009, Washington "owned" 60 percent of GM, almost 80 percent of AIG, and 34 percent of Citigroup, and has assumed total control of Fannie Mae and Freddie Mac, with the federal government effectively financing nine of every ten new housing mortgages in the United States.[47] This trend of direct government intervention in the private sector must be reversed quickly.

Government's role must revert back to making sure that no monopolistic practices are tolerated and that competition takes place on a level playing field. Trade protectionism will also be avoided because it tends to protect the least competitive industries at the expense of the most competitive and American consumers in general. Campaign finance reform will bring an end to crony capitalism and the special favors dispensed by politicians to privileged corporate and individual donors. No company will be considered too big to fail. Limited but effective financial regulation and supervision will focus on insuring no repeat of the subprime mortgage crisis or casino-type transactions geared toward short-term profits and bonuses at the expense of long-term business viability. If the United States can return to steady 3–4 percent real economic growth over the next few decades, many of its fiscal problems will become more manageable.

(10) Illegal immigration will be curtailed through the denial of jobs and strict surveillance of employer hiring practices. Illegals living in the United States will not be eligible for health care coverage, with the exception of emergency care. Generous allowances will be given to those illegals who voluntarily relocate to their home countries. The United States will also introduce an expansive guest worker project for those willing to come to the country and work on a temporary basis. A new constitutional amendment will deny U.S. citizenship to any future children born in the United States to illegal immigrants. Washington will increase legal immigration quotas and change qualifications to favor those with good educations and possessing skills in high demand by American companies.

(11) United States' troop withdrawals from Iraq and Afghanistan, selective cutbacks in the Navy and the Air Force, the termination of many private contracting schemes, and an end to building unwanted weapons in order to preserve jobs will combine to save the federal government's

budget over $200 billion a year and move overall defense spending toward the range of 3 percent of GDP, except during times of national emergency. All of these changes will still leave the United States with the most formidable military capability in the world. Even with this military superiority, the United States should refrain from major unilateral warfare in the future unless it is abundantly clear that America's vital interests are in dire jeopardy and other viable options have been exhausted.[48] In addition, the long-term military occupation of other countries, as well as laborious nation-building pursuits in these countries, should be avoided like the plague—never again should the United States repeat the grievous mistakes that have occurred in Vietnam, Iraq, and Afghanistan.

(12) A sea change will occur in the conduct of U.S. foreign policy. Statecraft will be reinvigorated and the State Department given a much more expansive role in the overall foreign policy arena. Diplomacy will be geared toward enhanced regional and international cooperation and the creation of what Gelb calls "power coalitions" in order to solve problems linked to political instability, energy, the environment, hunger and poverty, and the lack of human rights.[49] U.S. Foreign Service officers will be engaged more fully with the citizens of countries where they are posted and will no longer be sheltered behind the fortified walls of U.S. embassies and consulates. Foreigners will be encouraged to visit the United States and students from abroad will be welcomed in unprecedented numbers to U.S. schools. Americans will also be encouraged to travel abroad, and almost every person will hold a passport, up dramatically from the 30 percent who currently possess this document. American students will be urged to participate in study abroad and international internship programs. All aspects of international involvement will be strengthened, ranging from official government contacts to increased interaction by those in business, academia, and civil society in general.[50]

If this set of recommendations is actually implemented, the United States will succeed in reestablishing a strong foundation based on steady economic growth and a vibrant and responsive system of governance. By 2050, America's status in the world will have declined modestly in relative terms, but the United States will continue to be a major force in global politics.

However, are the American people up to the formidable task of making changes that will arrest America's steady decline, or will the United

States continue to rot from within and endure an accelerated downward slide lasting for several decades? One must always keep in mind that when there is no penalty for failure, failure proliferates. Some noted scholars are convinced that the American people are simply not up to the task of preserving America's superpower role. Zbigniew Brzezinski, for one, suggests that Americans are too fixated on mass entertainment, personal hedonism, and "socially escapist themes," rendering them incapable of bolstering the worldwide greatness and influence of the United States.[51] Will extreme partisanship, niche media, Beltway greed and ineptitude, and citizen apathy combine to doom the prospects for necessary reforms? Remember once again Benjamin Franklin's admonition as the new Constitution was proclaimed, you have "a Republic, if you can keep it." Americans now have to respond to another great challenge. They have been a part of the most powerful nation-state on the face of the earth. How much of its greatness are they willing to fight for and preserve for the benefit of their own posterity and humanity in general?[52]

Notes

Chapter 1

1. Some scholars such as Fareed Zakaria argue that the United States was the greatest superpower since Rome. See his thought-provoking book *The Post-American World* (New York: W.W. Norton, 2008), 2. George G. Herring, in his almost 1000-page tome devoted to the history of U.S. foreign relations, contends that in America's unipolar moment, "comparisons were drawn with ancient Rome, the only historical example that seemed adequately to describe America's global preëminence." See his book *From Colony to Superpower: U.S. Foreign Relations Since 1776* (New York: Oxford University Press, 2008), 1 and 917. Amy Chua, in her book *Day of Empire: How Hyperpowers Rise to Global Dominance—And Why They Fail* (New York: Doubleday, 2007), depicts the United States as a "hyperpower" in the same league as the Persian empire, the Roman empire, China's Golden Age, the Great Mongol empire, Spain under Ferdinand and Isabella, the Dutch empire, the Ottoman empire, the Ming empire, the Mughal empire, and the British empire. Cullen Murphy entitled his book *Are We Rome?* (Boston: Houghton Mifflin, 2007) and compares and contrasts Pax Romana and Pax Americana. In his volume *The Grand Chessboard: American Primacy and Its Geostrategic Imperatives* (New York: Basic Books, 1997), 215, Zbigniew Brzezinski accurately refers to the United States as "the first, only, and last truly global superpower." Leslie H. Gelb, in his insightful book *Power Rules: How Common Sense Can Rescue American Foreign Policy* (New York: HarperCollins, 2009), 3, describes the U.S. as "probably the most powerful nation in history." In *At War with Ourselves* (Oxford: Oxford University Press, 2003), 25, Michael Hirsh labels the United States the "überpower" that almost single-handedly built the current global system, adding that "we are a shining success, the supreme power on earth. And we are entangled everywhere." Walter Russell Mead asserts that unprecedented globalization and technological advancements solidified America's position as the most influential nation in history: "only a few countries and cultures have had anything like the impact of the United States on religion, politics, technology, and culture," adding that "because the American era coincided with (and indeed helped cause) the technological and economic revolutions of the twentieth century, the impact of the United States has spread faster and deeper than did the impact of its predecessors." See his article "Hegemon's Coming of Age," *Foreign Affairs* 88 (July/August 2009): 138–139.

2. U.S. National Intelligence Council, *Global Trends 2025: A Transformed World* (Washington, D.C.: U.S. Government Printing Office, 2008), vi.

3. *Ibid.* In his article "The Shrinking Superpower," *theatlantic.com*, 9 March 2009, Robert D. Kaplan concurs with this assessment, stating that the U.S. is headed toward a "multipolar world and the end of American dominance."

4. Soros is quoted in Diane Francis, "Worries about Rescue Plan," *National Post*, 24 March 2009. In his remarks, Soros is lamenting the collapse of the U.S. financial system.

5. Kishore Mahbubani, "Can America Fail?" *The Wilson Quarterly* 33 (Spring 2009): 48–54. He suggests that Americans suffer from groupthink when they cannot perceive that their country may be in decline or that unregulated financial markets do not serve the interests of most citizens. Other problems he identifies include erosion in the notion of individual responsibility, abuse of American power abroad, such as in Iraq, collapse of the social contract at home, and ascendancy of the special interest over the public interest in Washington, D.C.

6. Department of the Treasury/Federal Reserve Board, "Major Foreign Holders of Treasury Securities," 15 June 2009. This is up from less than 30 percent in 2001.

7. Keith Bradsher, "China Losing Taste for Debt From U.S.," *New York Times*, 8 January 2009.

8. In Zakaria, *Post-American*, 4, he argues the following: "At the politico-military level, we remain in a single-superpower world. But in every other dimension—industrial, financial, educational, social, cultural—the distribution of power is shifting, moving away from American dominance."

9. Jason DeParle and Robert Gebeloff, "Food Stamp Use Soars, and Stigma Fades," *New York Times*, 29 November 2009, and "Indicators of Welfare Dependence," *ASPE Research Brief*, September 2007. The U.S. Department of Agriculture also reported that in 2008 forty-nine million Americans experienced "food insecurity," lacking at one time or another "dependable access to adequate food." This is the highest number ever recorded since the annual tabulation of food insecurity was first released in 1995. See Amy Goldstein, "Report: More Americans Going Hungry," *Washington Post*, 16 November 2009.

10. Carmen DeNavas-Walt, Bernadette D. Proctor, and Jessica C. Smith, *Income, Poverty, and Health Insurance Coverage in the United States, 2008* (Washington, D.C.: U.S. Census Bureau, 2009), 13, 22, 29, 44, 59–60, and U.S. Bureau of Labor Statistics, "Employment, Hours, and Earnings from the Current Employment Statistics Survey (National)," at *http://data.bls.gov/PDQ/servlet/SurveyOutputServlet*. The poverty rate was 13.2 percent in 2008, the highest since 1997. In addition, 19.0 percent of children under the age of eighteen lived in poverty at the end of 2008, compared with 16.2 percent at the end of 2000. In 2008, 46.3 million people had no health insurance, representing 15.4 percent of the entire population. In comparison, 38.4 million were without health insurance in 2000, accounting for 13.7 percent of the population. The real median household income in 2008 was $50,303 versus $52,500 in 2000. There were also fewer private-sector jobs in September 2009 than in October 1999.

11. Henry R. Luce, "The American Century," *Life Magazine*, 17 February 1941.

12. German Marshall Fund of the United States, *Transatlantic Trends*, 10 September 2008.

13. CBC News, "15 Percent Would Rather Vote in U.S. Election: Survey," 4 February 2008, and Ronald Wright, *What Is America? A Short History of the New World Order* (Toronto: Alfred A. Knopf Canada, 2008), 221.

14. Pew Global Attitudes Project, "Confidence in Obama Lifts U.S. Image around the World: Muslim Publics Not So Easily Moved," 23 July 2009, at *www.pewglobal.org*.

15. Tom Brokaw, *The Greatest Generation* (New York: Random House, 1998).

16. David Boren, *A Letter to America* (Norman: University of Oklahoma Press, 2008), 7.

17. Isabel Sawhill and Ron Haskins, "Five Myths about Our Land of Opportunity," *Washington Post*, 1 November 2009.

18. S. Jay Olshansky *et al.*, "A Potential Decline in Life Expectancy in the United States in the Twenty-First Century," *New England Journal of Medicine*, 17 March 2005, 1138–1145. For example, diabetes, with its attendant complications, is expected to double among the U.S. population over the next quarter century. See Elbert S. Huang, Anirban Basu, Michael O'Grady, and James C. Capretta, "Projecting the Future Diabetes Population Size and Related Costs for the U.S.," *Diabetes Care* 32 (December 2009): 2228.

19. William Christeson, Amy Dawson Taggart, and Soren Messner-Zidell, *Ready, Willing, and Unable to Serve* (Washington, D.C.: Mission: Readiness, 2009), 1–3. Twenty-seven percent of young people in this age group are too overweight to join the military

services, 32 percent have health problems not directly related to being overweight, 25 percent lack a high school diploma, and 10 percent have been convicted of felonies or serious misdemeanors. Some individuals fall within more than one of these categories.

20. Noah Shachtman, "75 Percent of Potential Recruits Too Fat, Too Sickly, Too Dumb to Serve," *Wired*, 4 November 2009. Curt Gilroy, director of accessions at the Pentagon, observes that "kids are just not able to do push-ups. And they don't do pull-ups. And they can't run." See William H. McMichael, "Most U.S. Youths Unfit to Serve, Data Show," *Army Times*, 5 November 2009.

21. U.S. Department of Commerce, Bureau of Economic Analysis, "Current-Dollar and 'Real' Gross Domestic Product," at *www.bea.gov/national/index.htm#gdp*. The period covered is between 1961 and the end of 2008.

22. Bill Gates, *Business @ the Speed of Thought* (New York: Warner Books, 1999), xiii. He also predicted business during the first decade of the twenty-first century would endure more rapid change than it had in the previous half century.

23. Creative destruction was coined by Joseph A. Schumpeter in his book *Capitalism, Socialism and Democracy* (London: Routledge, 1994), Chapter VII, 81–86. The book was first published in the United States in 1942 by Harper & Row.

24. William L. Silber, *When Washington Shut Down Wall Street* (Princeton: Princeton University Press, 2007), 160–161.

25. Walt Kelly first used this phrase to commemorate Earth Day in 1970.

26. The survey was sponsored by NBC News and the *Wall Street Journal*. See "He's Got Some Numbers to Back Him Up," *PolitiFact.com*, 24 June 2008.

Chapter 2

1. Chris Edwards, "The Simple (Tax) Life," *Salt Lake Tribune*, 6 April 2006. See also Steven Malanga, "Geithner and Our Incomprehensible Tax System," *RealClearMarkets.com*, 21 January 2009, and Norton Garfinkle, *The American Dream vs. the Gospel of Wealth: The Fight for a Productive Middle-Class Economy* (New Haven: Yale University Press, 2007), 191.

2. "Members of Congress Increasingly Use Revolving Door to Launch Lucrative Lobbying Careers," *Public Citizen*, 28 July 2005. These statistics were for the period 1998 to 2005.

3. Byron York, "How Did Daschle Realize He Had a Limo Problem?," *nationalreviewonline.com*, 3 February 2009.

4. Norman J. Ornstein, Thomas E. Mann, and Michael J. Malbin, *Vital Statistics on Congress, 2001–2002* (Washington, D.C.: AEI Press, 2002), 20–21.

5. Derek Wyatt, MP, "The Changing Role of an MP," at *www.derekwyatt.co.uk/*.

6. Mildred Amer and Jennifer E. Manning, *Membership of the 111th Congress: A Profile* (Washington, D.C.: Congressional Research Service, 2008), 1, 4–6.

7. James J. Gosling, *Economics, Politics, and American Public Policy* (Armonk, NY: M.E. Sharpe, 2008), 108.

8. Congressional Budget Office, "The Budget and Economic Outlook: An Update," July 2000.

9. Statistics compiled by the Citizens Against Government Waste, a non-partisan organization, and quoted in Caroline Baum, "Americans Went to Polls with the GOP They've Got," *Bloomberg.com*, 13 November 2006. Some on Capitol Hill argue the costs for earmarks in fiscal year 2006 may have been several billion dollars lower than the organization estimated. See Ronald Brownstein, "Bush's Tax Cuts Far Outweigh Congressional Pork," *Los Angeles Times*, 14 May 2006.

10. "The Other Defense Budget," *Washington Post*, 6 February 2007, and R. Jeffrey Smith, "Defense Bill, Lauded by White House, Contains Billions in Earmarks," *Washington Post*, 29 September 2009.

11. Kaiser's book was published by New York-based Random House in 2009.

12. Kaiser's comments to Bill Moyers on *Bill Moyers Journal*, PBS, 20 February 2009.

13. Research by Jeffrey Birnbaum discussed in Drew Lindsay, "How Big Money Has Changed Washington," *Washingtonian*, November 2006, 5.

14. Center for Responsive Politics, "Lobbying Database," at *www.opensecrets.org/lobbyists/*.

15. This estimate is made by James Thurber of American University. See Eliza Newlin Carney, "What You Don't See," *National Journal*, 21 March 2008.

16. Robert J. Samuelson, "Lobbying Is Democracy in Action," *Newsweek*, 22 December 2008.

17. Reed quoted in David Cay Johnston, *Perfectly Legal: The Covert Campaign to Rig Our Tax System to Benefit the Super Rich* (New York: Portfolio, 2003), 305.

18. "The Whir of the Political Casino," *New York Times*, 29 June 2006.

19. Hightower quoted in Mort Rosenblum, *Escaping Plato's Cave: How America's Blindness to the Rest of the World Threatens Our Survival* (New York: St. Martin's Press, 2007), 239.

20. Norman Ornstein, "District of Corruption," *New Republic*, 4 February 2009.

21. Scott McClellan, *What Happened? Inside the Bush White House and Washington's Culture of Deception* (New York: Public Affairs, 2008), 311. In his book *Homo Politicus: The Strange and Barbaric Tribes of the Beltway* (New York: Doubleday, 2008), 5–6, Dana Milbank gives his somewhat lighthearted interpretation of "Potomac Land" which has "a status system that is both hierarchical and byzantine." The highest caste consists of the top appointees and advisers to the president, congressional leaders, and Supreme Court justices. The second caste is comprised of rank-and-file members of Congress. The third caste includes journalists, lobbyists, and bureaucrats. The lowest caste is composed of the vast number of people who live in or around Potomac Land and have no interest in politics. They are by far the most numerous but are essentially invisible to the upper castes.

22. Ornstein, "District of Corruption."

23. *Ibid.*, and Thomas E. Mann and Norman J. Ornstein, *The Broken Branch: How Congress Is Failing America and How to Get It Back on Track* (Oxford: Oxford University Press, 2006), 231.

24. Thomas Frank, *The Wrecking Crew: How Conservatives Rule* (New York: Metropolitan Books, 2008), 2.

25. "House GOP and the Favor Factory," *Christian Science Monitor*, 1 February 2006.

26. Mann and Ornstein, *Broken Branch*, 238.

27. Eliza Newlin Carney, "Murtha Scandals Keep Eyes on Earmarks," *National Journal Online*, 1 June 2009, and Paul Kane and Carol Leonnig, "A Congressman, a Lobbying Firm and a Swift Path to Earmarks," *Washington Post*, 26 October 2009.

28. Robert B. Reich, *Supercapitalism* (New York: Alfred A. Knopf, 2007), 211.

29. John Newhouse, "Diplomacy, Inc.," *Foreign Affairs* 88 (May/June 2009): 73.

30. Alex Knott, "New Study Details Contacts between Foreign Interests and Lawmakers," *CQ Politics*, 18 August 2009. The study was completed by the Sunlight Foundation and ProPublica and based on an analysis of filings required by the Foreign Agent Registration Act.

31. In his book *Politics Lost* (New York: Random House, 2006), 223, Joe Klein refers to the United States as being plagued with a system of "permanent campaigns."

32. *Ibid.*, 240.

33. Center for Responsive Politics, "2008 Overview," at *OpenSecrets.org*.

34. Micah L. Sifry and Nancy Watzman, *Is That a Politician in Your Pocket?* (Hoboken, NJ: John Wiley & Sons, 2004), 211.

35. *Ibid.*, 1.

36. Jacob Hacker and Paul Pierson are quoted in Frank, *The Wrecking Crew*, 269.

37. Richard L. Berke, "Cash of Campaigns Can Go Elsewhere," *New York Times*, 22 January 1989.

38. Peter Yost, "Inside Washington: PACs as Personal Slush Funds?," *newsvine.com*, 14 May 2009.

39. *Ibid.*

40. Brady Mullins and Brad Haynes, "Some PACs Run After Politicians Drop Out," *Wall Street Journal*, 6 May 2009, and Kevin Diaz, "Leadership PACs Helping Politicians Help Themselves," *Minneapolis Star Tribune*, 26 May 2008.

41. Barack Obama, John McCain, Hillary Clinton, and John Edwards were the senators seeking the presidency.

42. Norman Ornstein, "Our Broken Senate," *The American*, March/April 2008.

43. *Ibid.*

44. Ivy J. Sellers, "Robert Byrd Breaks Down, Admits to Hold—And Withdraws It," *Human Events*, 31 August 2006.

45. Lee Hamilton, who served in the House for over thirty years and is currently president of the Woodrow Wilson International Center for Scholars, laments the loss of civility in Congress. He says that "civility means that legislators respect the rights and dignity of others. It does not mean that they need to agree with one another—far from it. Rather, treating one another civilly is how people who don't agree still manage to weigh issues carefully and find common ground." Hamilton is quoted in Sunil Ahuja, *Congress Behaving Badly: The Rise of Partisanship and Incivility and the Death of Public Trust* (Westport, CN: Praeger, 2008), 2 and 15. Gerald Ford, long-time member of the House and former U.S. president, stated that he hoped his legacy would be "that I was a dedicated, hardworking, honest person who served constructively in Congress and in the White House." Others have called Ford "a politician of rare amiability" and "an ordinary guy in the noblest sense of the term." Where are the Gerald Fords on Capitol Hill today? See Thomas M. DeFrank, *Write It When I'm Gone: Remarkable Off-the-Record Conversations with Gerald F. Ford* (New York: G.P. Putnam's Sons, 2007), 107, 217, and 242.

46. See *www.allgreatquotes.com/peanuts_quotes3.shtml*.

47. Andrew Chamberlain, "Twenty Years Later: The Tax Reform Act of 1986," *Tax Foundation's Tax Policy Blog*, 23 October 2006.

48. Tom Herman, "What I Learned in My 16 Years on the Tax Beat," *Wall Street Journal*, 15 April 2009.

49. *Ibid.* This is an estimate made by Joel Slemrod, economics professor at the University of Michigan.

50. *Ibid.*

51. Thomas B. Edsall, "Obama Seeks to Kill Hedge Fund Tax Break," *Huffington Post*, 2 February 2009.

52. *Ibid.*

53. Robert Reich, "Why Democrats Are Afraid to Raise Taxes on the Rich," *salon.com*, 25 October 2007.

54. Floyd Norris, "Tax Break for Profits Went Awry," *New York Times*, 4 June 2009. The study is entitled "Watch What I Do, Not What I Say: The Unintended Consequences of the Homeland Investment Act," and is written by Dhammika Dharmapala, C. Fritz Foley, and Kristin J. Forbes for the National Bureau of Economic Research. It was published in June 2009.

55. *Ibid.*

56. Roger Lowenstein, "Who Needs the Mortgage-Interest Deduction," *New York Times*, 5 March 2006, and Sebastian Mallaby, "Attacking Inequality," *Washington Post,* 4 September 2006.

57. Lowenstein "Who Needs," and Konrad Yakabuski, "Ghosts of Housing Bubble Still Haunt U.S.," *Globe and Mail*, 7 May 2009.

58. Lowenstein, "Who Needs."

59. *Ibid.*

60. Christopher Swann, "Tax Panel Seeks Cap on Break for Homeowners," *Financial Times*, 11 October 2005, and Justin Fox, "Get Homes off Welfare," *Time Magazine*, 12 October 2009.

61. Leonard E. Burman, William G. Gale, Matthew Hall, and Peter Orszag, "Distributional Effects of Defined Contribution Plans and Individual Retirement Accounts," *Urban Institute TPC Discussion Paper No. 16*, 19 August 2004.

62. Mallaby, "Attacking Inequality."

63. The European Union also indulges in an ultra-expensive and dysfunctional Common Agricultural Program (CAP), which doles out $75 billion per year in subsidies. See Stephen Castle and Doreen Carvajal, "Subsidies Spur Fraud in European Sugar," *New York Times*, 27 October 2009.

64. "A Lot More to Cut," *New York Times*, 11 May 2009. Much of the problem is linked to cost-plus contracts that have been in use for almost a century.

65. Lehman quoted in David Dietz, "Hidden Bonuses Enrich Government Contractors at Taxpayer Expense," *Bloomberg.com*, 29 January 2009.

66. Foon Rhee, "McCain Allies with Obama on F-22s," *boston.com*, 13 July 2009.

67. See Olga Pierce, "Medicare Drug Planners Now Lobbyists, with Billions at Stake," *Huffington Post*, 22 October 2009. Pierce highlights the influence of Billy Tauzin from Louisiana, former chair of the House Energy and Commerce Committee, who left Congress to become president of PhRMA, the drug industry's chief lobbying group. He reportedly earns ten times more with PhRMA than he earned as a member of the U.S. Congress.

68. Quoted in Mark Lange, "A Tumor at the Heart of Medicare," *New York Times*, 21 March 2009. See also Frank R. Lichtenberg and Shawn X. Sun, "The Impact of Medicare Part D on Prescription Drug Use by the Elderly," *Health Affairs* 26 (#6 2007): 1735–1744.

69. Robert Kuttner, "Who Killed Off the GOP Deficit Hawks?," *Business Week*, 27 December 2004.

70. Paul Krugman, "The Green-Zoning of America," *New York Times*, 5 February 2007.

71. Dietz, "Hidden Bonuses."

72. Paul C. Light, *A Government Ill Executed: The Decline of the Federal Service and How to Reverse It* (Cambridge, MA: Harvard University Press, 2008), 202.

73. Rajiv Chandrasekaran, *Imperial Life in the Emerald City: Inside Iraq's Green Zone* (New York: Random House, 2006), 91.

74. This issue will be discussed in greater detail in the next chapter. The chairman of the New York Fed, Stephen Friedman, served simultaneously on the board of Goldman Sachs and was a big shareholder in that company.

75. Michael Barone, "Why Did AIG's Counterparties Get 100 Percent Repayment?," *U.S. News and World Report*, 19 March 2009.

76. Gretchen Morgenson, "AIG Bailout Priorities Are in Critics' Cross Hairs," *New York Times*, 17 March 2009.

77. Will Rogers' quotes at *www.cmgww.com/historic/rogers/quotes2.htm*.

Chapter 3

1. Leslie Gelb warns that "every great nation or empire ultimately rots from within" and that the U.S. is on the way to becoming just "another great power, a nation barely worth fearing or following." See his article "Necessity, Choice, and Common Sense," *Foreign Affairs* 88 (May/June 2009): 72.

2. Reagan quote at *www.famous-quotes.com*.

3. For fiscal year 2008, Washington spent $451 billion on interest payments, the fourth largest expenditure after defense, Social Security, and Health and Human Services, which administers the Medicare and Medicaid programs. See Kerry Young, "Paying It Forward: A Look at the Looming National Debt," *CQ Today*, 12 December 2008. The Congressional Budget Office predicts a quadrupling of these interest payments over the next decade, as noted in Graham Bowley and Jack Healy, "Worries Rise on the Size of the U.S. Debt," *New York Times*, 3 May 2009.

4. Martin Wolf, *Fixing Global Finance* (Baltimore: Johns Hopkins University, 2008), 76.

5. Some baby boomers are already retiring, but they are collecting only partial Social Security and no Medicare benefits until they reach age sixty-five.

6. The Board of Trustees, *The 2009 Annual Report of the Board of Trustees of the Federal Old-Age and Survivors Insurance and Federal Disability Insurance Trust Funds* (Washington, D.C.: U.S. Government Printing Office, 2009), 3.

7. U.S. Congressional Budget Office, *The Budget and Economic Outlook: Fiscal Years 2002–2011* (Washington, D.C.: Government Printing Office, 2001), xiii.

8. David M. Walker, comptroller general of the United States, "Fiscal, Social Security, and Health Care Challenges," presentation at the Awakening Conference, Sea Island, Georgia, 7 January 2007. Also see David S. Broder, "Red Ink Run Amok," *Washington Post*, 13 April 2006.

9. Walker, "Fiscal."

10. *Ibid.*

11. One should not take comfort in the fact that the current deficits as a percentage of GDP are still far below World War II levels. The Second World War was an exceptional period, because in 1945, defense was the sole cause of the U.S. government's deficit and actually accounted for 90 percent of total federal government spending. Once the war was over and troops were quickly demobilized, Washington moved to a budget surplus of 1.2 percent in 1947. There is no comparable quick panacea for the onerous deficit problems currently facing the federal government. See "False Analogy," *Washington Post*, 21 October 2009.

12. Robert J. Samuelson, "Obama's Risky Debt," *Washington Post*, 18 May 2009.

13. Warren E. Buffett, "The Greenback Effect," *New York Times*, 18 August 2009. As Buffett concludes, "fiscally, we are in uncharted territory."

14. World Bank, "Gross Domestic Product 2008," at *http://siteresources.worldbank.org/ DATASTATISICS*. GDP percentage increases or decreases were used to calculate 2009 figures.

15. Matthew Leising, "Fed Seeks End to Wall Street Lock on OTC Derivatives," *Bloomberg.com*, 6 May 2009.

16. David Walker, "America's Triple A Rating Is at Risk," *ft.com*, 12 May 2009. For more information about these staggering future liabilities, see the web sites of the Concord Coalition and the Peterson Foundation.

17. Bowley and Healey, "Worries."

18. Elena L. Nguyen, "The International Investment Position of the United States at Year-end 2008," *Survey of Current Business*, July 2009, 10.

19. Bureau of Economic Analysis, U.S. Department of Commerce, "International Investment Position of the United States at Yearend, 1976–2007," and Nguyen, "The International Investment Position," 10.

20. Department of the Treasury/Federal Reserve Board, "Major Foreign Holders," and Ernest S. Christian and Gary A. Robbins, "Obama's Plan for a Debt-Ridden Future," *ibdeditorials.com*, 5 June 2009.

21. Department of the Treasury/Federal Reserve Board, "Major Foreign Holders."

22. David M. Smick, "Geithner's Last Laugh," *Washington Post*, 9 June 2009.

23. Even Robert Zoellick, current World Bank president and former U.S. Trade representative, has warned that Americans must prepare for the dollar being usurped as the world's reserve currency and the creation of "a radically different world economic order." See Heather Stewart, "U.S. Dollar Set to Be Eclipsed, World Bank President Predicts," *guardian.co.uk*, 28 September 2009.

24. David Malpass, "The Weak Dollar Threat to Prosperity," *wsj.com*, 7 October 2009.

25. Barry Eichengreen, in "The Dollar Dilemma," *Foreign Affairs* 88 (September/October 2009): 67–68, predicts the dollar will still be first among equals, but there will emerge an international reserve system based on multiple currencies.

26. Anthony Faiola, "Fading of the Dollar's Dominance," *Washington Post*, 24 June 2009.

27. *Ibid.*

28. Edmund Conway, "UN Wants New Global Currency to Replace Dollar," *telegraph. co.uk*, 7 September 2009.

29. Faiola, "Fading of the Dollar's Dominance." Bergsten adds, "Like it or not, the dollar is going to lose some of its global status. So maybe it's time we just accepted that and figure out the best and most orderly way to make that happen."

30. Wolf, *Fixing Global Finance*, 76. The current account is the broadest measure of trade in goods and services and also includes various transfer payments between the United States and other countries.

31. George P. Shultz and John B. Shoven, *Putting Our House in Order: A Guide to Social Security and Health Care Reform* (New York: W.W. Norton, 2008), ix.

32. The oldest baby boomers will become eligible for Medicare coverage in 2011 and full Social Security benefits in 2012.

33. Addison Wiggin and Kate Incontrera, *I.O.U.S.A.* (New York: John Wiley & Sons, 2008), 139.

34. "A Thought for Tax Day: The Real Fiscal Crisis Is Yet to Come," *Knowledge @ Wharton*, 15 April 2009.

35. The Board of Trustees, *Federal Old-Age*, 10.

36. *Ibid.*

37. These benefits accounted for 16.2 percent of all personal income in the first quarter of 2009, according to the U.S. Bureau of Economic Analysis. This is the largest percentage since the government started keeping records in 1929. See Dennis Cauchon, "Benefit Spending Soars to New High," *USA Today*, 4 June 2009.

38. Robert J. Samuelson, "A 'Crisis' America Needs," *Washington Post*, 25 May 2009.

39. The Boards of Trustees, *2009 Annual Report of the Boards of Trustees of the Federal Hospital Insurance and Federal Supplementary Medicare Insurance Trust Funds* (Washington, D.C.: U.S. Government Printing Office, 2009), 3 and 201–202.

40. Tom Daschle, "A Public Plan Will Reduce Costs and Improve Access," *Newsweek*, 18 May 2009, and Executive Office of the President, Council of Economic Advisers (CEA), *The Economic Case for Health Care Reform* (Washington, D.C.: U.S. Government Printing Office, 2009), ii.

41. Andrew P. Wilper, Steffie Woolhandler, Karen E. Lasser, Danny McCormick, David H. Bor, and David U. Himmelstein, "Health Insurance and Mortality in U.S. Adults," *American Journal of Public Health* 99 (December 2009): 4 and 6. Also see Nicholas D. Kristof, "The Body Count at Home," *New York Times*, 12 September 2009.

42. The OECD's most recent data for health-care spending as a percentage of GDP, using 2005 statistics, indicates the U.S. spent 15.3 percent, Switzerland 11.6 percent, Canada 9.8 percent, the United Kingdom 8.3 percent, and Japan 8.0 percent. The average for all OECD countries was 9.0 percent. Also see CEA, *The Economic Case*, 2. In 1980, the United States spent the same amount as Germany on health care as a percentage of GDP, and only slightly more than Canada and France. The gap has grown dramatically since that time. See Arnold Kling, *Crisis of Abundance: Rethinking How We Pay for Health Care* (Washington, D.C.: Cato Institute, 2006), 3.

43. National Coalition on Health Care, "Health Insurance Costs," at *www.nchc.org*.

44. David U. Himmelstein, Deborah Thorne, Elizabeth Warren, and Steffie Woolhandler, "Medical Bankruptcy in the United States 2007: Results of a National Study," *American Journal of Medicine* 122 (2009): 741. This estimate is limited to the age group from eighteen to sixty-four years old. The number dying because of the lack of health insurance is actually greater than those who succumb each year to kidney disease (about forty-three thousand).

45. CEA, *The Economic Case*, 2.

46. *Ibid.*, 4.

47. Peter R. Orzag, "That's Why President Obama Is Making Health-Care Reform a Priority," *Wall Street Journal*, 15 May 2009.

48. *Ibid.* Lauran Neergaard, in "Better Care, Pay Less: Some Communities Find a Way," *New York Times*, 7 September 2009, points out that according to the *Dartmouth Atlas of Health Care*, Medicare is currently paying double or triple the price to treat people with similar illnesses, yet the patients in the more expensive areas do not receive higher quality care. The author also provides specific examples of American cities where high quality but affordable health care is available.

49. Uwe E. Reinhardt, "What Is 'Socialized Medicine'?: A Taxonomy of Health Care Systems," *New York Times*, 8 May 2009.

50. *Ibid.*

51. *Ibid.*

52. *Ibid.*

53. Atul Gawande, "Getting There from Here," *The New Yorker*, 26 January 2009.

54. *Ibid.*

55. *Ibid.*

56. Ian Austen, "How Does Canada's Health System Actually Work?" *New York Times*, 7 July 2009.

57. *Ibid.* For comparative studies of the Canadian and U.S. health systems, see Gordon H. Guyatt *et al.*, "A Systematic Review of Studies Comparing Health Outcomes in Canada and the United States," *Open Medicine* 1 (No. 1 2007): 27–36, and Robert G. Evans, "Extravagant Americans, Healthier Canadians: The Bottom Line in North American Health Care," in *Canada and the United States: Differences That Count*, third edition, ed. David M. Thomas and Barbara Boyle Torrey (Toronto: University of Toronto Press, 2008), 135–164.

58. Austen, "How Does Canada's Health System Actually Work?"

59. CEA, *The Economic Case*, 12.

60. T.R. Reid, "Five Myths about Health Care around the World," *Washington Post*, 23 August 2009, and T.R. Reid, *The Healing of America: A Global Quest for Better, Cheaper, and Fairer Health Care* (New York: Penguin Press, 2009).

61. U.S. Central Intelligence Agency, *World Factbook 2008* (Washington, D.C.,: U.S. Government Printing Office, 2008). In World Health Organization, *World Health Statistics 2009* (Geneva: World Health Organization, 2009), the United States ranks 31st in life expectancy, tied with Chile and Kuwait, 37th in infant mortality, and 34th in maternal mortality. See also Nicholas D. Kristof, "Unhealthy America," *New York Times*, 5 November 2009.

62. Jeff Green, "U.S. Has Second Worst Newborn Death Rate in Modern World, Report Says," *CNN.com*, 10 May 2006. The report was released by the Save the Children organization.

63. *Ibid.*

64. World Health Organization, *The World Health Report 2000—Health Systems: Improving Performance* (Geneva: World Health Organization, 2000).

65. National Coalition on Health Care, "Health Insurance Costs."

66. Kaiser Family Foundation, "Employer Health Benefits: 2009 Summary of Findings," 15 September 2009, 1, at *www.kff.org*.

67. CEA, *The Economic Case*, 8.

68. *Ibid.*, 4.

69. Robert Frank, "Global Wealth Gap Widens," *Wall Street Journal*, 3 October 2007.

70. U.S. Bureau of Labor Statistics, "Employment, Hours, and Earnings."

71. S. Mitra Kalita, "Americans See 18 Percent of Wealth Vanish," *Wall Street Journal*, 13 March 2009. Wealth calculations were provided by the Federal Reserve.

72. Erik Eckholm, "Last Year's Poverty Rate Was Highest in 12 Years," *New York Times*, 11 September 2009. Data were compiled by the U.S. Census Bureau.

73. *Ibid.*

74. Carlos Torres, "Jobless Gender Gap Widest Since 'Riveter' Rosie: Chart of the Day," *Bloomberg.com*, 8 May 2009. A good share of these men will eventually find new jobs, but often these jobs will have lower wages and fringe benefits than they had received in their previous manufacturing or construction jobs.

75. DeParle and Gebeloff, "Food Stamp Use Soars."

76. The median price of an existing home was $143,600 in 2000, $230,300 in July 2006, and $175,000 at the end of 2009. See Andy Serwer, "The '00s': Goodbye (at Last) to the Decade From Hell," *Time Magazine*, 24 November 2009.

77. Ruth Simon and James R. Hagerty, "House-Price Drops Leave More Underwater," *Wall Street Journal*, 5 May 2009.

78. Janet L. Yellen, president and CEO, Federal Reserve Bank of San Francisco, "The Outlook for Recovery in the U.S. Economy," presentation to the San Francisco Society of Certified Financial Analysts, San Francisco, 14 September 2009.

79. Eric Dash and Andrew Martin, "Banks Brace for Credit Card Write-Offs," *New York Times*, 10 May 2009. The credit card debt burdens were estimates from *Moody's Economy.com*.

80. Meizhu Lui, "The Wealth Gap Gets Wider," *Washington Post*, 23 March 2009.

81. Dennis Cauchon, "Why Home Values May Take Decades to Recover," *USA Today*, 15 December 2008.

82. Reuters, "U.S. Home Size Shrinks to Fit Smaller Wallets," *Investors.com*, 25 June 2009.

83. Gosling, *Economics*, 214.

84. "Counting the Hours," *OECD Observer*, March 2008. For example, on average Americans take fourteen vacation days a year versus thirty-seven for the French.

85. "The Cost of Staying Home Sick," *New York Times*, 4 May 2009. Statistics were provided by Dr. Jody Heymann, director of the Institute for Health and Social Policy at McGill University.

86. David Ignatius, "Boomers Going Bust," *Washington Post*, 7 May 2009, and Teresa Ghilarducci and Christian E. Weller, eds., *Employee Pensions: Policies, Problems, and Possibilities* (Champaign, Ill.: Land and Employment Relations Association, 2007), 1.

87. *Ibid.*

88. *Ibid.*, with data obtained from the U.S. Department of Labor.

89. Randall W. Forsyth, "The Market's Formula: A Square-Root Rally," *Barron's*, 4 June 2009.

90. Michael Kranish, "Pension Insurer Shifted to Stocks," *Boston Globe*, 30 March 2009.

91. *Ibid.*

92. Roger Lowenstine, *While America Aged: How Pension Debts Ruined General Motors, Stopped the NYC Subways, Bankrupted San Diego, and Loom as the Next Financial Crisis* (New York: Penguin Press, 2008), 1. Lowenstine argues that "America now faces a crisis of epidemic proportions" with unfunded or underfunded pension funds, at a time when the number of seniors in society will increase from 38 million today to 72 million by 2030. In terms of state government problems, see Robert Novy-Marx and Joshua D. Rauh, "The Intergenerational Transfer of Public Pension Providers," *NBER Working Paper No. 14343*, September 2008.

93. Philip M. Dine, *State of the Unions* (New York: McGraw-Hill, 2008), ix.

94. *Ibid.*, 254.

95. Jacob S. Hacker and Elisabeth Jacobs, "Take Off," *New Republic*, 15 April 2009.

96. See Jacob S. Hacker, *The Great Risk Shift: The Assault on American Jobs, Families, Health Care, and Retirement and How You Can Fight Back* (Oxford: Oxford University Press, 2006), x and 128. Hacker argues that the message today is "you are on your own," and "social insecurity" has now become the watchword of the day.

97. Sawhill and Haskins, "Five Myths."

98. In 2006, consumer spending reached 76 percent of nominal GDP, the highest ever recorded since quarterly data began to be tabulated back in 1947. See Peter Schrank, "American Consumers Struggle with Their Debts," *Economist.com*, 6 May 2009.

99. In the 1960s and 1970s, Americans saved almost 10 percent of their income. It would not be surprising for them to return to saving rates in the 7 to 10 percent range.

100. In his book *Free Lunch: How the Wealthiest Americans Enrich Themselves at Government Expense (And Stick You with the Bill)* (New York: Portfolio, 2007), 10, David Cay Johnston argues that the bottom 90 percent of Americans have seen their incomes on a mostly downhill slide for more than three decades.

101. Paul Krugman, "America the Tarnished," *New York Times*, 30 March 2009.

102. Thomas L. Friedman, "The Great Unraveling," *New York Times*, 17 December 2008.

103. Andrew Clark, "Buffett Says: Act or Face 'Economic Pearl Harbor.'" *The Guardian*, 25 September 2008.

104. Nouriel Roubini, "The United States of Ponzi," *Forbes.com*, 19 March 2009. See also two books by Kevin Phillips, *Bad Money: Reckless Finance, Failed Politics, and the Global Crisis of American Capitalism* (New York: Viking Press, 2008) and *American Theocracy: The Peril and Politics of Radical Religion, Oil, and Borrowed Money in the Twenty-First Century* (New York: Viking Press, 2006).

105. Historically, subprime mortgages are foreclosed at ten times the rate of prime mortgages. See Souphala Chomsisengphet and Anthony Pennington-Cross, "The Evolution of the Subprime Mortgage Market," *Federal Reserve Bank of St. Louis Review* 88 (February 2006): 31–56.

106. Kai Wright, "More Mortgage Madness," *The Nation*, 29 April 2009.

107. The purpose of securitization was to expand investment pools and spread the risk of making loans by packaging the mortgages and selling them at home and abroad as collateralized debt obligations.

108. Robert Rosenkranz, "Let's Write the Rating Agencies Out of Our Law," *Wall Street Journal*, 2 January 2009.

109. Adam Davidson, "How AIG Fell Apart," *Reuters*, 18 September 2008. AIG provided insurance for roughly $440 billion in bonds. See also Michael Hirsh, "Last Chance for Justice," *Newsweek Web Exclusive*, 17 September 2009.

110. Simon Johnson, "The Quiet Coup," *Atlantic Online*, May 2009. In addition, consult Lisa A. Keister, *Wealth in America: Trends in Wealth Inequality* (Cambridge: Cambridge University Press, 2000).

111. Robert Frank, *Richistan: A Journey through the American Wealth Boom and the Lives of the New Rich* (New York: Crown Publishers, 2007), 11.

112. Edward N. Wolff, "Recent Trends in Household Wealth in the United States: Rising Debt and the Middle-Class Squeeze," *Levy Economics Institute Working Paper #502* (New York: Levy Economics Institute of Bard College, 2007), 11.

113. Robert B. Reich, "Obamanomics Isn't About Big Government," *wsj.com*, 28 March 2009.

114. Bob Herbert, "Safety Nets for the Rich," *New York Times*, 20 October 2009.

115. Johnston, *Free Lunch*, 272 and 275.

116. Sarah Burd-Sharps, Kristen Lewis, and Eduardo Borges Martins, *The Measure of America: American Human Development Report 2008–2009* (New York: Columbia University Press, 2008), 136. On page 133, the authors point out that real mean income has more than doubled since 1947, but the distribution of that income across society is increasingly top-heavy.

117. Brandeis' quote at *www.brainyquote.com/quotes/quotes/l/louisbra105452.html*.

118. Paul Krugman, *The Conscience of a Liberal* (New York: W.W. Norton, 2007), 128.

119. Sarah Anderson and Sam Pizzzigati, "Ending Plutocracy: A Twelve-Step Program," *The Nation*, 11 June 2008.

120. Nicole Tichon, *Tax Shell Game: The Taxpayer Cost of Offshore Corporate Tax Havens* (Washington, D.C.: U.S. Public Interest Research Group Education Fund, 2009), 1.

121. "The Swiss and Their Secrets," *New York Times*, 2 May 2009, Devlin Barrett, "IRS Squeezes Swiss Bank Clients for Evidence," *Yahoo!News*, 26 March 2009, and David Voreacos and Mort Lucoff, "U.S., UBS Agree to Delay Hearing on 52,000 Accounts," *Bloomberg.com*, 12 July 2009.

122. Tichon, *Tax Shell Game*, 1, and "Isles of Plenty," *The Guardian*, 13 February 2009. One of the offshore tax havens is the Cayman Islands, a British Overseas Territory. It has a population of fifty-two thousand but ranks as the fifth-largest financial center in the world. One-tenth of its population is comprised of lawyers and accountants.

123. David Brooks, "Greed and Stupidity," *New York Times*, 3 April 2009.

124. William Greider, "Fixing the Fed," *The Nation*, 13 March 2009.

125. In his book *House of Cards: A Tale of Hubris and Wretched Excess on Wall Street* (New York: Doubleday, 2009), 3, William D. Cohan stresses that many of the bosses simply did not know or understand what was going on downstairs in their own companies.

126. Andrew Ross Sorkin, "A Back to Basics Weekend with Warren Buffett," *New York Times*, 5 May 2009.

127. Joe Nocera, "Risk Management," *New York Times*, 4 January 2009. The model ignored the possibility of massive losses, or what Nassim Nicholas Taleb referred to as the "Black Swan" scenario. Eventually the model became "garbage in, garbage out," and the resulting catastrophe was a combination of human failure and the imperfections in risk modeling.

128. In his article "Not Quite a Confession, But a Good Start," *Washington Post*, 8 April 2009, Steven Pearlstein concludes that pay in the shadow banking sector was "ridiculously out of line with that of similarly skilled and equally successful people in other industries."

129. Alistair Barr and Matt Andrejczak, "Pay Dirt: The Executive Pay System Is Broken," *MarketWatch*, 12 May 2009. CEO compensation statistics were compiled by the organization United for a Fair Economy.

130. Philip Klein, "Wrestling with Capitalist Pigs," *American Spectator*, April 2009.

131. Ben Levishon, "Bear Stearns Big Shots Reaped Big Paydays," *BusinessWeek.com*, 19 March 2008, and Cohan, *House of Cards*.

132. Cohan, *House of Cards*.

133. Gabriel Sherman, "The Wail of the One Percent," *New Yorker*, 19 April 2009.

134. "Seventy-Three AIG Bonuses Hit Million-Dollar Mark," *www.cbsnews.com*, 17 March 2009.

135. Jake Tapper, "High-Flying Citigroup Grounds Plans for $50M Jet," *abcnews.go.com*, 27 January 2009.

136. Karen Freifeld, "Cuomo Seeks to Force Thain to Reveal Merrill Bonuses," *Bloomberg.com*, 23 February 2009, and Heidi N. Moore, "John Thain's $35,000 'Commode on Legs' Outrage," *WSJ Blogs*, 23 January 2009.

137. Kate Kelly and Jon Hilsenrath, "New York Fed Chairman's Ties to Goldman Raise Questions," *Wall Street Journal*, 4 May 2009. As soon as this information became public, Friedman resigned his position on the New York Fed.

138. In his article, "Diminished Returns," *New York Times*, 15 May 2009, Niall Ferguson correctly concludes that "the reality is that crises are more often caused by bad regulation than deregulation."

139. Joseph Stiglitz labeled the bailout of Wall Street a huge Rube Goldberg project to transfer money to Wall Street from the taxpayers. He is quoted in Frank Rich, "Awake and Sing!," *New York Times*, 11 April 2009.

140. Shoshana Zuboff, "Wall Street's Economic Crimes against Humanity," *Business Week*, 20 March 2009.

141. As John C. Bogle, founder of the Vanguard mutual fund giant, laments: "The banks are too big to fail and the man in the street is too small to bail." Quoted in Gretchen Morgenson, "Borrowers and Bankers: A Great Divide," *New York Times*, 20 July 2008. In his book *Falling Behind: How Rising Inequality Harms the Middle Class* (Berkeley: University of California Press, 2007), 78–79, Robert H. Frank argues that in an effort to try to keep up, middle-class households often expand to two earners and work longer hours.

142. In his article "The Looting of America's Coffers," *New York Times*, 11 March 2009, David Leonhardt concludes that "given the incentive to loot, Wall Street did so," and credit derivatives became the vehicle for this looting.

143. Dawn Kopecki and Robert Schmidt, "Geithner Seeks 'Difficult-to-Evade' Derivatives Laws," *Bloomberg.com*, 10 July 2009.

144. The high of 381.2 was reached on September 3, 1929, and was not surpassed until 1954.

Chapter 4

1. Peter Lyman and Hal R. Varian, "How Much Information?" 2003, at *www.sims.berkeley.edu/how-much-info-2003*.

2. Claudia Golding and Lawrence F. Katz, *Race between Education and Technology* (Cambridge, MA: Belknap Press of Harvard University, 2008), 1–2.

3. *Ibid.*, 353.

4. National Center on Education and the Economy, *Tough Choices, Tough Times: The Report of the New Commission on the Skills of the American Workplace: Executive Summary*, at *www.skillscommission.org*, 6.

5. Irwin Kirsch, Henry Braun, Kentaro Yamamoto, and Andrew Sum, *America's Perfect Storm: Three Forces Changing Our Nation's Future* (Princeton, NJ: Educational Testing Service, 2007), 14.

6. *Ibid.*

7. David C. Miller, Anindita Sen, Lydia B. Malley, Stephanie D. Burns, and Eugene Owen, *Comparative Indicators of Education in the United States and Other G-8 Countries* (Washington, D.C.: U.S. Department of Education, 2009), iii–iv.

8. Bob Herbert, "Clueless in America," *New York Times*, 22 April 2008, and Miller *et al.*, *Comparative Indicators*, vi.

9. Herbert, "Clueless."

10. *Ibid.*

11. Clive Crook, "America's Classroom Equality Battle," *Financial Times*, 10 May 2009. The data cited were compiled by the Organization for Economic Cooperation and Development in a report entitled *Programme for International Student Assessment*. Crook adds that on the OECD PISA tests "the U.S. lags far behind the industrial-country average in a standardized measure of math and science skills among fifteen-year olds. It sits among low-achievers such as Portugal and Italy, and way behind the best performers, such as South Korea, Finland, Canada and the Netherlands. It scores worse than the UK, which is about average on both measures."

12. Fred Hiatt, "How Bill Gates Would Repair Our Schools," *Washington Post*, 30 March, 2009.

13. "UC Professor Takes on School Spending," *Los Angeles Times*, 6 April 2009.

14. Jonathan Kozol, *The Shame of the Nation* (New York: Random House, 2005), 135.

15. *Ibid.*, 49.

16. Hiatt, "How Bill Gates."

17. Tim Rutten, "By All Accounts a Failure," *Los Angeles Times*, 19 July 2008.

18. Clive R. Belfield and Henry M. Levin, "The Economic Losses from High School Dropouts in California," *California Dropout Research Project*, August 2007, 1.

19. Michael Hitzik, "Cutting School? When Will the State Learn?," *Los Angeles Times*, 5 March 2009.

20. All of these statistics come from Teach for America, "Our Nation's Greatest Injustice," at *www.teachforamerica.org/mission/greatest_injustice.htm*.

21. John Ibbitson, "Boomers and Whites Will Soon be America's New Minorities," *Globe and Mail*, 25 June 2009.

22. "Top 200 World Universities," *Times of London*, 7 October 2009, and Phil Baty, "UK Boosts Standing but Asian Countries 'Snap at Our Heels,'" *Times of London*, 8 October 2009.

23. A College Board report estimates that the average annual cost of attending a public four-year college in 2008, including room and board, was $15,213. The cost of attending private nonprofit colleges, which enroll 20 percent of all students nationally, was $35,636. The real median annual household income in 2008 was $50,303. Overall college costs have been escalating at a rate well above the increase in the consumer price index, especially over the past decade. See Tamara Lewin, "College Costs Are on Rise, As Is Concern about Effect," *New York Times*, 21 October 2009, and Carmen DeNavas-Walt *et al.*, *Income, Poverty, and Health Insurance*, 29.

24. Zakaria, *Post-American*, 198.

25. *Ibid.*

26. Daniel Lyons, "Silicon Valley Wants to Stay on the Road to Prosperity," *Washington Post*, 27 January 2009.

27. National Center on Education, "Tough Choices," 8–9.

28. Burd-Sharps *et al.*, *The Measure of America*, 119.

29. *Ibid.*, 8, and Miller *et al.*, *Comparative Indicators*, 8. Bill Gates adds that "our performance at every level—primary and secondary school achievement, high school graduation, college entry, college completion—is dropping against the rest of the world." Gates is quoted in Bob Herbert, "Peering at the Future," *New York Times*, 29 September 2009.

30. Amity Shales, "The Perils of a Cement Tsunami," *Washington Post*, 10 December 2008.

31. Thomas L. Friedman, "Time to Reboot America," *New York Times*, 23 December 2008.

32. *Ibid.*

33. Quoted in Bob Herbert, "Risking the Future," *New York Times*, 3 February 2009.

34. *Ibid.*

35. "Akami: U.S. 33rd Fastest Broadband Country," 9 July 2009 at *www.dslreports*; James Kantor, "Europe Says It Leads U.S. in Broadband Use," *New York Times*, 4 August 2009; and "U.S. Ranks 20th in Global Broadband Household Penetration," 22 June 2009 at *www.telecompaper.com*. The latter report was prepared by Strategy Analytics.

36. Quoted in Matt Richtel, "Tech Recruiting Clashes with Immigration Rules," *New York Times*, 12 April 2009.

37. Robert J. Samuelson, "A Path to Downward Mobility," *Washington Post*, 12 October 2009. Samuelson contends that "every generation of Americans should live better than its predecessors. That's Americans' core definition of economic 'progress.' But for today's young, it may be a mirage."

38. Robert J. Samuelson, "The Consequences of Big Government," *Washington Post*, 13 July 2009.

39. *Ibid.*

40. Board of Trustees, *Federal Old-Age*, 51.

41. Mark R. Rank and Thomas A. Hirschl, "Estimating the Risk of Food Stamp Use and Impoverishment during Childhood," *Archives of Pediatrics and Adolescent Medicine* 163 (November 2009): 997.

42. *Ibid.*, 998.

43. Burd-Sharps *et al.*, *The Measure of America*, 17.

44. Jeffrey Passel and D'Vera Cohn, *U.S. Population Projections: 2005–2050* (Washington, D.C.: Pew Research Center, 2009), i.

45. *Ibid.*

46. Pew Hispanic Center, "Statistical Portrait of the Foreign-born Population in the United States, 2006," 23 January 2008, at *http://pewhispanic.org/factsheets/*.

47. Passel and Cohn, *U.S. Population*, 2.

48. *Ibid.*, i.

49. *Ibid.*

50. *Ibid.*

51. Pew Hispanic Center, "Mexican Immigrants in the United States, 2008," 15 April 2008, 1, at *http://pewhispanic.org/files/factsheets/47.pdf*.

52. Randall Monger and Nancy Rytina, "U.S. Legal Permanent Residents: 2008," *Office of Immigration Statistics Annual Report*, March 2009, 1.

53. Jeffrey S. Passel and D'Vera Cohn, *A Portrait of Unauthorized Immigrants in the United States* (Washington, D.C.: Pew Hispanic Center, 2009), 1–2.

54. *Ibid.*, 1.

55. *Ibid.*

56. *Ibid.*, 1–2.

57. *Ibid.*, 17.

58. *Ibid.*, 18.

59. *Ibid.*

60. *Ibid.*, 19.

61. Pew Hispanic Center, "Mexican Immigrants," 3.

62. Richtel, "Tech Recruiting." These statistics were compiled by Vivek Wadhwa, an immigration scholar from Duke and Harvard. See also Bernard P. Wong, *The Chinese in Silicon Valley: Globalization, Social Networks, and Ethnic Identity* (Lanham, MD: Rowman & Littlefield, 2006).

63. Richtel, "Tech Recruiting."

64. David M. Hart and Spencer L. Tracy, Jr., "High-tech Immigrant Entrepreneurship in the United States," July 2009, at *www.sba.gov/advo*.

65. Richtel, "Tech Recruiting."

66. *Ibid.* Twenty thousand additional visas are available for foreign residents who obtain graduate degrees from U.S. universities.

67. *Ibid.*

68. Moira Herbst, "Immigration: When Only 'Geniuses' Need Apply," *Business Week*, 7 May 2009.

69. *Ibid.* Dirk Nowitzki of the Dallas Mavericks is an O–1 recipient.
70. Moira Herbst, "Skilled Immigrants on Why They're Leaving the U.S.," *Business Week*, 26 July 2009.
71. *Ibid.*
72. Hua Hsu, "The End of White America?," *The Atlantic*, January/February 2009, 50.
73. Patrick J. Buchanan, *State of Emergency: The Third World Invasion and Conquest of America* (New York: St. Martin's, 2007). See also Mark Krikorian, *The New Case Against Immigration, Both Legal and Illegal* (New York: Penguin Group, 2008).
74. The most consistent and enthusiastic supporter of "open borders" for the United States has been the *Wall Street Journal* editorial page.
75. In 2009, the *National Journal* labeled New York as the most dysfunctional state government based on the following criteria: the quality of leadership; the amount of "criminality" in the state's top political leadership; the severity of the state's policy challenges; and the intensity of the media circus surrounding state government. New York was followed by Nevada, Illinois, Alaska, South Carolina, and California. See Louis Jacobsen, "The Six Most Dysfunctional State Governments," *NationalJournal. com*, 13 July 2009.
76. Ann O'M. Bowman, "American Federalism on the Horizon," *Publius* 32 (Spring 2002): 20.
77. Erich Steinman, "American Federalism and Intergovernmental Innovation in State-Tribal Relations," *Publius* 34 (Spring 2004): 113–114. Within the court system, *Cherokee Nation v. Georgia* (1831) provides significant insights on future intergovernmental relations involving tribal groups.
78. A more detailed discussion of democracy and federalism is provided in Kevin Arceneaux, "Does Federalism Weaken Democratic Representation in the United States?" *Publius* 35 (Spring 2005): 297–312.
79. A discussion of the Tenth Amendment is found in Mark R. Killenbeck, ed., *The Tenth Amendment and State Sovereignty: Constitutional History and Contemporary Issues* (Lanham, MD: Rowman & Littlefield, 2002).
80. Kavan Peterson, "Governors Lose in Power Struggle over National Guard," *Stateline. org*, 12 January 2007.
81. David S. Broder, "Governors Wary of Change on Troops," *Washington Post*, 6 August 2006.
82. *Ibid.*
83. Joel Kotkin, "Sundown for California," *The American*, 12 November 2008.
84. Donn Esmonde, "Budget Pain Not Shared by Politicians," *Buffalo News*, 3 April 2009.
85. New York Public Interest Research Group, "Reform New York: Redistricting," at *www. nypirg.org/goodgov/reformny/redist.html*, and Scott Jordan, *Advantage, Incumbent* (Helena, MT: Institute on Money in State Politics, 2008). In a piece entitled "The Fog of Ethics in Albany," 27 October 2009, the *New York Times* editorial board laments that over the past five years members of the New York legislature have been convicted of extortion, bribery, and racketeering, and that ethical standards in Albany are virtually non-existent.
86. "Illinois Has Long Legacy of Public Corruption," *msnbc.com*, 9 December 2008.
87. Mike Hughlett and Wailin Wong, "The Cost of Corruption," *Chicago Tribune*, 14 December 2008.
88. Charles Olivier, "Labyrinth of Incentives," *Financial Times*, 2 December 2002.
89. Earl H. Fry, *The Expanding Role of State and Local Governments in U.S. Foreign Affairs* (New York: Council on Foreign Relations Press, 1998), 117.

90. Nguyen, "The International Investment Position," 16.
91. Thomas Anderson, "U.S. Affiliates of Foreign Companies," *Survey of Current Business*, August 2008, 186. At the end of 2006, 5.33 million worked for foreign-owned companies in the United States. This figure is well below the total number of workers because it excludes the banking sector altogether and only includes majority-owned foreign affiliates. The U.S. Department of Commerce considers any investment by an overseas firm that gives the firm at least 10 percent of the shares in a U.S. publicly traded company as constituting a foreign direct investment, not 50 percent.
92. Peter Fisher and Alan Peters, "The Failure of Economic Development Incentives," *Journal of the American Planning Association* 70 (#1 2004), and Dennis Cauchon, "Business Incentives Lose Luster for States," *USA Today*, 22 August 2007. In *DaimlerChrysler Corp. v. Cuno* and *Wilkins (Ohio Tax Comm.) v. Cuno*, the U.S. Supreme Court ruled 9–0 that Ohio taxpayers had no right to challenge the state government's granting of $300 million in tax breaks to entice DaimlerChrysler to build a new assembly plant in Toledo.
93. Neil Brenner and Roger Keil, "Editors' Introduction," in *The Global Cities Reader*, eds. Neil Brenner and Roger Keil (London: Routledge, 2006), 4.
94. Population Reference Bureau, "Human Population: Fundamentals of Growth Patterns of World Urbanization," 2003, at *www.prb.org*.
95. United States Conference of Mayors, *Strong Cities . . . Strong Families . . . for a Strong America: Mayors' Ten-Point Plan* (Washington, D.C.: United States Conference of Mayors, 2008), 1.
96. United States Conference of Mayors, *U.S. Metro Economies: GMP—The Engines of America's Growth* (Lexington, KY: Global Insight, 2006), 37.
97. Burd-Sharps *et al.*, *The Measure of America*, 11.
98. *Ibid.*, 3.
99. *Ibid.*
100. *Ibid.*, 37.
101. Evan Ben-Joseph, "Double Standards, Single Goal: Private Communities and Design Innovation," *Journal of Urban Design* 9 (June 2004): 132.
102. As Tom Friedman laments in "Where Do 'We' Go?," *New York Times*, 29 September 2009, Americans are tolerating "the wild excess of money in politics; the gerrymandering of political districts, making them permanently Republican or Democratic and erasing the political middle; a 24/7 cable news cycle that makes all politics a daily battle of tactics that overwhelm strategic thinking; and a blogosphere that at its best enriches our debates, adding new checks on the establishment, and at its worst coarsens our debates to a whole new level, giving a new power to anonymous slanderers to send lies around the world. Finally, on top of it all, we now have a permanent presidential campaign that encourages all partisanship, all the time among our leading politicians."
103. Chris Cillizza, "Post/ABC Poll: McCain's Structural Problems," *Washington Post*, 13 October 2008.
104. "Poll: More Disapprove of Bush than Any Other President," *CNNpolitics.com*, 1 May 2008.
105. Lydia Saad, "Congressional Approval Rating Hits Record-Low 14 Percent," at *www.gallup.com*, 16 July 2008.
106. Gelb, "Necessity," 56.
107. Intercollegiate Studies Institute, "Our Fading Heritage: Americans Fail a Basic Test on Their History and Institutions: 2008–2009," at *www.americancivilization.org/2008/summary_summary.html*.

108. Anthony Lutkus and Andrew R. Weiss, *The Nation's Report Card: Civics 2006* (Washington, D.C.: National Assessment of Education Progress, 2007).

109. *Ibid.*, and Mark Bauerlein, "History, Civics Courses Failing Students and Our Democracy," *Atlanta Journal-Constitution*, 8 June 2007.

110. Intercollegiate Studies Institute, *The Coming Crisis in Citizenship* (Wilmington, DE: Intercollegiate Studies Institute, 2006). Elite universities were identified as the highest-rated institutions in the 2006 rankings by *U.S. News & World Report*.

111. Burke's quote at *www.quotationspage.com*.

112. Twain's interview with the *Boston Transcript*, 6 November 1905, at *www.twainquotes.com*.

113. *Ibid.*, quote from *Traveling with a Reformer*.

114. Rogers' quote at *www.cmgww.com*.

115. Brandeis' quote at *www.brainyquote.com/quotes/quotes/l/louisbra105452.html*.

116. This quote attributable to Franklin is found in the notes of Dr. James McHenry, a Maryland delegate to the convention. See *www.bartleby.com*.

Chapter 5

1. Gelb, "Necessity," 57.

2. Paul Kennedy, *The Rise and Fall of the Great Powers* (New York: Random House, 1987).

3. Based on his twelve-volume study entitled *A Study of History*, which focuses on the rise and decline of twenty-three civilizations, Arnold Toynbee reached the conclusion that all empires are susceptible to "the mirage of immortality." Toynbee is quoted in Parag Khanna, *The Second World: Empires and Influence in the New Global Order* (New York: Random House, 2008), xiv. Toynbee's twelve volumes were written between 1934 and 1961.

4. The World Bank estimates Iraq's GDP in 2005 was $12.6 billion, compared with the U.S. Department of Commerce's estimate of a $23 billion GDP for Vermont.

5. Richard Reeves, *President Kennedy: Profile of Power* (New York: Simon & Schuster, 1994), Chapter 1.

6. Pat Schroeder, "The Burden-Sharing Numbers Racket," *New York Times*, 6 April 1988.

7. Stockholm International Peace Research Institute, *SIPRI Yearbook 2009: Summary* (Stockholm: Stockholm International Peace Research Institute, 2009), 10–11.

8. Steven W. Hook and John Spanier, *American Foreign Policy Since World War II*, 17th edition (Washington, D.C.: CQ Press, 2007), 324–327.

9. *Ibid.*, 327.

10. Gary Wills, "Entangled Giant," *New York Review of Books*, 8 October 2009, and Chalmers Johnson, "Empire vs. Democracy: Why Nemesis Is at Our Door," *TomDispatch.com*, 30 January 2007.

11. Johnson, "Empire vs. Democracy."

12. David A. Lake, "American Hegemony and the Future of East-West Relations," *International Studies Perspectives* 7 (no. 1, 2006): 23–30.

13. Michael Dobbs and John M. Goshko, "Albright's Personal Odyssey Shaped Foreign Policy Beliefs," *Washington Post*, 6 December 1996. She used this phrase in her remarks after being nominated by President Clinton to be America's first female Secretary of State in December 1996.

14. Joseph E. Stiglitz and Linda J. Bilmes, *The Three Trillion Dollar War: The True Cost of the Iraq Conflict* (New York: W.W. Norton, 2008), 31.

15. Jimmy Carter, *Beyond the White House* (New York: Simon & Schuster, 2007), 250.

16. Jean-Marie Colombani, "Nous sommes tous Américains," *Le Monde*, 12 Septembre 2001.

17. Burnett's call was quoted in Peggy Noonan, *Patriotic Grace* (New York: HarperCollins, 2008), 65.

18. *Ibid.*, 117. In Peggy Noonan's words, the TSA treats us "like cattle."

19. Thomas Frank, "Report Blasts TSA Air Cargo Security," *USA Today*, 6 September 2007, and Joan Goodchild, "What New Air Cargo Security Rules Mean for Business," *CSO Online*, 29 January 2009.

20. For example, 220 million sea containers move 90 percent of the world's merchandise trade every year, but only 10 percent of the containers are inspected. See Jerome C. Glenn, "Scanning the Global Situation and Prospects for the Future," *The Futurist*, January/February 2008, 44.

21. An essential understanding of al-Qaeda should begin with a thorough reading of Lawrence Wright, *The Looming Tower: Al-Qaeda and the Road to 9/11* (New York: Alfred A. Knopf, 2006).

22. This is based on the author's own interviews. For years, Texas and Utah combined to bring Brazilian business representatives to their states in an effort to build trade and investment linkages. The program was suddenly shut down because the U.S. embassy in Brazil would no longer offer visas in a timely fashion.

23. Author's interviews with representatives of the Las Vegas Convention and Visitors Authority.

24. World Tourism Organization, "Testing Times for International Tourism," 2 July 2009, at *www.unwto.org/media/news* and its data bank at *www.unwto.org.*

25. Department of Commerce, International Trade Administration, "International Visitation to the United States: A Statistical Summary of U.S. Arrivals (2008)," at *www.tinet. ita.doc.gov/outreach pages*, and Department of Commerce, International Trade Administration, "U.S. Travel and Tourism Trends: International Visitor Spending," at *www.tinet.ita.doc.gov/outreachpages.*

26. Glenn Haussman, "U.S. Ceding World Tourism Market Share," *Hotel Interactive*, 19 June 2007.

27. Department of Commerce, "International Visitation" and "U.S. Travel and Tourism Trends."

28. Department of Commerce, "U.S. Travel and Tourism Trends."

29. Zakaria, *Post-American*, 14.

30. John Mueller, *Overblown: How Politicians and the Terrorism Industry Inflate National Security Threats, and Why We Believe Them* (New York: Free Press, 2006), 8, and Peter N. Stearns, *American Fear* (New York: Routledge, 2006), 217.

31. Jane Mayer, *The Dark Side: The Inside Story of How the War on Terror Turned into a War on American Ideals* (New York: Doubleday, 2008), 326–329.

32. In this case, Washington practiced "exemptionalism," unilaterally exempting itself from a number of international conventions it had helped craft in the first place. See John Gerald Ruggie, "Doctrinal Unilateralism and Its Limits: America and Global Governance in the New Century," in *American Foreign Policy in a Globalized World*, eds. David P. Forsythe, Patrice C. McMahon, and Andrew Wedeman (New York: Routledge, 2006), 37.

33. Quoted in Michael Scheuer, *Marching toward Hell: America and Islam after Iraq* (New York: Free Press, 2008), xi.

34. Zakaria, *Post-American*, 251.

35. *Ibid.*

36. Jules Jusserand, French ambassador to the U.S. from 1902 to 1925, is quoted in Thomas A. Bailey, *Diplomatic History of the American People*, 6th edition (New York: Appleton-Century-Crofts, 1958), 4.

37. "Quebec Firetrucks Rushing to U.S. Fire Stopped at Border," *Vancouver Sun*, 15 November 2007.

38. Sheldon Albert, "Border Changes Needed: Report," *Ottawa Citizen*, 22 July 2009.

39. Jeffrey Davidow, *The Bear and the Porcupine: The U.S. and Mexico* (Princeton: Marcus Wiener Publishers, 2007), 263–264, Shannon O'Neil, "The Real War in Mexico," *Foreign Affairs* 88 (July/August 2009):76–77, and Denise Dresser and Veronica Wilson, *U.S.–Mexico Relations: Permeable Borders, Transnational Communities* (Los Angeles: Pacific Council on International Policy, 2006), 6–35.

40. Adams' quote is found at *www.brainyquote.com*.

41. Rice stated that "the problem here is that there will always be some uncertainty about how quickly he can acquire nuclear weapons. But we don't want the smoking gun to be a mushroom cloud." She made these remarks on CNN's *Late Edition* on 8 September 2002.

42. Kishore Mahbubani asserts that "the Iraq War had such a shattering impact on America's standing in the world. When America decided to go to war despite having failed to get an enabling UN resolution, America tore a hole in the very consensus that had been an American gift to the world." See his book *Beyond the Age of Innocence: Rebuilding Trust between America and the World* (New York: Public Affairs, 2005), 209. In Patrick Tyler, *A World of Trouble: The White House and the Middle East—From the Cold War to the War on Terror* (New York: Farrar Straus Giroux, 2009), 545, the author labels the Iraq War as "a forced and fraudulent act of militarism that weakened America's moral profile."

43. Elizabeth Drew, "The Neocons in Power," *New York Review of Books*, 12 June 2003.

44. Daniel Pipes, "The Caliphate," *danielpipes.org*, 12 December 2005.

45. "U.S. Embassy in Iraq Largest, Most Expensive Ever," *FoxNews.com*, 5 January 2009. The embassy cost over $700 million to build.

46. *Ibid.*

47. Fred Kaplan asserts that the mix of neoconservatism and evangelism proved to be disastrous. See his book *Daydream Believers: How a Few Grand Ideas Wrecked American Power* (Hoboken, NJ: John Wiley & Sons, 2008), 195. See also Hal Brands, *From Berlin to Baghdad: America's Search for Purpose in the Post-Cold War World* (Lexington: University of Kentucky Press, 2008), 301. In Craig Unger, *The Fall of the House of Bush* (New York: Scribner, 2007), 45, the author suggests that the neocons' message coincided with Bush's image of the United States as the "Redeemer Nation." In Strobe Talbott, *The Great Experiment: The Story of Ancient Empires, Modern States, and the Quest for a Global Nation* (New York: Simon & Schuster, 2008), 375 and 377, the author labels Bush as Manichean and insists that "Bush's evangelism undergirded his certitude."

48. Andrew Sullivan, "Neocons Caught in Their Very Own Civil War," *Sunday Times*, 23 July 2006.

49. A thorough overview of the Iraq War is provided in the following books and articles: James A. Baker, III and Lee H. Hamilton, *The Iraq Study Group Report* (New York: Vintage Books, 2006); Dexter Filkins, *The Forever War: Dispatches from the War on Terror* (London: The Bodley Head, 2008); Lawrence J. Korb, Sean Duggan, and Laura Conley, "Lessons from Six Years in Iraq," *RealClearPolitics*, 20 March 2009; Peter W. Galbraith, *The End of Iraq* (New York: Simon & Schuster, 2006); Anthony Shadid, *Night Draws Near: Iraq's People in the Shadow of America's War* (New York: Henry Holt, 2005); Michael R. Gordon and General Bernard E. Trainor, *Cobra II* (New York: Pantheon Books, 2006); Scheuer, *Marching toward Hell*; Chandrasekaran, *Imperial Life in the Emerald City*; Michael Isikoff and David Corn, *Hubris: The Inside Story of Spin, Scandal, and the Selling of the Iraq War* (New York: Crown Publishers, 2006); Charles W. Kegley, Jr. and Gregory A. Raymond, *After Iraq: The Imperiled American Imperium* (New York: Oxford University Press, 2007); Philip H. Gordon, *Winning the Right War* (New York: Times Books, 2007); and Larry Diamond, *Squandered Victory* (New York: Times Books, 2006).

50. For example, the draft report of the Office of the Special Inspector General for Iraq Reconstruction roundly criticizes the U.S. government for its efforts to reconstruct Iraq after the occupation. It blames poor planning, bureaucratic infighting, widespread

violence, and general ignorance about Iraqi society and infrastructure. Through mid-2008, the total bill for these largely ineffective reconstruction projects approached $117 billion, of which $50 billion came from the United States. See James Glanz and T. Christian Miller, "Official History Spotlights Iraq Rebuilding Blunders," *New York Times*, 13 December 2008.

In another incident, Paul Bremer, the head of the Coalition Provisional Authority, was granted his request to have $12 billion in hundred-dollar bills, wrapped in plastic bundles and placed on pallets in huge troop-carrying aircraft, shipped to Iraq in order to influence individuals and groups in Iraqi society and facilitate reconstruction efforts. Almost $9 billion of that money is currently unaccountable, according to Representative Henry Waxman, chair of the House Committee on Oversight and Government Reform. See Jackie Northam, "What Went Wrong with the Rebuilding of Iraq?" *National Public Radio Report*, 17 May 2007.

51. Juan Cole, "Iraq: The Necessary Withdrawal," *The Nation*, 23 December 2008. See also Hassan M. Fattah, "Uneasy Havens Await Those Who Flee Iraq," *New York Times*, 8 December 2006.

52. Peter Beinart, *The Good Fight* (New York: HarperCollins, 2006), 206.

53. Topeditor, "Should Bush Tell America to Go Shopping Again?," *wsj.com*, 7 October 2008.

54. *Ibid*.

55. Karen Leigh, "For Soldiers, Stress After War May Be the Biggest Enemy," *Medill Reports Washington*, 2 June 2009.

56. Richard Holbrooke, "The Longest War," *Washington Post*, 31 March 2008.

57. Santayana's quote is found at *http://thinkexist.com/quotation/those_who_do_not_learn_ from_history_are_doomed_to/170710.html*.

58. Tony Judt, *Reappraisals: Reflections on the Forgotten Twentieth Century* (New York: Penguin Press, 2008), 2 and 19.

59. Graham Allison and John Deutch, "The Real Afghan Issue Is Pakistan," *Wall Street Journal*, 30 March 2009. They argue that Pakistan is a more pressing problem than Afghanistan because Pakistan possesses nuclear weapons.

60. Roxana Tiron, "U.S. Spending $3.6 Billion a Month in Afghanistan, According to CRS Report," *The Hill's Blog Briefing Room*, 14 October 2009. Steve Daggett of the Congressional Research Service calculated the $1 million estimate for each U.S. soldier.

61. Bradley made these remarks during his congressional testimony on 15 May 1951.

62. Pew Global Attitudes Project, *Twenty-five-Nation Pew Global Attitudes Survey* (Washington, D.C.; Pew Research Center, 2009), 1 and 43. The polls were taken in twenty-four nations and the Palestinian territories. Attitudes in Muslim nations were only slightly more positive, and Israeli attitudes were slightly more negative. Elsewhere, public attitudes were generally more positive toward the United States. The poll was released in July 2009. See also Peter J. Katzenstein and Robert O. Keohane, eds., *Anti-Americanisms in World Politics* (Ithaca: Cornell University Press, 2007), and Richard L. Armitage and Joseph S. Nye, Jr., *CSIS Commission on Smart Power: A Smarter, More Secure America* (Washington, D.C.: Center for Strategic and International Studies, 2007), 19.

63. Armitage and Nye, *CSIS Commission*, 7. The authors advocate "smart power," which combines the attributes of hard power, such as military, economic, and political clout, with soft power.

64. Joseph S. Nye, Jr., *Soft Power: The Means to Success in World Politics* (New York: Basic Books, 2004), 5–11. Ironically, some of the policy recommendations in this chapter actually echo what George W. Bush pledged to do during the 2000 presidential campaign, namely be very suspicious of nation-building projects abroad and emphasize a "more humble" U.S. foreign policy.

In the intelligence arena, the director of National Intelligence should be given more authority over all intelligence budgets, including the huge intelligence budget controlled by the Pentagon. See Richard A. Clarke, *Your Government Failed You: Breaking the Cycle of National Security Disasters* (New York: HarperCollins, 2008), 150–153.

65. American Foreign Service Association, "AFSANET: Telling Our Story," 17 October 2007, at *www.afsa.org*. Near the end of 2007, there were 6,500 Foreign Service Officers (FSOs), plus 5,000 Foreign Service specialists and 1,500 others, including representatives of USAID, the Foreign Commercial Service, the Foreign Agricultural Service, and the International Broadcasting Bureau. The U.S. active-duty military was 119 times larger than the entire Foreign Service, and total uniformed military, including the reserves, were 217 times larger.

66. Between fiscal year 2000 and 2006, organized crime cases that were prosecuted fell by 73 percent and white-collar crime cases fell by 63 percent. See Bob Rossiter, "As FBI Fights Terrorism, Other Prosecutions Drop," *Christian Science Monitor*, 21 June 2007.

67. John R. Wagley, *Transnational Organized Crime: Threats and U.S. Responses* (Washington, D.C.: Congressional Research Service, 2006), 5.

68. *Ibid.*

69. National Drug Intelligence Center, U.S. Department of Justice, "National Drug Threat Assessment, 2009," iv, at *www.usdoj.gov/dea/concern/18862/indi.c_2009*.

70. *Ibid.*, 45.

71. National Gang Intelligence Center, *National Gang Threat Assessment, 2009* (Washington, D.C.: U.S. Department of Justice, 2009), iii.

72. National Drug Intelligence Center, "National Drug Threat Assessment, 2009," 43.

73. R. Jeffrey Smith, "U.S. Efforts Against Mexican Cartels Called Lacking," *Washington Post*, 18 March 2009. The estimate is made by Denise Dresser.

74. *Ibid.*

75. Randal C. Archibold, "In Heartland Death, Traces of Heroin's Spread," *New York Times*, 30 May 2009.

76. National Drug Intelligence Center, U.S. Department of Justice, "National Drug Threat Assessment 2009," December 2008, and Ginger Thompson and Elisabeth Malkin, "Top U.S. Officials Meet with Mexicans to Quell Growing Drug-Related Border Violence," *New York Times*, 2 April 2009.

77. Bob Herbert, "A Culture Soaked in Blood," *New York Times*, 25 April 2009.

78. Cynthia Tucker, "Shootings Are Insane, But So Is Response," *Atlantic-Journal Constitution*, 21 April 2009.

79. Bob Herbert, "The American Way," *New York Times*, 13 April 2009.

80. Herbert, "A Culture."

81. Adam Liptak, "Inmate Count in U.S. Dwarfs Other Nations," *New York Times*, 23 April 2008, and Burd-Sharps *et al.*, *The Measure of America*, 142. On the same page, Burd-Sharps and her colleagues point out that the United States incarcerates people at a rate five to nine times higher than its peer Western countries.

82. National Drug Intelligence Center, "National Drug Threat," iii.

83. Kaplan, *Daydream*, 200, and Dennis Ross, *Statecraft* (New York: Farrar, Straus and Giroux, 2007), x.

84. Gelb, "Necessity," 57, Seyom Brown, *Higher Realism: A New Foreign Policy for the United States* (Boulder, CO: Paradigm Publishers, 2009), 4, and Seyom Brown, *The Illusion of Control: Force and Foreign Policy in the Twenty-First Century* (Washington: Brookings Institution, 2003), 142–177.

85. Fareed Zakaria, "Why Washington Worries," *Newsweek*, 23 March 2009.

86. For a thorough discussion of U.S. foreign energy policy over the past few decades, consult the following sources: Robert Bryce, *Gusher of Lies: The Dangerous Delusions*

of "Energy Independence" (New York: Public Affairs, 2008); Michael T. Klare, *Blood and Oil: The Dangers and Consequences of America's Growing Dependency on Imported Oil* (New York: Metropolitan Books, 2004); and Michael T. Klare, *Rising Powers, Shrinking Planet: The New Geopolitics of Energy* (New York: Metropolitan Books, 2008).

87. In his book *The War for Wealth* (New York: McGraw-Hill, 2008), ix, Gabor Steingart argues that fears of terrorism have spun out of control, emphasizing that the Taliban consists of "military dwarves and political pygmies," and that Iran has the GDP of Connecticut and the military budget of Sweden. He insists that world history is now being written in Shanghai, not Afghanistan, Iraq, or Iran. Thomas Friedman, in "The Losers Hang On," *New York Times*, 25 July 2009, exults that "the dominos you see falling in the Muslim world today are the extremist Islamist groups and governments. They have failed to persuade people by either their arguments or their performances in power that their puritanical versions of Islam are the answer. Having lost the argument, though, the radicals still hang on thanks to gun barrels and oil barrels—and they can for a while." He adds that "the only way to really dry up their support, though, is for the Arab and Muslim modernists to actually implement better ideas by producing less corrupt and more consensual governance, with better schools, more economic opportunities and a vision of Islam that is perceived as authentic yet embracing of modernity. That is where 'our' allies in Egypt, Palestine, Iraq, Afghanistan and Pakistan have so consistently failed. Until that happens, the Islamist radicals will be bankrupt, but not out of business." In effect, the Islamic world has the capacity to solve its own problems with help from its friends but not help in the form of U.S. troops who are expected to do most of the fighting and suffer most of the casualties.

88. Zbigniew Brzezinski and Brent Scowcroft, *America and the World* (New York: Basic Books, 2008), 2–3. Brzezinski contends that there is a shifting locus of power from the Atlantic to East Asia and that emerging global problem areas such as climate, environment, poverty, and injustice should move way up the foreign policy priority list.

89. Madeleine Albright, *Memo to the President Elect* (New York: HarperCollins, 2008), 177.

90. In Bryce, *Gusher*, 211, he refers to the United States as "the Saudi Arabia of coal."

91. Clifford Krauss, "New Ways to Tap Gas May Expand Global Supplies," *New York Times*, 9 October 2009.

92. For example, the leading foreign sources of crude oil for the United States are its two North American neighbors, Canada and Mexico.

93. In his book *The Limits of Power: The End of American Exceptionalism* (New York: Metropolitan Books, 2008), 169, Andrew J. Bacevich concludes that America does not need a bigger army; it needs a more modest foreign policy.

94. Statistics compiled by Global Security.Org at *www.globalsecurity.org/military/world/deploy.htm*.

95. U.S. Department of Defense, "Active Duty Military Personnel Strengths by Regional Area and by Country, 31 December 2007," at *www.globalsecurity.org/military/library/report/2007/hst0712.pdf*.

96. Roger Cohen, "America Agonistes," *New York Times*, 2 April 2009.

97. Brandon Griggs, "U.S. at Risk of Cyberattacks, Experts Say," *CNN.com*, 18 August 2008.

98. Patrice C. McMahon and Andrew Wederman, "Introduction," in *American Foreign Policy in a Globalized World*, 11, and U.S. Department of State, "2007 Annual Report on Implementation of the Moscow Treaty," 12 July 2007.

99. Clyde Prestowitz, *Rogue Nation* (New York: Basic Books, 2003), 1.

Chapter 6

1. Zakaria, *Post-American*, 1 and 3.

2. *Ibid.*, 4.

3. In international relations jargon, unipolar describes a world dominated by a single nation, and this term was used widely to describe the United States after the collapse of the Soviet Union in 1991. Hegemon also depicts an international system dominated by one great power. Both unipolar and hegemon have been used widely in the literature of international relations to describe the United States during the post–Cold War era. See Donald E. Nuechterlein, *Defiant Superpower: The New American Hegemony* (Washington, D.C.: Potomac Books, 2005), 5–10.

4. World Bank, "World Development Indicators Database," 1 July 2009, at *http://web. worldbank.org/wbsite/external/datastatistics*.

5. UNCTAD, *World Investment Report 2008* (New York: United Nations, 2008), Annex B, 257.

6. Thomas Anderson, "U.S. Affiliates of Foreign Companies: Operations in 2006," *Survey of Current Business*, August 2008, 186.

7. *CIA World Factbook*, 2009, at *www.cia.gov/publications/the-world-factbook/ rankorder/2078rank.html*. In 2008, Germany exported $1.53 trillion in goods, China $1.47 trillion, and the United States $1.38 trillion.

8. *Ibid.* The EU exported $1.95 trillion in goods in 2007, the latest year data are available.

9. *Ibid.*, and World Trade Organization's (WTO) annual data on merchandise exports.

10. Ray Uhalde and Jeff Strohl, *America in the Global Economy* (Washington, D.C.: National Center on Education and the Economy, 2006), 44.

11. *Ibid.*, 48.

12. Kenneth Rogoff, "No Grand Plans, but the Financial System Needs Fixing," *Financial Times*, 8 February 2007.

13. Nguyen, "International Investment," 10.

14. U.S. Bureau of Economic Analysis, "International Investment Position, Yearend Positions, 1976–2005." These figures are based on direct investment being computed on a current-cost basis.

15. Corporations are ranked in terms of revenues, and the statistics are based on *Fortune* Global 500 listings for the years indicated. The most recent listings are found in "Fortune Global 500, 2009," *Fortune*, 20 July 2009.

16. UNCTAD, *World Investment Report*, xvi.

17. *Ibid.*

18. Ian Bremmer, "State Capitalism Comes of Age," *Foreign Affairs* 88 (May/June 2009): 40.

19. *Ibid.*, 42.

20. *Ibid.*

21. *Ibid.*, 50.

22. *Ibid.*, 54.

23. International Monetary Fund estimates for central bank reserves quoted in "China's Central Bank Renews Call for New World Reserve Currency," *Bloomberg.com*, 27 June 2009, and Shalendra D. Sharma, "The Rising Euro and Sinking Dollar: Explanations and Implications," *Mediterranean Quarterly* 19 (Spring 2008): 11–18.

24. Brad Setser and Arpana Pandey, "China's 1.7 Trillion Dollar Bet: China's External Portfolio and Dollar Reserves," *Council on Foreign Relations Working Paper*, January 2009, 1 and 2.

25. "China's Central Bank."

26. Dominic Wilson and Roopa Purushothaman, "Dreaming with BRICs: The Path to

2050," *Goldman Sachs Global Economy Paper No. 99*, October 2003. Also consult Emilio Casetti, "Power Shifts and Economic Development: When Will China Overtake the USA?" *Journal of Peace Research* 40 (No. 6, 2003): 661–675.

27. Albert Keidel, "China's Economic Rise—Fact and Fiction," *Carnegie Endowment for International Peace Policy Brief 61* (Washington, D.C.: Carnegie Endowment for International Peace, 2008), 1.

28. National Intelligence Council, *Mapping the Global Future* (Washington, D.C.: Government Printing Office, 2004), 9.

29. Kegley and Raymond, *After Iraq*, 126.

30. Martin Jacque, "The Great Shift in Global Power Just Hit High Gear, Sparked by a Financial Crisis," *The Guardian*, 20 April 2009. Jacque is the author of *When China Rules the World: The Rise of the Middle Kingdom and the End of the Western World* (London: Allen Lane, 2009).

31. *Ibid.*

32. *Ibid.*

33. Nathan Gardels, "Niall Ferguson: Is U.S.–China Economic Marriage on the Rocks?," *Huffington Post*, 27 July 2009.

34. C. Fred Bergsten, Charles Freeman, Nicholas R. Lardy, and Derek J. Mitchell, *China's Rise: Challenges and Opportunities* (Washington, D.C.: Peterson Institute for International Economics, 2008), 2. Deng Xiaoping also launched the Four Modernizations: agriculture, industry, science and technology, and national defense.

35. World Bank, "Gross National Income Per Capita 2008, Atlas Method and PPP," at *http://siteresources.worldbank.org/DATASTATISTICS/Resources/GNIPC.pdf*, and David Pilling, "China's 'Warp-Speed' Industrial Revolution," *ft.com*, 17 December 2008.

36. Zakaria, *Post-American*, 92.

37. *Ibid.*, 89.

38. *Ibid.*, and Bergsten *et al.*, *China's Rise*, 2.

39. "General Motors' Car Sales Surge in China," *guardian.co.uk*, 9 October 2009, and Bergsten *et al.*, *China's Rise*, 115–116.

40. Rob Gifford, *China Road: A Journey into the Future of a Rising Power* (New York: Random House, 2007), 73.

41. *Ibid.*, 278.

42. *Ibid.*, 7.

43. Perry Luo, "45 Billion Invested in Shanghai World Expo," *Inside China Today*, 2 June 2009.

44. Stockholm International Peace Research Institute, *SIPRI Yearbook 2009*.

45. Andrei Chang, "Analysis: Ukraine Aids China Carrier Plan," *Space War*, 10 December 2008.

46. Anthony Kuhn, "China Aims High for Its Space Program," *NPR Morning Edition*, 22 July 2009.

47. In early October 2009, the prime minister of China met with the leaders of Japan and South Korea in Beijing and issued a joint statement stressing that they were "committed to the development of an East Asian community." See Associated Press, "Asia's Biggest Economies Promise Greater Cooperation," *New York Times*, 12 October 2009, and Evan A. Feigenbaum and Robert A. Manning, "The United States in the New Asia," *Council Special Reports No. 50* (New York: Council on Foreign Relations, 2009), 3, 18–21.

48. Zakaria, *Post-American*, 45. In his article "Globalization in Retreat," *Foreign Affairs* 88

(July/August 2009): 5 and 7, Roger C. Altman argues that "for thirty years, the Anglo-Saxon model of free-market capitalism spread across the globe. The role of the state was diminishing, and deregulation, privatization, and the openness of borders to capital and trade were rising." Now, he insists, the "Anglo-Saxon financial model" is seen as failing, and the far different "Chinese model" is on the rise.

49. Kishore Mahbubani, "The Dangers of Decadence: What the Rest Can Teach the West," *Foreign Affairs* 72 (September/October 1993): 14. Mahbubani often applies the Asian model to his own home country of Singapore, but he believes it is germane for various parts of East Asia.

50. T.R. Reid, *Confucius Lives Next Door: What Living in the East Teaches Us About Living in the West* (New York: Random House, 1999), 62 and 241.

51. Bates Gill, "China's Health Care and Pension Challenges," testimony before the U.S.–China Security and Economic Review Commission, Washington, D.C., 2 February 2006, 4 and 8.

52. As one solution to the growing demand for automobiles, China is striving to become the world's largest producer of electric cars. See Keith Bradsher, "China Outlines Plans for Electric Cars," *New York Times*, 11 April 2009.

53. Michael Wines, "Beijing's Air Is Cleaner, but Far from Clean," *New York Times*, 16 October 2009.

54. Gifford, *China Road*, 278–279. The author hypothesizes on page 282 that China may not become a superpower nor will it implode, but it may just muddle through. Political sclerosis could eventually end the economic miracle.

55. Ted C. Fishman, *China Inc.* (New York: Scribner, 2005), 231, and Keith Bradsher, "WTO Rules against China's Limits on Media Imports," *New York Times*, 12 August 2009.

56. Gifford, *China Road*, 284.

57. Jim Yardley, "After Thirty Years, Economic Perils on China's Path," *New York Times*, 18 December 2008.

58. Niall Ferguson, *The War of the Worlds: History's Age of Hatred* (London: Allen Lane, 2006), xxiv.

59. In his book *The European Union* (London: Routledge, 2008), xii, Clive Archer describes the EU as a "complex set of international and transnational bodies drawn together for the purpose of uniting Europe."

60. Mark Leonard, *Why Europe Will Run the Twenty-First Century* (London: Fourth Estate, 2005), 82.

61. *Ibid.*, 145.

62. European Commission, "Languages of Europe," at *http://ec.europa.eu/education/languages/languages-of-europe*.

63. George Voskopoulos, "A European Dwarf and an American Giant," *American Chronicle*, 21 July 2006.

64. The French political scientist Raymond Aron once complained that U.S. foreign policy lacked consistency as it swung "between the crusading spirit and a withdrawal into isolation far from a corrupt world that refused to heed the American Gospel." Aron is quoted in Leonard, *Why Europe*, 121.

65. Mira Kamdar, *Planet India* (New York: Scribner, 2007), 8.

66. Mark Sappenfield, "Moon Mission Takes India's Space Program in New Direction," *Christian Science Monitor*, 23 October 2008.

67. James Lamont, "India to Follow $2,000 Car with $20 Laptop," *ft.com*, 1 February 2009.

68. Zakaria, *Post-American*, 3, and Kamdar, *Planet India*, 65.

69. Kamdar, *Planet India*, 193.

70. World Bank statistics quoted in Shankar Acharya, "Asia Rises, One Economic Giant at a Time," *ft.com*, 28 July 2009.

71. *Ibid.*

72. *Ibid.*

73. Kamdar, *Planet India*, 199.

74. *Ibid.*, 251.

75. *Ibid.*, 203.

76. *Ibid.*, 253.

77. Acharya, "Asia Rises."

78. Michael Schwirtz, "Clashes Kill Over Twenty in Russia Region," *New York Times*, 14 August 2009.

79. Grace Wong, "Russia's Bleak Picture of Health," *CNN.com*, 19 May 2009.

80. *Ibid.*

81. Zakaria, *Post-American*, 210.

82. "An Orderly Landslide, Please, Say Japan's Politicians," *The Economist*, 15 December 1990.

83. Eric Weiner, "What the U.S. Can Learn from Japan's 'Lost Decade,'" *NPR News*, 13 March 2008.

84. World Bank, "Gross National Income."

85. Stockholm International Peace Research Institute, *SIPRI Yearbook*.

86. Topeditor, "Japanese Solution? Put off Retirement Until 70", *wsj*.com, 4 June 2008.

87. Vaclav Smil, "The Unprecedented Shift in Japan's Population: Numbers, Age, and Prospects," *Japan Focus Newsletter*, 2007, at *www.japanfocus.org/-Vaclav-Smil/2411*.

88. Unlike the United States, Japan can finance 93 percent of its huge debt domestically. Japan is also the second-largest foreign holder of U.S. debt. See Oxford Analytica, "Japan's Debt Financing Program Carries Risk," *Forbes.com*, 30 June 2009.

89. The FTAA, which began as an initiative of the first Bush administration and was actively pursued by both the Clinton and second Bush administrations, would have created a free trade area consisting of all the nations in the Western Hemisphere except for Cuba.

90. Alan Clendenning, "Offshore Discovery Could Make Brazil Major Oil Exporter," *USA Today*, 9 November 2007.

91. Mercosur is the Common Market of the South with Brazil, Argentina, Uruguay, and Paraguay having full membership, and Bolivia, Chile, Colombia, Ecuador, and Peru having associate membership. Venezuela has petitioned to become a full member of Mercosur, but all full member states must first ratify Venezuela's request. Mercosur is the fourth-largest regional trading bloc in terms of the value of trade, trailing the EU, NAFTA, and ASEAN.

Chapter 7

1. Fareed Zakaria, "The Capitalist Manifesto: Greed Is Good," *Newsweek*, 22 June 2009.

2. Anderson, "U.S. Affiliates," 191 and 196.

3. Jeffrey D. Sachs, *Common Wealth: Economics for a Crowded Planet* (New York: Penguin Press, 2008), 3. Bill Clinton has referred to globalization as "the best engine we know of

to lift living standards and build shared prosperity." Former UN Secretary General Kofi Annan echoes these sentiments: "I believe the poor are poor not because of too much globalization, but because of too little." Both Clinton and Annan are quoted in Tom d'Aquino, "Enhancing the Canada–United States Partnership," remarks to the Standing Committee on Foreign Affairs and International Development, House of Commons, Parliament of Canada, 25 February 2009.

4. Jerome C. Glenn, "Scanning the Global Situation and Prospects for the Future," *The Futurist*, January/February 2008, 44.

5. Thomas L. Friedman, *The World Is Flat, 3.0: A Brief History of the Twenty-First Century* (New York: Picador, 2007). See also Andrew Walter and Gautam Sen, *Analyzing the Global Political Economy* (Princeton: Princeton University Press, 2009); Thomas L. Friedman, *Hot, Flat, and Crowded: Why We Need a Green Revolution* (New York: Farrar, Straus and Giroux, 2008); Pankay Ghemawat, *Redefining Global Strategy* (Boston: Harvard Business School Press, 2007); Andrew P. Cortell, *Mediating Globalization* (Albany: State University Press of New York, 2006); Eric Rauchway, *Blessed Among Nations: How the World Made America* (New York: Hill and Wang, 2006); William H. Marling, *How "American" Is Globalization?* (Baltimore: Johns Hopkins University Press, 2006); David Held and Anthony Grew, eds., *Globalization Theory* (Cambridge, MA: Polity Press, 2007); and Barry K. Gills and William R. Thompson, eds., *Globalization and Global History* (London: Routledge, 2006).

6. Jane Fraser and Jeremy Oppenheim, "What's New about Globalization," *McKinsey Quarterly*, 22 March 1997.

7. Michael Veseth, in his book *Globaloney: Unraveling the Myths of Globalization* (Lanham, MD: Rowman & Littlefield, 2005), 231, points out that "the facts about globalization are messy, complicated, and constantly changing."

8. John Kincaid has concluded that "to date, globalization has had no impact on the constitutional design or basic institutional structure of the federal system of the United States of America, nor has it significantly altered domestic intergovernmental relations." See his article "Globalization and Federalism in the United States: Continuity in Adaptation," in *The Impact of Global and Regional Integration on Federal Systems: A Comparative Analysis,* eds. Harvey Lazar, Hamish Telford, and Ronald L. Watts (Montreal: McGill-Queen's University Press, 2003), 37. Kincaid is accurate in his appraisal. The big question will be whether more intensive globalization, combined with accelerated non-central government involvement internationally, will alter this appraisal within the next quarter century.

9. In his book *Making Globalization Work* (New York: W.W. Norton, 2007), 7 and 273, Joseph E. Stiglitz warns that there is a false notion that globalization will bring prosperity to everyone. In fact, he argues, many people will suffer losses because of globalization. Pat Choate is much more ominous in his alarmist book linking American losses directly to globalization, including a significant diminution in U.S. sovereignty. See his book *Dangerous Business: The Risks of Globalization for America* (New York: Alfred A. Knopf, 2008), 159. Parag Khanna also warns about the fragmentation of the international economy in "The Next Big Thing: Neomedievalism," *Foreign Policy*, May/June 2009, 91.

10. Bayless Manning, "The Congress, the Executive, and Intermestic Affairs: Three Proposals," *Foreign Affairs* 55 (January 1977): 309–310.

11. See the National Intelligence Council, *Mapping the Global Future*, for a discussion of some of the major challenges that will face the United States internationally over the next few decades. See also Stephen Aguilar-Millan, Joan E. Foltz, John Jackson, and Amy Oberg, "The Globalization of Crime," *The Futurist*, November/December 2008, 42 and 47.

12. Ferguson, *The War*, 646. H.G. Wells' book was published in 1898.

13. *Ibid.*, xxiv.

14. Stanley Schmidt, *The Coming Convergence: Surprising Ways Diverse Technologies Interact to Shape Our World and Change the Future* (Amherst, NY: Prometheus Books, 2008), 228. See also Thomas L. Friedman, "Mother Nature's Dow," *New York Times*, 29 March 2009.

15. Interview with Lisa Margonelli, author of *Oil on the Brain: Adventures from the Pump to the Pipeline* (New York: Nan A. Talese/Doubleday, 2007), "Weekend Edition Saturday," National Public Radio, 24 February 2007.

16. Jeffrey K. Taubenberger and David M. Moren, "1918 Influenza: The Mother of All Pandemics," *CDC Emerging Infectious Diseases*, January 2006, and Keith Bradsher, "Assessing the Danger of New Flu," *New York Times*, 28 April 2009.

17. "Ebola Fears After Woman Falls Ill," *The Independent*, 7 February 2001.

18. Taras George, "How to Handle an Invasive Species? Eat It," *New York Times*, 20 February 2008.

19. *Ibid.*, and Steve Pardo, "Asian Carp May Have Breached Great Lakes Barrier," *Detroit News*, 20 November 2009.

20. George, "How to Handle an Invasive Species?"

21. Alan Weisman, *The World Without Us* (New York: St Martin's Press, 2007), 274.

22. "The Amazing Story of Kudzu," at *www.maxshores.com/kudzu*.

23. WHO statistics quoted in Jerome C. Glenn, "Scanning the Global Situation and Prospects for the Future," *The Futurist*, January/February 2008, 42.

24. Weisman, *The World*, 272.

25. Glenn, "Scanning the Global Situation," 42.

26. *Ibid.*

27. *Ibid.*, 43.

28. Andrew Taylor, "OECD States Host 75 Million Immigrants," *ft.com*, 21 February 2008.

29. Bismarck's quote found at *www.quotationspage.com/quote/35200.html*.

30. Rosenblum, *Escaping Plato's Cave*, 5. Rosenblum warns that "soon our society, a four percent fringe of humanity, will no longer call the shots."

31. Larry Borsato, "Information Overload on the Web, and Searching for the Right Sifting Tool," *The Industry Standard*, 28 August 2008.

32. *Ibid.*, and Paul Coles, Tony Cox, Chris Mackey, and Simon Richardson, "The Toxic Terabyte: How Data-Dumping Threatens Business Efficiency," *IBM Global Technology Services*, July 2006, 2.

33. Elizabeth C. Hanson, *The Information Revolution and World Politics* (Lanham, MD: Rowman & Littlefield, 2008), 1–3.

34. Abraham Newman and John Zysman, "Transforming Politics in the Digital Era," in *How Revolutionary Was the Digital Revolution?*, eds. John Zysman and Abraham Newman (Stanford: Stanford University Press, 2006), 394.

35. Gingrich interviewed in "Assessing Global Trends for 2025," *The Futurist*, July–August 2009, at *www.wfs.org/May-June09/2025Trendspage.htm*.

36. Marvin J. Cetron and Owen Davies, "Trends Shaping Tomorrow's World, Part Two," *The Futurist*, May/June 2008, 39.

37. *Ibid.*, 36 and 39.

38. *Ibid.*, 41.

39. Peter Coy, "Help Wanted: Why That Sign's Bad," *Business Week*, 30 April 2009.

40. RAND Corporation, "Is the United States Losing Its Edge in Science and

Technology?," *Rand National Defense Research Institute Research Brief*, June 2008. The major RAND research report was written by Titus Galama and James Hosek and entitled "U.S. Competitiveness in Science and Technology."

41. *Ibid.*, 1.

42. *Ibid.*

43. *Ibid.* At that time, the EU consisted of fifteen countries.

44. *Ibid.*, 2–3.

45. Cetron and Davies, "Trends," 37.

46. *Ibid.*

47. *Ibid.*, 36.

48. Stephen Ezell, "America and the World: We're #40!," *Democracy: A Journal of Ideas*, Fall 2009, 13–14.

49. Schmidt, *The Coming Convergence*, 23 and 171.

50. Schumpeter, *Capitalism*.

51. Carolyn Dimitri, Anne Effland, and Neilson Conklin, *The Twentieth Century Transformation of U.S. Agriculture and Farm Policy* (Washington, D.C.: Economic Research Service, U.S. Department of Agriculture, 2005). Agriculture's contribution to total U.S. GDP also fell from 7.7 percent in 1930 to 0.7 percent in 2002.

52. Paul Kennedy's foreword in Jeffry A. Frieden, *Global Capitalism: Its Fall and Rise in the Twentieth Century* (New York: W.W. Norton, 2006), xiii.

53. U.S. Small Business Administration, *The Small Business Economy: A Report to the President, 2009* (Washington, D.C.: U.S. Government Printing Office, 2009), 8. Employer firms are businesses that hire employees in addition to the owner. See also Akbar Sadeghi, "The Birth and Death of Business Establishments in the United States," *Monthly Labor Review*, December 2008, 3–18.

54. U.S. Bureau of Labor Statistics, "Business Employment Dynamics Summary," *Economic News Release*, 24 February 2009.

55. Statistics for June 2009. See U.S. Bureau of Labor Statistics, "The Employment Situation: June 2009," 2 July 2009, at *www.bls.gov/news.release*.

56. Richard Foster and Sarah Kaplan, *Creative Destruction: Why Companies That Are Built to Last Underperform the Market and How to Successfully Transform Them* (New York: Doubleday/Currency, 2001), 7.

57. *Ibid.*, 8.

58. Brigid Schulte, "So Long, Snail Shells," *Washington Post*, 25 July 2009.

59. Bremmer, "State Capitalism," 40–55.

60. Foster and Kaplan, *Creative Destruction*, 9–10.

Chapter 8

1. As Richard Beeman describes in *Plain, Honest Men* (New York: Random House, 2009), 413, when Washington took the oath of office in New York City on 14 April 1789, the new nation faced substantial government debt, continuing jealousies among the states, and formidable challenges in dealing with the nations of Europe, "most of which remained contemptuous of America's weakness." For a very interesting account of life in America's Dust Bowl region during the Great Depression, see Timothy Egan, *The Worst Hard Time: The Untold Story of Those Who Survived the Great American Dust Bowl* (Boston: Houghton Mifflin, 2006).

2. Richard Florida, "How the Crash Will Reshape America," *www.theatlantic.com*, March 2009.

3. *Ibid.*

4. *Ibid.*

5. Zakaria, *Post-American*, 210.

6. Josef Joffe, "The Default Power," *New York Times*, 20 August 2009.

7. In his book *The American Ascendancy: How the United States Gained and Wielded Global Dominance* (Chapel Hill: University of North Carolina Press, 2007), 23, Michael W. Hunt estimates that the United States caught up to Great Britain's GDP by 1870 and may have had a two-to-one edge by 1913. The United States was also the world's leader in manufacturing by 1913.

8. U.S. Census Bureau, "U.S. Interim Projections by Age, Sex, Race, and Hispanic Origin," 18 March 2004.

9. Neil Howe and Richard Jackson, "Rising Populations Breed Rising Powers," *Financial Times*, 9 February 2007.

10. U.S. Bureau of Labor Statistics, Series ID LNS12000000.

11. James P. Moore, Jr., "Five Myths About Our Sputtering Economy," *Washington Post*, 14 December 2008.

12. Zachary Karabell, "The Economic News Isn't All Bleak," *Wall Street Journal*, 26 December 2008.

13. Hachigian and Sutphen, *Next American Century*, 119.

14. U.S. Census Bureau, Current Population Survey, *Annual Geographical Mobility Rates, By Type of Movement: 1947–2008*, April 2009, A–1.

15. Interestingly enough, the mobility of Americans is also paralleled by their religious commitments, with 44 percent stating that they have changed religious faiths at least once. See Amy Sullivan, "Church-Shopping: Why Do Americans Change Faiths?," *Time Magazine*, 28 April 2009. Data are derived from a survey sponsored by the Pew Forum on Religion and Public Life.

16. Timothy Egan, "The Distant Mirror," *New York Times*, 15 August 2009.

17. *Ibid.*

18. *Ibid.*, and Lizette Alvarez, "G.I. Jane Breaks the Combat Barrier," *New York Times*, 15 August 2009.

19. Churchill's quote found in Howard Gardner, "The Next Big Thing: Personalized Education," *Foreign Policy*, May/June 2009, 86.

20. David Levey and Stuart Brown, "The Overstretch Myth," *Foreign Affairs* 84 (March/April 2005): 2–7.

21. Walter Russell Mead, "Only Makes You Stronger," *New Republic*, 4 February 2009.

22. Shaw's quote at *www.quotationspage.com/quotes/George_Bernard_Shaw/31.*

23. Peter G. Peterson, "Why I Am Giving Away $1 Billion," *Newsweek*, 30 May 2009.

24. Clayton D. Peoples, "Campaign Finance in Canada and the U.S.: Policies, Powers, and Prospects," *ACSUS Occasional Papers on Public Policy*, 2009, 1. The most notable case of a rich person trying to buy an election was Michael Bloomberg's spending of $102 million of his own fortune, or $183 for every vote he received, to secure a third term as New York City's mayor in 2009. See Michael Barbaro, "Bloomberg Spent 102 Million Dollars to Win Third Term," *New York Times*, 17 November 2009.

25. Ciara Torres-Spelliscy, "The Incumbency Problem Has Everything to Do with Money," *Brennan Center for Justice at NYU School of Law Blog*, 20 May 2009. The two dozen states that permit the election of judges should also end this practice in favor of the selection of judges on a merit basis. These judges would then serve for a fixed

maximum number of years on the court to which they are appointed. Currently, some state elections for judges involve millions of dollars in donations from contributors who may later have cases heard by these judges. See Gene Johnson, "Sandra Day O'Connor: Stop Electing Judges," *Huffington Post*, 14 September 2009.

26. Center for Governmental Studies, "Mapping Public Financing in American Elections," January 2009, at *www.csg.org*. At the same web site, Steven M. Levin, in his article "Keeping It Clean: Public Financing in American Elections," 2006, asserts that public financing will (1) free candidates from the pressure of fundraising, (2) reduce the perception that special interests and wealthy contributors exert undue influence over candidates, (3) create opportunities for women, minority representatives, and new candidates to participate in the political process, (4) reduce funding disparities between candidates and help new candidates become more competitive, and (5) increase opportunities for voters to become more engaged in the political process by lowering contribution levels and improving voter education.

27. Common Cause, "The Fair Elections Now Act," at *www.commoncause.org/*. For a comparison of U.S. and Canadian campaign financing, see Peoples, "Campaign Finance," 1–7.

28. Jose Antonia Vargas, "Obama Raised Half a Billion Online," *Washington Post*, 20 November 2008.

29. In his article "A Collapse of the Campaign Finance Regime?," *The Forum* 6 (April 2008), Thomas E. Mann insists that "encouraging electoral competition, strengthening transparency, promoting political equality, and reducing conflicts of interest in our electoral system require continuing attention to the role of money."

30. Redistricting occurs after the official U.S. census is completed every ten years. In 2000, Democrats in California paid consultant Michael Berman $2 million to design safe districts, with each incumbent Democratic House member chipping in $20,000. As Democratic Representative Loretta Sanchez emphasized, "Twenty thousand is nothing to keep your seat. If my colleagues are smart, they'll pay $20,000 and Michael will draw the district they can win. Those who have refused to pay, God help them." See Albert R. Hunt, "Washington's Substance Deficit Fuels Civility Gap," *Bloomberg.com*, 21 September 2009.

31. Lobbyists are also omnipresent on the nearly one thousand advisory committees that "advise agencies on trade rules, troop levels, environmental regulations, consumer protection and thousands of other government policies." To his credit, President Obama is attempting through executive orders to remove registered lobbyists from all federal advisory panels. See Dan Eggen, "Lobbyists Pushed Off Advisory Panels," *Washington Post*, 27 November 2009.

32. As John Newhouse suggests in "Diplomacy, Inc.," 73–92, most of the hundred or so foreign governments that feel compelled to hire Beltway lobbyists would also welcome an end to congressional deference to special-interest money.

33. Reich, *Supercapitalism*, 212. He asserts that "many politicians and lobbyists want to continue to extort money from the private sector."

34. *Ibid.*, 210–211, Reich provides several very useful recommendations related to campaign financing and lobbying: (1) publicly finance campaigns for all major offices, (2) require broadcasters to donate time for campaigns, (3) prohibit lobbyists from soliciting and bundling big-check donations from their business clients, (4) ban corporate gifts to members of Congress, (5) prohibit privately financed trips for members of Congress and their aides, (6) ban parties funded by corporations to "honor" lawmakers, (7) prohibit former lawmakers from lobbying for at least five years after

leaving Capitol Hill, (8) require lobbyists to disclose all lobbying expenses, (9) mandate all expert witnesses in legislative or regulatory hearings to disclose their financial relationships with interested parties, and (10) create an independent inspector general to monitor and enforce rules, investigate allegations of misconduct, and levy penalties.

35. Larry Diamond, *The Spirit of Democracy* (New York: Times Books, 2008), 350.

36. David Walker, "America's Triple A Rating Is at Risk," *ft.com*, 12 May 2009.

37. Stephen Moore, "It's Time to Legislate a Spending Cap," *Wall Street Journal*, 6 August 2009.

38. See *www.pgpf.org*.

39. Joseph J. DioGuardi, "Time to Bring Truth in Budgeting and Accounting to Washington," *Association of Government Accountants Weblog*, 3 August 2009.

40. Jackie Calmes, "Obama Bans Gimmicks, and Deficits Will Rise," *New York Times*, 19 February 2009.

41. DioGuardi, "Time."

42. *Ibid.*

43. Term used by David Walker and quoted in Addison Wiggin and Kate Incontrera, *I.O.U.S.A.* (New York: John Wiley and Sons, 2008), 19.

44. The Concord Coalition, "Designing a Framework for Economic Recovery and Fiscal Sustainability," 28 January 2009, at *www.concordcoalition.org*.

45. U.S. Department of Agriculture, Economic Research Service, *Data Sets*, 30 June 2009, and James Pethokoukis, "U.S. Farm Subsidies: Billions and Billions Served," *Policy Today*, 15 September 2006.

46. "How to Spend an Extra $15 Billion," *Washington Post*, 15 October 2006. The article provides an overview of several other investigative reports published earlier in October 2006.

47. Vikas Bajal, "India Gets Caught Short as Sugar Prices Soar," *New York Times*, 4 August 2009.

48. *Ibid.*

49. Rick Moran, "Time to Phase Out Farm Subsidies," *American Issues Project*, 7 July 2009. Over the past decade, 75 percent of the $177 billion in total subsidy payments were ladled out to the top 10 percent of subsidy recipients. See Amanda France, "Mr. President, End This Farm Subsidy Boondoggle," *TCS Daily*, 27 February 2009.

50. David M. Herszenhorn, "Obama's Farm Subsidy Cuts Meet Stiff Resistance," *New York Times*, 3 April 2009.

51. David Dietz, "Hidden Bonuses Enrich Government Contractors at Taxpayer Cost," *Bloomberg.com*, 29 January 2009. Senator Tom Coburn has estimated that about $100 billion is wasted each year in the bidding process.

52. Brody Mullins and August Cole, "Pentagon Takes Aim at Jets for Congressional Travel," *Wall Street Journal*, 8 August 2009.

53. Moore, "It's Time."

54. The Balanced Budget Act of 1997 provides a good example of how bipartisan cooperation on Capitol Hill can achieve worthwhile results. See John L. Hilley, *The Challenge of Legislation: Bipartisanship in a Partisan World* (Washington, D.C.: Brookings Institution, 2008), xi. See also Jeffrey Scheuer, *The Big Picture: Why Democracies Need Journalistic Excellence* (New York: Routledge, 2008), xviii and 32.

55. Norman Ornstein has made this suggestion, although he recommends two weeks in Washington and then two weeks back home. See his article "Five-day Workweek Is Key

to Restoring a Vibrant Congress," *Roll Call*, 20 February 2007.

56. "Reviving the Motor Voter Law," *New York Times*, 11 April 2009.

57. These statistics were compiled by the public policy group Demos. See "Election Day Registration," *Washington Post*, 27 July, 2009.

58. R. Michael Alvarez *et al.*, "2008 Survey of the Performance of American Elections: Final Report Executive Summary," *Caltech/MIT Voting Technology Project*, 2009. In the 2008 election, 18 percent of those surveyed reported voting in-person absentee prior to election day, and 19 percent voted by mail.

59. See Tova Andrea Wang, "A Right to Vote: Modernizing Voter Registration," *Demos Blog*, 1 October 2009.

60. Beeman, *Plain, Honest Men*, 422.

61. *Ibid.*, 423. Larry J. Sabato, in *A More Perfect Constitution: Twenty-Three Proposals to Revitalize Our Constitution and Make America a Fairer Country* (New York: Walker & Company, 2007), 6, argues that Washington, Madison, and Jefferson would be the first "to insist that the words that ended up in the Constitution are not the final word. . . ."

62. In both 2000 and 2004, over 60 percent of respondents favored this path. See Darren K. Carlson, "Public Flunks Electoral College System," *Gallup.com*, 2 November 2004.

63. Pamela M. Prah, "States Aim to End the Electoral College," *Stateline.org*, 9 June 2008.

64. Sabato, *A More Perfect Constitution*.

65. William G, Gale, "Fixing the Tax System," in *Opportunity 08: Independent Ideas for America's Next President*, ed. Michael E. O'Hanlon (Washington, D.C.: Brookings Institution Press, 2007), 322.

66. Andrew Chamberlain, "Twenty Years Later: The Tax Reform Act of 1986," *Tax Foundation News*, 23 October 2006.

67. UBS has pleaded guilty in U.S. courts to promoting tax evasion. See Devlin Barrett, "IRS Squeezes Swiss Bank Clients for Evidence," *Yahoo!News*, 26 March 2009, and Lynnley Browning, "UBS and Prosecutors Seek Hearing Delay," *New York Times*, 12 July 2009.

68. Nicole Tichon, *Tax-Shell Game: The Taxpayer Cost of Offshore Corporate Tax Havens* (Washington, D.C.: U.S. Public Interest Research Group, 2009), 1.

69. Nina E. Olson, "We Still Need a Simpler Tax Code," *Wall Street Journal*, 10 April 2009.

70. The biggest tax burden for three-quarters of Americans is not the income tax, but rather the Social Security tax, when the employer's portion of the contribution is included.

71. Newt Gingrich, *Real Change* (Washington, D.C.: Regnery Publishing, 2008), 150.

72. A good primer covering a variety of health-care solutions is found in Jason Furman, ed., *Who Has the Cure? Hamilton Project Ideas on Health Care* (Washington, D.C.: Brookings Institution Press, 2008).

73. Kaiser Family Foundation, "Employer Health Benefits." See also Henry J. Aaron and Joseph P. Newhouse, "Meeting the Dilemma of Health Care Access," in *Opportunity 08*, 281. The federal hourly minimum wage in 2009 was $7.25.

74. National Coalition on Health Care, "Health Insurance Costs," at *www.nchc.org/facts/cost.shtml*.

75. Elizabeth Cohen, "What You Need to Know About Health Care Reform," *CNN.com*, 18 June 2008, and Roger Cohen, "Get Real on Health Care," *New York Times*, 14 September 2009.

76. Atul Gawande, "The Cost Conundrum," *The New Yorker*, 1 June 2009.

77. Kay Lazar, "High Healthcare Costs Taking Toll on Insured," *Boston Globe*, 2 May 2009.

78. Atul Gawande, "Getting There."

79. Edward Cody, "For French, U.S. Health Debate Hard to Imagine," *Washington Post*, 23 September 2009. France spends about 11 percent of its GDP on health care and covers 99 percent of its population. On average, the French live almost three years longer than Americans.

80. Gawande, "Getting There."

81. Gawande, "The Cost." Patient outcomes were based on a list of twenty-five metrics of care that Medicare uses to rank hospitals.

82. *Ibid*. Two economists at Dartmouth, Katherine Baicker and Amitabh Chandra, found that the more money Medicare spent per person in a given state, the lower that state's quality rating for patient care tended to be.

83. Gingrich, *Real Change*, 225.

84. David Ignatius, in "A Medical Revolution via the Cleveland Clinic," *Washington Post*, 6 September 2009, also trumpets the model provided by the Cleveland Clinic, a health-care facility visited by President Obama in July 2009. This model is based on not-for-profit health care, group practice, salaried doctors rather than fee for service, and rigorous annual professional review of all facets of the clinic's operations and cost structures. In her article, "Better Care, Pay Less: Some Communities Find a Way," *New York Times*, 7 September 2009, Lauran Neergaard highlights the Geisinger Health System in Pennsylvania, which charges flat fees and guarantees high-quality care at below-average prices.

85. Gawande, "The Cost."

86. For lower price suggestions, see Arnold Cling, *Crisis of Abundance*. Also consult Theodore R. Marmor and Jonathan Oberlander, "Health Reform: The Fateful Moment," *New York Review of Books*, 13 August 2009, and Arnold Relman, "The Health Reform We Need and Are Not Getting," *New York Review of Books*, 2 July 2009.

87. Gawande, "The Cost." As a cardiac surgeon in McAllen admitted, "We took a wrong turn when doctors stopped being doctors and became businessmen."

88. David Leonhardt, "Making Health Care Better," *New York Times Magazine*, 8 November 2009.

89. William R. Brody, "A Fed for Health-Care Costs," *Washington Post*, 25 September 2009.

90. A *New England Journal of Medicine* study published in 2006 found that for every dollar in compensation resulting from successful lawsuits against doctors, fifty-four cents was eaten up by legal and administrative costs. See Nicholas D. Kristof, "The Prescription from Obama's Own Doctor," *New York Times*, 24 June 2009, and David Leonhardt, "Medical Malpractice System Breeds More Waste," *New York Times*, 23 September 2009.

91. Paul Roberts, *The End of Food* (Boston: Houghton Mifflin, 2008), 93 and 301.

92. Nani Hellmich, "Childhood Obesity: A Lifetime of Danger," *USA Today*, 14 January 2008.

93. *Ibid*., and "Preschool Obesity Rate Stabilizing, Study Finds," *Reuters*, 24 July 2009.

94. Daniel Akst, "Death by Uninsurance," *theatlantic.com*, 18 September 2009. He argues that death due to being uninsured "still pales in comparison with the more than one million Americans who die annually by their own hands—which they use to light cigarettes, lift forks and convey too many alcoholic beverages to their lips." He argues that many in American society need to change behavior, "whether by exhortation, better education or sumptuary taxes."

95. Susanne L. King, "Massachusetts Healthcare Reform Is Failing Us," *Boston Globe*, 2 March 2009.

96. This is a sensitive issue but one that cannot be ignored, especially in view of the fact that Medicare spends one-third of its budget during the last year of a beneficiary's life and that one percent of the population in general accounts for 35 percent of all health-care expenditures. See Mortimer Zuckerman, "Time for Some Hard Choices on Health Reform," *U.S. News and World Report*, 21 September 2009, and Timothy Egan, "The Way We Die Now," *New York Times*, 23 September 2009.

97. David Brooks, "No Picnic for Me Either," *New York Times*, 13 March 2009.

98. "Weights and Measures," *CIA World Factbook 2009*, Appendix G.

99. Zogby quoted in Slaughter, "America's Edge."

100. Nicholas D. Kristof, "Our Greatest National Shame," *New York Times*, 15 February 2009.

101. John Kao, *Innovation Nation* (New York: Free Press, 2007), 93. Kao states that "it's a crime against our children that half of the math teachers in the United States have no formal training in mathematics and are sometimes recruited from the bottom third of their high school graduating class."

102. National Center on Education and the Economy, "Tough Choices," 8–9.

103. "Dropout Factories."

104. Brooks, "No Picnic."

105. See, for example, "To Reform Albany: Start Here," *New York Times*, 7 August 2009.

106. Florida, "How the Crash."

107. "The Second Presidential Debate," *PBS Online NewsHour*, 11 October 2000.

108. Walter Pincus, "Analysts Expect Long-Term, Costly U.S. Campaign in Afghanistan," *Washington Post*, 9 August 2009.

109. *Ibid.*

110. *Ibid.*

111. Andrew F. Krepinevich, Jr., "The Pentagon's Wasting Assets," *Foreign Affairs* 88 (July/August 2009): 28. The author suggests that in Afghanistan, the U.S. focus on fielding indigenous forces and withdrawing U.S. combat units.

112. Boston University historian Robert Dallek told President Obama at a White House meeting in 2009 that "war kills off great reform movements," citing the impact World War I had on the progressive movement, World War II on the New Deal, the Korean War on Harry Truman's Fair Deal, and the Vietnam War on Lyndon Johnson's Great Society programs. See Bruce Bartlett, "The Cost of War," *Forbes.com*, 28 November 2009.

113. Gordon M. Goldstein, *Lessons in Disaster* (New York: Times Books, 2008), 237.

114. *Ibid.*

115. *Ibid.*, 97, 144, 186, and 248.

116. J. Peter Scoblic, "The Hawkish Case for Nuclear Disarmament," *Los Angeles Times*, 16 August 2009.

117. "How to Pay for a Twenty-First Century Military," *New York Times*, 20 December 2008.

118. Richard Reeves, "The New Hessians and American Decline," *RealClearPolitics*, 15 September 2009.

119. Dan Balz, "The Challenge of Moving Beyond America Alone," *Washington Post*, 23 September 2009.

120. Bennett, "Sea Power," and Mark Thompson, "A New Kind of 'Top Gun' for a New Kind of War," *Time Magazine*, 5 October 2009.

121. In his article "Necessity," 71, Leslie Gelb offers several common-sense guidelines for U.S. foreign policy, including (1) making the U.S. strong again by restoring its economic

dynamism and pragmatic, can-do spirit, (2) understanding that mutual indispensability is the fundamental operating principle for power in the twenty-first century, (3) focusing U.S. policy and the power coalitions that must be formed on the greatest threats—terrorism, economic crises, nuclear proliferation, climate change, and global pandemics, (4) comprehending that international power works best when used to confront challenges before they become major threats, and (5) learning that the strong can no longer command the weak as in the past, because most major problems exist within nations rather than between them. In *CSIS Commission*, 1 and 70, Armitage and Nye add that the United States should focus on five critical areas: (1) alliances, partnerships, and institutions, (2) global development, (3) public diplomacy, (4) economic integration, and (5) technology and innovation, including energy security and climate change. They emphasize that "America has all the capacity to be a smart power. It has a social culture of tolerance. It has wonderful universities and colleges. It has an open and free political climate. It has a booming economy. And it has a legacy of idealism that channeled our enormous hard power in a way that the world accepted and wanted. We can become a smart power again."

122. David Frum, *Comeback: Conservatism That Can Win Again* (New York: Doubleday, 2008), 75.

123. *Ibid.*

124. In Friedman, "Time to Reboot," the columnist engages in a justifiable harangue about a number of subjects, including the immigration issue: "We've indulged ourselves for too long with tax cuts we can't afford, bailouts of auto companies that have become giant wealth-destruction machines, energy prices that do not encourage investment in twenty-first century renewable power systems or efficient cars, public schools with no national standards to prevent illiterates from graduation, and immigration policies that have our colleges educating the world's best scientists and engineers and then, when these foreigners graduate, instead of stapling green cards to their diplomas, we order them to go home and start companies to compete against ours."

125. Kao, *Innovation Nation*, 65.

126. *Ibid.*, 69–70.

127. *Ibid.*, 274. El Capitan refers to the majestic vertical rock formation in Yosemite National Park.

128. U.S. Bureau of Labor Statistics, "Employment Situation Summary," *Economic News Release*, 8 January 2010.

129. Richard Wilner, "The Dead End Kids," *New York Post*, 14 October 2009.

130. Heidi Shierholz, "Nine Years of Job Growth Wiped Out," *Economic Policy Institute Report*, 2 July 2009.

131. Katherine Newman calls this group the "missing class." See Bill Moyers, *Moyers on Democracy* (New York: Doubleday, 2008), 12.

132. A Deutsche Bank study predicts that up to 48 percent of homeowners could owe more than their house is worth by 2011, up from 26 percent at the end of March 2009. See Al Yoon, "About Half of U.S. Mortgages Seen Underwater by 2011," *Reuters*, 5 August 2009.

133. Lew Daly, "The Case for Paid Family Leave," *Newsweek*, 3 August 2009.

134. In 1993, 61 percent of small businesses provided health insurance for their employees, but this had fallen to 38 percent by 2009. See Fareed Zakaria, "More Crises Needed?" *Washington Post*, 17 August 2009.

135. Ron Haskins and Isabel Sawhill, *Creating an Opportunity Society* (Washington, D.C.: Brookings Institution, 2009), 9.

136. *Ibid.*

137. Steve Jobs and Steve Wozniak formed Apple Computer Company in 1976 in a garage in Los Altos, California. William Hewlett and David Packard also started their company in a garage in Palo Alto in 1938. These are true examples of entrepreneurs. See Christopher Lecuyer, *Making Silicon Valley: Innovation and the Growth of High Tech, 1930–1970* (Cambridge: MIT Press, 2006), 1–12.

138. Unionization in the private sector in 2008 was 7.6 percent. See U.S. Bureau of Labor Statistics, "Union Members Summary," *BLS Economic News Release*, 28 January 2009.

139. Reich, *Supercapitalism*, 108.

140. Sinclair Stewart, "Let Us Prey," *Globe and Mail*, 24 March 2009.

141. Susan Jacoby, *The Age of American Unreason* (New York: Pantheon Books, 2008), 301.

142. "Americans Spend Eight Hours a Day on Screens," *Breitbart.com*, 27 March 2009. This survey of adult habits was done for the Nielsen Company.

143. Robert D. Putnam and Lewis M. Feldstein, *Better Together: Restoring the American Community* (New York: Simon & Schuster, 2003), 1 and 294. The authors add that Americans need to develop "dense webs of encounter and participation so vital to the health of ourselves, our families, and our politics."

144. Francis Fukuyama, *Trust: The Social Virtues and the Creation of Prosperity* (New York: Free Press, 1995), 4 and 11.

145. Moyers quoted in Rosenblum, *Escaping Plato's Cave*, 254.

146. John M. Broder, "Climate Change Seen as Threat to U.S. Security," *New York Times*, 9 August 2009.

147. *Ibid.*

148. Adams quoted in Thomas J. Sugrue, "The New American Dream: Renting," *Wall Street Journal*, 15 August 2009.

149. Brian M. Carney, "Bye, Bye Light Bulbs," *Wall Street Journal*, 2 January 2008, and Friedman, "Mother Nature's Dow."

150. This is a major theme throughout Friedman's *Hot, Flat.*

Chapter 9

1. Zakaria, *Post-American*, 217.

2. Population Reference Bureau, "2009 World Population Data Sheet," August 2009, at www.prb.org, 2. In his book *Plan B 4.0: Mobilizing to Save Civilization* (New York: W.W. Norton, 2009), 24, Lester R. Brown predicts the global population will not reach 9.4 billion people by 2050, because inhabitants in developing countries will be forced to have smaller families or risk unprecedented loss of life through famine, thirst, disease, and environmental degradation.

3. *Ibid.*, 3.

4. Hachigian and Sutphen, *Next American Century*, 235, and James Kurth, "Pillars of the Next American Century," *The American Interest Online*, November/December 2009.

5. Kurth, "Pillars of the Next American Century."

6. Michael Krepon, "Target Practice in the Final Frontier," *Washington Post*, 4 February 2007.

7. Scoblic, "The Hawkish Case."

8. Keidel, "China's Economic Rise," 1.

9. John Hawksworth, *The World in 2050: How Big Will the Major Emerging Market Economies Get and How Can the OECD Compete?* (London: PricewaterhouseCoopers, 2006), 5, István Zsoldos and Anna Zadornova, "New EU Member States—A Fifth BRIC?," *Goldman Sachs Global Economics Paper No. 173*, 26 September 2008,

3 and 13, and Jim O'Neill and Tushar Poddar, "Ten Things for India to Achieve Its 2050 Potential," *Goldman Sachs Global Economics Paper No. 169*, 16 June 2008, 4. O'Neill and Poddar predict India has the capacity to match U.S. GDP on a purchasing power parity (PPP) basis. See also Jack A. Goldstone, "The New Population Bomb," *Foreign Affairs* 89 (January/February 2010): 31–43. In this article, Goldstone discusses the potential ramifications of the unprecedented shift over the next four decades of population, GDP, and workers away from North America and Europe and toward Asia and the developing world in general.

10. Quoted in Arthur M. Schlesinger, Jr., "Folly's Antidote," *New York Times*, 1 January 2007.

11. Using current projections, the U.S. share of the global population may actually increase slightly from 2010 to 2050, from 4.5 percent to almost 4.7 percent.

12. Fareed Zakaria, "Zakaria: Preview of a Post-U.S. World," *MSNBC.com*, 5 February 2007.

13. In their article "Twilight of Pax Americana," *Los Angeles Times*, 29 September 2009, Christopher Layne and Benjamin Schwarz contend that "the entire fabric of world order that the United States established after 1945—the Pax Americana—rested on the foundation of U.S. military and economic preponderance. Remove the foundation and the structure crumbles. The decline of American power means the end of U.S. dominance in world politics and the beginning of the transition to a new constellation of world powers. The result will be profound changes in world politics." See also David S. Mason, *The End of the American Century* (Lanham, MD: Rowman and Littlefield, 2009), 224.

14. Charles A. Kupchan, *The End of the American Era: U.S. Foreign Policy and the Geopolitics of the Twenty-First Century* (New York: Alfred A. Knopf, 2002), 305.

15. Michael Mandelbaum, *The Case for Goliath* (New York: PublicAffairs, 2005), 10.

16. In Zakaria, "Zakaria," the author expresses some concerns about a post–U.S. world: "We are certainly in a trough for America—with Bush in his last years, with the United States mired in Iraq, with hostility toward Washington still high almost everywhere. But if so, we might also be getting a glimpse of what a world without America would look like. It will be free of American domination, but perhaps also free of leadership—a world in which problems fester and the buck is endlessly passed, until problems explode."

17. This means Americans must have a growing awareness of what is transpiring in the world and understand that foreign policy should be a pivotal priority of government. In his book *From Colony to Superpower*, 937, Herring describes how Americans believed they were triumphant at the turn of the twenty-first century but still manifested scant concern for what was occurring around the world: "The American mood at the end of the century was one of triumphalism and smug, insular complacency. According to a January 2000 poll, Americans ranked foreign policy twentieth in terms of importance." Such a deadly combination of smugness and insularity would badly tarnish America's global standing in the decades ahead.

18. National Intelligence Council, *Global Trends 2025*, 51.

19. *Ibid.*

20. *Ibid.*

21. Sarah Forrest *et al.*, "Change Is Coming: A Framework for Climate Change—A Defining Issue of the Twenty-First Century," *Goldman Sachs GS Sustain Report,* 21 May 2009, 1–2.

22. Population Reference Bureau, "2009 World Population," 6.

23. John M. Broder, "Climate Change Seen as Threat to U.S. Security," *New York Times*, 9 August 2009.

24. Dan Farber, "Imagining the Tech World in 2050," *cnet.news*, 2 May 2008.

25. Hilary Rosner, "The Future of Farming: Eight Solutions for a Hungry World," *popsci. com*, 7 August 2009. See also Edward Gresser, "GEO-Politics," *Democracy: A Journal of Ideas*, Fall 2009, 49–61.

26. Boren, *A Letter to America*, 7. In his article "'Mad Men' Crashes Woodstock's Birthday," *New York Times*, 16 August 2009, Frank Rich captures some of this *ennui*: "'It's the economy, the fact that millions of people have lost their jobs and millions of others are afraid of losing theirs,' theorizes one heckled senator, Arlen Specter. That's surely part of it. So is fear of more home foreclosures and credit card bankruptcies. So is fear of China, whose economic ascension stands in sharp contrast to the collapse of traditional American industries from automobiles to newspapers. So is fear of Barack Obama, whose political ascension dramatizes the coming demographic order that will relegate whites to the American minority. In our uncharted new frontier, the most reliable fixture for a half-century of American public life, the Kennedy family, is crumbling."

27. Boren, *A Letter to America*, 56.

28. In Linda J. Bilmes and Joseph E. Stiglitz, "The $10 Trillion Hangover: Paying the Price for Eight Years of Bush," *Harper's Magazine*, January 2009, 35, the authors point out that "the worst legacy of the past eight years is that despite colossal government spending most Americans are worse off than they were in 2001." They add that in the period 2002–2006, the wealthiest 10 percent of households "saw more than 95 percent of the gains in income." Bruce Bartlett, in the "GOP's Misplaced Rage," *Daily Beast*, 13 August 2009, also points out that real GDP grew almost 35 percent during the Clinton presidency but only 16 percent during the George W. Bush presidency. Real gross private investment almost doubled under Clinton but actually fell under Bush. Employment increased by more than twenty-three million under Clinton but only 2.5 million under Bush. Clinton also left office with a budget surplus, whereas Bush left office with what was then the largest deficit in American history. Clinton abolished a major federal entitlement program, welfare, while Bush established a new one, prescription drugs for the elderly. In Ronald Brownstein, "Closing the Book on the Bush Legacy," *theatlantic.com*, 11 September 2009, the author concludes that "on every major measurement, the Census Bureau report shows that the country lost ground during Bush's two terms. While Bush was in office, the median household income declined, poverty increased, childhood poverty increased even more, and the number of Americans without health insurance spiked. By contrast, the country's condition improved on each of those measures during Bill Clinton's two terms, often substantially."

29. Joseph E. Stiglitz, "Wall Street's Toxic Message," *Vanity Fair*, July 2009, 82, and Carl Schramm and Robert E. Litan, "The End of American Capitalism?," *The American*, 6 February 2009.

30. Michael Beschloss, *Presidential Courage: Brave Leaders and How They Changed America 1789–1989* (New York: Simon & Schuster, 2007), ix.

31. *Ibid.*

32. Jean Edward Smith, *FDR* (New York: Random House, 2007), xii.

33. As T.R. Reid stresses in *Confucius*, 245–249, Asians value hard work, honesty, thrift, and a commitment to education, similar to what he was taught growing up in the United States. He urges a return to "Yankee virtues" and the traditional tenets of Western culture.

34. Zakaria, who arrived in the United States as an eighteen-year-old student from India in the fall of 1982, praises the United States for being such an open, welcoming, tolerant society. See *Post-American*, 257.

35. Robert J. Shapiro, *Futurecast: How Superpowers, Populations, and Globalization Will Change the Way You Live and Work* (New York: St. Martin's Press, 2008), 6.

36. According to a 2008 report released by the accounting firm KPMG, within the next five years China "should become the most influential country in IT and telecom." See Harold Meyerson, "Just One Word: Factories," *Washington Post*, 12 August 2009.

37. GAO report quoted in Mort Zuckerman, "Drowning in Debt: Obama's Spending and Borrowing Leaves U.S. Gasping for Air," *New York Daily News*, 9 August 2009.

38. Shapiro, *Futurecast*, 1–2.

39. Peter F. Drucker, *Management Challenges for the Twenty-First Century* (New York: HarperBusiness, 1999), 61. Also see Shapiro, *Futurecast*, 313.

40. Some eminent economists, such as Nobel Prize winners Joseph Stiglitz and Amartya Sen, argue the concept of GDP should be altered substantially to include measures of sustainability and human well-being. See David Jolly, "Commission Calls for New Economic Yardstick," *New York Times*, 15 September 2009.

41. United Nations Development Program, "Human Development Indices: A Statistical Update 2008—HDI Rankings," at *http://origin-hdr.undp.org/en/statistics/*. In Burd-Sharps et al., *The Measure of America*, 10, Amartya Sen emphasizes that "human development is concerned with what I take to be the basic development idea: namely, advancing the richness of human life, rather than the richness of the economy in which human beings live, which is only a part of it."

42. In Will Hutton, *The Writing on the Wall: Why We Must Embrace China as a Partner or Face It as an Enemy* (New York: Free Press, 2006), 2–4, the author asserts that China must embrace the economic and political pluralism of the West in order to sustain vigorous economic growth in the future. If this occurs, China will not be a threat to the United States and indeed a growing trans-Pacific "partnership" may evolve between the U.S. and China.

43. Ian Rowley, "Japan's Population Decline Is Gathering Momentum," *Business Week*, 11 August 2009.

44. These changes will dramatically alter the current system of lobbying, and as David Brooks emphasizes in "The Next Culture War," *New York Times*, 29 September 2009, the "lobbyist ethos" will be shattered, an ethos or "righteous conviction held by everybody from AARP to the agribusinesses that their groups are entitled to every possible appropriation, regardless of the larger public cost."

45. Reid, *Confucius*, 246.

46. Rosenblum, *Escaping Plato's Cave*, 222.

47. Edmund L. Andrews and David E. Sanger, "U.S. Is Finding Its Role in Business Hard to Unwind," *New York Times*, 14 September 2009.

48. Every president in the future should take note of the comments made by Robert McNamara and McGeorge Bundy concerning the war in Vietnam. McNamara was Secretary of Defense during much of the war period, and Bundy was National Security Adviser. They both lament the role they played in the decision to escalate the war effort under President Johnson. Tragically, they emphasize that Johnson never considered the broad range of available options and allowed the national interest of the country to take a backseat to his own reelection aspirations. Bundy stated that "LBJ isn't deeply concerned about . . . who governs South Vietnam—he's deeply concerned with what the average American voter is going to think about how he did in the ballgame of the Cold War. The great Cold War Championship gets played in the largest stadium in the United States, and he, Lyndon Johnson, is the quarterback, and

if he loses, how does he do in the next election? So don't lose. . . . He's living with his own political survival every time he looks at these questions." In the meantime, while Johnson was fixated on his reelection prospects, 2.6 million young Americans would serve in Vietnam, with over fifty-eight thousand killed and 300,000 wounded. See the chilling account provided by McNamara and Bundy before their deaths in Bob Woodward and Gordon M. Goldstein, "The Anguish of Decision," *Washington Post*, 18 October 2008.

49. Gelb uses the term "power coalitions" of key states in *Power Rules*, 119–121. Later in 297–299, he emphasizes that the United States will need "indispensable partners," especially among what he refers to as second-tier powers such as China, Japan, India, Russia, the UK, France, Germany, and Brazil, to solve the vexing challenges of the next several decades. Although Gelb does not suggest this, the United States must also work more collaboratively with Canada and Mexico and other North American nations to strengthen the competitiveness and vitality of the entire North American continent.

50. The rest of the world has much to learn from the United States, but Americans also have much to learn from the rest of the world, and this will require a mind-set change on the part of U.S. leaders and the general public. As Mahbubani observes in "Can America Fail?," 51, "virtually all analysis by American intellectuals rests on the assumption that *problems* come from outside America and America provides only *solutions*. Yet the rest of the world can see clearly that American power has created many of the world's major problems. American thinkers and policymakers cannot see this because they are engaged in an incestuous, self-referential, and self-congratulatory discourse. They have lost the ability to listen to other voices on the planet because they cannot conceive of the possibility that they are not already listening. But until they begin to open their ears, America's problems with the world will continue."

51. Brzezinski, *The Grand Chessboard*, 212.

52. In "The End," Schramm and Litan emphasize that "the most important citizen is not the politician, nor the big businessman, nor the bankers on Wall Street. They are important but not central to the renewal of democratic capitalism. That role, that burden, that honor falls to our fellow citizens who in the face of the challenges we see all around us are ready to pursue what it is the entrepreneurs do—birth the new, create our jobs, and make the wealth that will be more necessary than ever to purchase a prosperous future."

Bibliography

Ahuja, Sunil. *Congress Behaving Badly: The Rise of Partisanship and Incivility and the Death of Public Trust*. Westport, CN: Praeger, 2008.

Albright, Madeleine. *Memo to the President Elect*. New York: HarperCollins, 2008.

Alvarez, R. Michael, Stephen Ansolabehere, Adam Berinsky, Gabriel Lenz, Charles Stewart III, and Thad Hall. "2008 Survey of the Performance of American Elections: Final Report Executive Summary," *Caltech/MIT Voting Technology Project*, 2009.

Amer, Mildred and Jennifer E. Manning. *Membership of the 111th Congress: A Profile*. Washington, D.C.: Congressional Research Service, 2008.

Arceneaux, Kevin. "Does Federalism Weaken Democratic Representation in the United States?" *Publius* 35 (Spring 2005): 297–312.

Archer, Clive. *The European Union*. London: Routledge, 2008.

Armitage, Richard L. and Joseph S. Nye, Jr., *CSIS Commission on Smart Power: A Smarter, More Secure America*. Washington, D.C.: Center for Strategic and International Studies, 2007.

Bacevich, Andrew. *The Limits of Power: The End of American Exceptionalism*. New York: Metropolitan Books, 2008.

Bailey, Thomas A. *Diplomatic History of the American People*, 6th edition. New York: Appleton-Century-Crofts, 1958.

Baker, James A. and Lee H. Hamilton, *The Iraq Study Group Report*. New York: Vintage Books, 2006.

Beeman, Richard. *Plain, Honest Men*. New York: Random House, 2009.

Beinart, Peter. *The Good Fight*. New York: HarperCollins, 2006.

Ben-Joseph, Eran. "Double Standards, Single Goal: Private Communities and Design Innovation," *Journal of Urban Design* 9 (June 2004): 131–151.

Bergsten, C. Fred, Charles Freeman, Nicholas R. Lardy, and Derek J. Mitchell. *China's Rise: Challenges and Opportunities*. Washington, D.C.: Peterson Institute for International Economics, 2008.

Beschloss, Michael. *Presidential Courage: Brave Leaders and How They Changed America 1789–1989*. New York: Simon & Schuster, 2007.

Board of Trustees. *The 2009 Annual Report of the Board of Trustees of the Federal Old-Age and Survivors Insurance and Federal Disability Insurance Trust Funds*. Washington, D.C.: U.S. Government Printing Office, 2009.

Boards of Trustees. *2009 Annual Report of the Boards of Trustees of the Federal Hospital Insurance and Federal Supplementary Medicare Insurance Trust Funds*. Washington, D.C.: U.S. Government Printing Office, 2009.

Boren, David. *A Letter to America*. Norman: University of Oklahoma Press, 2008.

Brands, Hal. *From Berlin to Baghdad: America's Search for Purpose in the Post-Cold War World*. Lexington: University of Kentucky Press, 2008.

Brenner, Neil and Roger Keil. "Editors' Introduction." In *The Global Cities Reader*. Edited by Neil Brenner and Roger Keil. London: Routledge, 2006.

Brokaw, Tom. *The Greatest Generation*. New York: Random House, 1998.

Brown, Lester R. *Plan B 4.0: Mobilizing to Save Civilization*. New York: W.W. Norton, 2009.

Brown, Seyom. *Higher Realism: A New Foreign Policy for the United States*. Boulder, CO: Paradigm Publishers, 2009.

Brown, Seyom. *The Illusion of Control: Force and Foreign Policy in the Twenty-First Century*. Washington, D.C.: Brookings Institution, 2003.

Bryce, Robert. *Gusher of Lies: The Dangerous Delusions of "Energy Independence."* New York: Public Affairs, 2008.

Brzezinski, Zbigniew. *The Grand Chessboard: American Primacy and Its Geostrategic Imperatives*. New York: Basic Books, 1997.

Brzezinski, Zbigniew and Brent Scowcroft. *America and the World*. New York: Basic Books, 2008.

Buchanan, Patrick J. *State of Emergency: The Third World Invasion and Conquest of America*. New York: St. Martin's, 2007.

Burd-Sharps, Sarah, Kristen Lewis, and Eduardo Borges Martins. *The Measure of America: American Human Development Report 2008–2009*. New York: Columbia University Press, 2008.

Bureau of Economic Analysis, U.S. Department of Commerce. "International Investment Position of the United States at Yearend, 1976–2008." *www.bea.gov/intinv08_t2.xls*.

Burman, Leonard E.,William G. Gale, Matthew Hall, and Peter Orszag, "Distributional Effects of Defined Contribution Plans and Individual Retirement Accounts," *Urban Institute TPC Discussion Paper No. 16*, August 19, 2004.

Carter, Jimmy. *Beyond the White House*. New York: Simon & Schuster, 2007.

Casetti, Emilio. "Power Shifts and Economic Development: When Will China Overtake the USA?" *Journal of Peace Research* 40 (no. 6, 2003): 661–675.

Center for Governmental Studies. "Mapping Public Financing in American Elections, January 2009." *www.csg.org*.

Center for Responsive Politics. "Lobbying Database." *www.opensecrets.org/lobbyists*.

Center for Responsive Politics. "2008 Overview." *www.OpenSecrets.org*.

Chandrasekaran, Rajiv. *Imperial Life in the Emerald City: Inside Iraq's Green Zone*. New York: Random House, 2006.

Chau, Amy. *Day of Empire: How Hyperpowers Rise to Global Dominance—And Why They Fail*. New York: Doubleday, 2007.

Choate, Pat. *Dangerous Business: The Risks of Globalization for America*. New York: Alfred A. Knopf, 2008.

Chomsisengphet, Souphala and Anthony Pennington-Cross. "The Evolution of the Subprime Mortgage Market." *Federal Reserve Bank of St. Louis Review* 88. February 2006: 31–56.

Christeson, William, Amy Dawson Taggart, and Soren Messner-Zidell, *Ready, Willing, and Unable to Serve*. Washington, D.C.: Mission: Readiness, 2009.

Clarke, Richard A. *Your Government Failed You: Breaking the Cycle of National Security Disasters*. New York: HarperCollins, 2008.

Cling, Arnold. *Crisis of Abundance: Rethinking How We Pay for Health Care*. Washington, D.C.: Cato Institute, 2006.

Cohan, William D. *House of Cards: A Tale of Hubris and Wretched Excess on Wall Street*. NewYork: Doubleday, 2009.

Common Cause. "The Fair Elections Now Act." *www.commoncause.org*.

Congressional Budget Office. "The Budget and Economic Outlook: An Update," July 2000. *www.cbo.gov.*

Corn, David. *Hubris: The Inside Story of Spin, Scandal, and the Selling of the Iraq War.* New York: Crown Publishers, 2006.

Cortell, Andrew P. *Mediating Globalization.* Albany: State University Press of New York, 2006.

D'Aquino, Tom. "Enhancing the Canada–United States Partnership," remarks to the Standing Committee on Foreign Affairs and International Development, House of Commons, Parliament of Canada, 25 February 2009.

Davidow, Jeffrey. *The Bear and the Porcupine: The U.S. and Mexico.* Princeton: Marcus Wiener Publishers, 2007.

DeFrank, Thomas M. *Write It When I'm Gone: Remarkable Off-the-Record Conversations with Gerald F. Ford.* New York: G.P. Putnam's Sons, 2007.

DeNavas-Walt, Carmen, Bernadette D. Proctor, and Jessica C. Smith. *Income, Poverty, and Health Insurance Coverage in the United States, 2008.* Washington, D.C.: U.S. Census Bureau, 2009.

Department of Commerce. International Trade Administration. "U.S. Travel and Tourism Trends: International Visitor Spending." *www.tinet.ita.doc.gov/outreachpages.*

Department of Commerce. "International Visitation" and "U.S. Travel and Tourism Trends." *http://tinet.ita.doc.gov/outreachpages/inbound.general_information.inbound_overview.html.*

Department of the Treasury/Federal Reserve Board. "Major Foreign Holders of Treasury Securities," 15 June 2009. *www.treasury.gov/tic/mfh.txt.*

Diamond, Larry. *Squandered Victory.* New York: Times Books, 2006.

Diamond, Larry. *The Spirit of Democracy.* New York: Times Books, 2008.

Dimitri, Carolyn, Anne Effland, and Neilson Conklin. *The Twentieth Century Transformation of U.S. Agriculture and Farm Policy.* Washington, D.C.: Economic Research Service, U.S. Department of Agriculture, 2005.

Dine, Philip M. *State of the Unions.* New York: McGraw-Hill, 2008.

Dresser, Denise and Veronica Wilson. *U.S.–Mexico Relations: Permeable Borders, Transnational Communities.* Los Angeles: Pacific Council on International Policy, 2006.

Drucker, Peter F. *Management Challenges for the Twenty-First Century.* New York: HarperBusiness, 1999.

Egan, Timothy. *The Worst Hard Time: The Untold Story of Those Who Survived the Great American Dust Bowl.* Boston: Houghton Mifflin, 2006.

Evans, Robert G. "Extravagant Americans, Healthier Canadians: The Bottom Line in North American Health Care." In *Canada and the United States: Differences That Count,* third edition. Edited by David M. Thomas and Barbara Boyle Torrey. Toronto: University of Toronto Press, 2008, 135–164.

Executive Office of the President, Council of Economic Advisers (CEA). *The Economic Case for Health Care Reform.* Washington, D.C.: U.S. Government Printing Office, 2009.

Ezell, Stephen. "America and the World: We're #40!" *Democracy: A Journal of Ideas* (Fall 2009): 13–14.

Feigenbaum, Evan A. and Robert A. Manning. "The United States in the New Asia." *Council Special Reports No. 50.* New York: Council on Foreign Relations, 2009.

Ferguson, Niall. *The War of the Worlds: History's Age of Hatred.* London: Allen Lane, 2006.

Filkins, Dexter. *The Forever War: Dispatches from the War on Terror.* London: The Bodley Head, 2008.

Fisher, Peter and Alan Peters. "The Failure of Economic Development Incentives." *Journal of the American Planning Association* 70 (no. 1, 2004): 27–37.

Fishman, Ted C. *China Inc.* New York: Scribner, 2005.

Foster, Richard and Sarah Kaplan. *Creative Destruction: Why Companies That Are Built to Last Underperform the Market and How to Successfully Transform Them.* New York: Doubleday/Currency, 2001.

Frank, Robert. *Richistan: A Journey through the American Wealth Boom and the Lives of the New Rich.* New York: Crown Publishers, 2007.

Frank, Robert H. *Falling Behind: How Rising Inequality Harms the Middle Class.* Berkeley: University of California Press, 2007.

Frank, Thomas. *The Wrecking Crew: How Conservatives Rule.* New York: Metropolitan Books, 2008.

Frieden, Jeffry A. *Global Capitalism: Its Fall and Rise in the Twentieth Century.* New York: W.W. Norton, 2006.

Friedman, Thomas L. *Hot, Flat, and Crowded: Why We Need a Green Revolution.* New York: Farrar, Straus and Giroux, 2008.

Friedman, Thomas L. *The World Is Flat, 3.0: A Brief History of the Twenty-First Century.* New York: Picador, 2007.

Frum, David. *Comeback: Conservatism That Can Win Again.* New York: Doubleday, 2008.

Fry, Earl H. *The Expanding Role of State and Local Governments in U.S. Foreign Affairs.* New York: Council on Foreign Relations Press, 1998.

Fry, Earl H. "The United States of America." In *A Global Dialogue on Federalism*, volume 5. Edited by Hans Michelmann. Montreal and Kingston: McGill-Queen's University Press, 2009, 296–323.

Fukuyama, Francis. *Trust: The Social Virtues and the Creation of Prosperity.* New York: Free Press, 1995.

Furman, Jason. ed., *Who Has the Cure? Hamilton Project Ideas on Health Care.* Washington, D.C.: Brookings Institution Press, 2008.

Galbraith, Peter W. *The End of Iraq.* New York: Simon & Schuster, 2006.

Gale, William G. "Fixing the Tax System." In *Opportunity 08: Independent Ideas for America's Next President.* Edited by Michael E. O'Hanlon. Washington, D.C.: Brookings Institution Press, 2007, 331–341.

Garfinkle, Norton. *The American Dream vs. the Gospel of Wealth: The Fight for a Productive Middle-Class Economy.* New Haven: Yale University Press, 2007.

Gates, Bill. *Business @ the Speed of Thought.* New York: Warner Books, 1999.

Gelb, Leslie H. *Power Rules: How Common Sense Can Rescue American Foreign Policy.* New York: HarperCollins, 2009.

Ghemawat, Pankaj. *Redefining Global Strategy.* Boston: Harvard Business School Press, 2007.

Ghilarducci, Teresa and Christian E. Weller, eds. *Employee Pensions: Policies, Problems, and Possibilities.* Champaign, Ill.: Land and Employment Relations Association, 2007.

Gifford, Rob. *China Road: A Journey into the Future of a Rising Power.* New York: Random House, 2007.

Gill, Bates. "China's Health Care and Pension Challenges." Testimony before the U.S.–China Security and Economic Review Commission, Washington, D.C., 2 February 2006.

Gills, Barry K. and William R. Thompson, eds., *Globalization and Global History*. London: Routledge, 2006.

Gingrich, Newt. *Real Change*. Washington, D.C.: Regnery Publishing, 2008.

Golding, Claudia and Lawrence F. Katz, *Race between Education and Technology*. Cambridge, MA: Belknap Press of Harvard University, 2008.

Goldstein, Gordon M. *Lessons in Disaster*. New York: Times Books, 2008.

Gordon, Michael R. and General Bernard E. Trainor. *Cobra II*. New York: Pantheon Books, 2006.

Gordon, Philip H. *Winning the Right War*. New York: Times Books, 2007.

Gosling, James J. *Economics, Politics, and American Public Policy*. Armonk, NY: M.E. Sharpe, 2008.

Guyatt, Gordon H., P.J. Devereaux, Joel Lexchin, Samuel B. Stone, Armine Yalnizyan, David Himmelstein, Steffie Woolhandler, Qi Zhou, Laurie J. Goldsmith, Deborah J. Cook, Ted Haines, Christina Lacchetti, John N. Lavis, Terrence Sullivan, Ed Mills, Shelley Kraus, and Neera Bhatnagar. "A Systematic Review of Studies Comparing Health Outcomes in Canada and the United States." *Open Medicine* 1 (no. 1, 2007): 27–36.

Hacker, Jacob S. *The Great Risk Shift: The Assault on American Jobs, Families, Health Care, and Retirement and How You Can Fight Back*. Oxford: Oxford University Press, 2006.

Hanson, Elizabeth C. *The Information Revolution and World Politics*. Lanham, MD: Rowman & Littlefield, 2008.

Haskins, Ron and Isabel Sawhill, *Creating an Opportunity Society*. Washington, D.C.: Brookings Institution, 2009.

Hawksworth, John. *The World in 2050: How Big Will the Major Emerging Market Economies Get and How Can the OECD Compete?* London: PricewaterhouseCoopers, 2006.

Held, David and Anthony Grew, eds., *Globalization Theory*. Cambridge, MA: Polity Press, 2007.

Herring, George G. *From Colony to Superpower: U.S. Foreign Relations Since 1776*. New York: Oxford University Press, 2008.

Hilley, John L. *The Challenge of Legislation: Bipartisanship in a Partisan World*. Washington, D.C.: Brookings Institution, 2008.

Himmelstein, David U., Deborah Thorne, Elizabeth Warren, and Steffie Woolhandler. "Medical Bankruptcy in the United States 2007: Results of a National Study." *American Journal of Medicine* 122 (no. 8, 2009): 741–746.

Hirsh, Michael. *At War with Ourselves*. Oxford: Oxford University Press, 2003.

Hook, Steven W. and John Spanier. *American Foreign Policy Since World War II*, 17th edition. Washington, D.C.: CQ Press, 2007.

Huang, Elbert S., Anirban Basu, Michael O'Grady, and James C. Capretta, "Projecting the Future Diabetes Population Size and Related Costs for the U.S.," *Diabetes Care* 32 (December 2009): 2225–2229.

Hunt, Michael W. *The American Ascendancy: How the United States Gained and Wielded Global Dominance*. Chapel Hill: University of North Carolina Press, 2007.

Intercollegiate Studies Institute. "Our Fading Heritage: Americans Fail a Basic Test on Their History and Institutions: 2008–2009." *www.americancivilization.org/2008/summary_ summary.html*.

Intercollegiate Studies Institute. *The Coming Crisis in Citizenship*. Wilmington, DE: Intercollegiate Studies Institute, 2006.

"International Visitation to the United States: A Statistical Summary of U.S. Arrivals (2008)." *www.tinet.ita.doc.gov/outreach pages.*

Jacoby, Susan. *The Age of American Unreason.* New York: Pantheon Books, 2008.

Jacque, Martin. *When China Rules the World: The Rise of the Middle Kingdom and the End of the Western World.* London: Allen Lane, 2009.

Johnston, David Cay. *Free Lunch: How the Wealthiest Americans Enrich Themselves at Government Expense (And Stick You with the Bill).* New York: Portfolio, 2007.

Johnston, David Cay. *Perfectly Legal: The Covert Campaign to Rig Our Tax System to Benefit the Super Rich.* New York: Portfolio, 2003.

Judt, Tony. *Reappraisals: Reflections on the Forgotten Twentieth Century.* New York: Penguin Press, 2008.

Kaiser, Robert G. *So Damn Much Money: The Triumph of Lobbying and the Corrosion of American Government.* New York: Random House, 2009.

Kamdar, Mira. *Planet India.* New York: Scribner, 2007.

Kao, John. *Innovation Nation.* New York: Free Press, 2007.

Kaplan, Fred. *Daydream Believers: How a Few Grand Ideas Wrecked American Power.* Hoboken, NJ: John Wiley & Sons, 2008.

Katzenstein, Peter J. and Robert O. Keohane, eds. *Anti-Americanisms in World Politics.* Ithaca: Cornell University Press, 2007.

Kegley, Charles W. and Gregory A. Raymond. *After Iraq: The Imperiled American Imperium.* New York: Oxford University Press, 2007.

Keidel, Albert. "China's Economic Rise—Fact and Fiction." *Carnegie Endowment for International Peace Policy Brief 61.* Washington, D.C.: Carnegie Endowment for International Peace, 2008.

Keister, Lisa A. *Wealth in America: Trends in Wealth Inequality.* Cambridge: Cambridge University Press, 2000.

Kennedy, Paul. *The Rise and Fall of the Great Powers.* New York: Random House, 1987.

Khanna, Parag. *The Second World: Empires and Influence in the New Global Order.* New York: Random House, 2008.

Killenbeck, Mark R., ed. *The Tenth Amendment and State Sovereignty: Constitutional History and Contemporary Issues.* Lanham, MD: Rowman & Littlefield, 2002.

Kincaid, John. "Globalization and Federalism in the United States: Continuity in Adaptation." In *The Impact of Global and Regional Integration on Federal Systems: A Comparative Analysis.* Edited by Harvey Lazar, Hamish Telford, and Ronald L. Watts. Montreal: McGill-Queen's University Press, 2003, 37–85.

Kirsch, Irwin, Henry Braun, Kentaro Yamamoto, and Andrew Sum. *America's Perfect Storm: Three Forces Changing Our Nation's Future.* Princeton, NJ: Educational Testing Service, 2007.

Klare, Michael T. *Blood and Oil: The Dangers and Consequences of America's Growing Dependency on Imported Oil.* New York: Metropolitan Books, 2004.

Klare, Michael T. *Rising Powers, Shrinking Planet: The New Geopolitics of Energy.* New York: Metropolitan Books, 2008.

Klein, Joe. *Politics Lost: How American Democracy Was Trivialized by People Who Think You're Stupid.* New York: Random House, 2006.

Kling, Arnold. *Crisis of Abundance: Rethinking How We Pay for Health Care.* Washington, D.C.: Cato Institute, 2006.

Kozol, Jonathan. *The Shame of the Nation*. New York: Random House, 2005.

Krikorian, Mark. *The New Case Against Immigration, Both Legal and Illegal*. New York: Penguin Group, 2008.

Kupchan, Charles A. *The End of the American Era: U.S. Foreign Policy and the Geopolitics of the Twenty-First Century*. New York: Alfred A. Knopf, 2002.

Lake, David A. "American Hegemony and the Future of East-West Relations." *International Studies Perspectives* 7 (no. 1, 2006): 23–30.

Lecuyer, Christopher. *Making Silicon Valley: Innovation and the Growth of High Tech, 1930–1970*. Cambridge: MIT Press, 2006.

Leonard, Mark. *Why Europe Will Run the Twenty-First Century*. London: Fourth Estate, 2005.

Levin, Steven M. "Keeping It Clean: Public Financing in American Elections." Center for Governmental Studies, 2006. *www.cgs.org/index.php?view=article&id=64%3APUBLICATI ONS&option=com_content&Itemid=72*.

Lichtenberg, Frank R., and Shawn X. Sun. "The Impact of Medicare Part D on Prescription Drug Use by the Elderly." *Health Affairs* 26 (no. 6, 2007): 1735-1744.

Light, Paul C. *A Government Ill Executed: The Decline of the Federal Service and How to Reverse It*. Cambridge, MA: Harvard University Press, 2008.

Lowenstine, Roger. *While America Aged: How Pension Debts Ruined General Motors, Stopped the NYC Subways, Bankrupted San Diego, and Loom as the Next Financial Crisis*. New York: Penguin Press, 2008.

Lutkus, Anthony and Andrew R. Weiss. *The Nation's Report Card: Civics 2006*. Washington, D.C.: National Assessment of Education Progress, 2007.

Mahbubani, Kishore. *Beyond the Age of Innocence: Rebuilding Trust between America and the World*. New York: Public Affairs, 2005.

Mahbubani, Kishore. "Can America Fail?" *The Wilson Quarterly* 33 (Spring 2009): 48–54.

Mandelbaum, Michael. *The Case for Goliath*. New York: PublicAffairs, 2005.

Mann, Thomas E. and Norman J. Ornstein. *The Broken Branch: How Congress Is Failing America and How to Get It Back on Track*. Oxford: Oxford University Press, 2006.

Marling, William H. *How "American" Is Globalization?* Baltimore: Johns Hopkins University Press, 2006.

Mayer, Jane. *The Dark Side: The Inside Story of How the War on Terror Turned into a War on American Ideals*. New York: Doubleday, 2008.

McClellan, Scott. *What Happened? Inside the Bush White House and Washington's Culture of Deception*. New York: Public Affairs, 2008.

Milbank, Dana. *Homo Politicus: The Strange and Barbaric Tribes of the Beltway*. New York: Doubleday, 2008.

Miller, David C., Anindita Sen, Lydia B. Malley, Stephanie D. Burns, and Eugene Owen. *Comparative Indicators of Education in the United States and Other G-8 Countries*. Washington, D.C.: U.S. Department of Education, 2009.

Monger, Randall and Nancy Rytina. "U.S. Legal Permanent Residents: 2008." *Office of Immigration Statistics Annual Report*. Washington, D.C.: U.S. Department of Homeland Security, 2009.

Moyers, Bill. *Moyers on Democracy*. New York: Doubleday, 2008.

Mueller, John. *Overblown: How Politicians and the Terrorism Industry Inflate National Security Threats, and Why We Believe Them*. New York: Free Press, 2006.

Murphy, Cullen. *Are We Rome?* Boston: Houghton Mifflin, 2007.

National Center on Education and the Economy. *Tough Choices, Tough Times: The Report of the New Commission on the Skills of the American Workplace: Executive Summary*, 2007. www.skillscommission.org

National Drug Intelligence Center, U.S. Department of Justice. "National Drug Threat Assessment, 2009." *www.usdoj.gov/dea/concern/18862/indi.c_2009*.

National Gang Intelligence Center. *National Gang Threat Assessment, 2009*. Washington, D.C.: U.S. Department of Justice, 2009.

National Intelligence Council. *Mapping the Global Future*. Washington, D.C.: Government Printing Office, 2004.

Newman, Abraham and John Zysman. "Transforming Politics in the Digital Era." In *How Revolutionary Was the Digital Revolution?* Edited by John Zysman and Abraham Newman. Stanford: Stanford University Press, 2006, 403–424.

Noonan, Peggy. *Patriotic Grace*. New York: HarperCollins, 2008.

Nuechterlein, Donald E. *Defiant Superpower: The New American Hegemony*. Washington, D.C.: Potomac Books, 2005.

Nye, Joseph S., Jr. *Soft Power: The Means to Success in World Politics*. New York: Basic Books, 2004.

Office of the Assistant Secretary for Planning and Evaluation, U.S. Department of Health and Human Services. "September 2007 ASPE Research Brief: Indicators of Welfare Dependence." *http://aspe.hhs.gov/hsp/Indicators07/rb.htm*.

Olshansky, S. Jay, Douglas J. Passaro, Ronald C. Hershow, and Jennifer Layden. "A Potential Decline in Life Expectancy in the United States in the Twenty-First Century," *New England Journal of Medicine* 352 (no. 11, 17 March 2005): 1138–1145.

O'Neill, Jim and Tushar Poddar. "Ten Things for India to Achieve Its 2050 Potential." *Goldman Sachs Global Economics Paper*, no. 169, 16 June 2008.

Ornstein, Norman J., Thomas E. Mann, and Michael J. Malbin. *Vital Statistics on Congress, 2001–2002*. Washington, D.C.: AEI Press, 2002.

Passel, Jeffrey S. and D'Vera Cohn. *A Portrait of Unauthorized Immigrants in the United States*. Washington, D.C.: Pew Hispanic Center, 2009.

Passel, Jeffrey and D'Vera Cohn. *U.S. Population Projections: 2005–2050*. Washington, D.C.: Pew Research Center, 2009.

Peoples, Clayton D. "Campaign Finance in Canada and the U.S.: Policies, Powers, and Prospects." In *ACSUS Occasional Papers on Public Policy*, 2009.

Pew Global Attitudes Project, "Confidence in Obama Lifts U.S. Image around the World: Muslim Publics Not So Easily Moved," 23 July 2009. *www.pewglobal.org*.

Pew Hispanic Center. "Mexican Immigrants in the United States, 2008." *http://pewhispanic. org/files/factsheets/47.pdf*.

Pew Hispanic Center, "Statistical Portrait of the Foreign-born Population in the United States, 2006." *http://pewhispanic.org/factsheets*.

Phillips, Kevin. *American Theocracy: The Peril and Politics of Radical Religion, Oil, and Borrowed Money in the Twenty-First Century*. New York: Viking Press, 2006.

Phillips, Kevin. *Bad Money: Reckless Finance, Failed Politics, and the Global Crisis of American Capitalism*. New York: Viking Press, 2008.

Population Reference Bureau. "Human Population: Fundamentals of Growth Patterns of World Urbanization," 2009. *www.prb.org*.

Population Reference Bureau. "2009 World Population Data Sheet." *www.prb.org*.

Prestowitz, Clyde. *Rogue Nation*. New York: Basic Books, 2003.

Putnam, Robert D. and Lewis M. Feldstein. *Better Together: Restoring the American Community*. New York: Simon & Schuster, 2003.

RAND Corporation. "Is the United States Losing Its Edge in Science and Technology?" *Rand National Defense Research Institute Research Brief*, June 2008.

Rank, Mark R. and Thomas A. Hirschl. "Estimating the Risk of Food Stamp Use and Impoverishment during Childhood." *Archives of Pediatrics and Adolescent Medicine* 163 (November 2009): 994–999.

Rauchway, Eric. *Blessed Among Nations: How the World Made America*. New York: Hill and Wang, 2006.

Reid, T.R. *Confucius Lives Next Door: What Living in the East Teaches Us About Living in the West*. New York: Random House, 1999.

Reid, T.R. *The Healing of America: A Global Quest for Better, Cheaper, and Fairer Health Care*. New York: Penguin Press, 2009.

Reeves, Richard. *President Kennedy: Profile of Power*. New York: Simon & Schuster, 1994.

Reich, Robert B. *Supercapitalism*. New York: Alfred A. Knopf, 2007.

Roberts, Paul. *The End of Food*. Boston: Houghton Mifflin, 2008.

Rosenblum, Mort. *Escaping Plato's Cave: How America's Blindness to the Rest of the World Threatens Our Survival*. New York: St. Martin's Press, 2007.

Ross, Dennis. *Statecraft*. New York: Farrar, Straus and Giroux, 2007.

Ruggie, John Gerald. "Doctrinal Unilateralism and Its Limits: America and Global Governance in the New Century." In *American Foreign Policy in a Globalized World*. Edited by David P. Forsythe, Patrice C. McMahon, and Andrew Wedeman. New York: Routledge, 2006, 31–50.

Sabato, Larry J. *A More Perfect Constitution: 23 Proposals to Revitalize Our Constitution and Make America a Fairer Country*. New York: Walker & Company, 2007.

Sachs, Jeffrey D. *Common Wealth: Economics for a Crowded Planet*. New York: Penguin Press, 2008.

Scheuer, Jeffrey. *The Big Picture: Why Democracies Need Journalistic Excellence*. New York: Routledge, 2008.

Scheuer, Michael. *Marching toward Hell: America and Islam after Iraq*. New York: Free Press, 2008.

Schmidt, Stanley. *The Coming Convergence: Surprising Ways Diverse Technologies Interact to Shape Our World and Change the Future*. Amherst, NY: Prometheus Books, 2008.

Schultz, George P. and John B. Shoven. *Putting Our House in Order: A Guide to Social Security and Health Care Reform*. New York: W.W. Norton, 2008.

Schumpeter, Joseph A. *Capitalism, Socialism and Democracy*. London: Routledge, 1994.

Setser, Brad, and Arpana Pandey. "China's 1.7 Trillion Dollar Bet: China's External Portfolio and Dollar Reserves." *Council on Foreign Relations Working Paper*, January 2009.

Shadid, Anthony. *Night Draws Near: Iraq's People in the Shadow of America's War*. New York: Henry Holt, 2005.

Shapiro, Robert J. *Futurecast: How Superpowers, Populations, and Globalization Will Change the Way You Live and Work*. New York: St. Martin's Press, 2008.

Sharma, Shalendra D. "The Rising Euro and Sinking Dollar: Explanations and Implications." *Mediterranean Quarterly* 19 (Spring 2008): 11–18.

Shierholz, Heidi. "Nine Years of Job Growth Wiped Out." *Economic Policy Institute Report,* July 2009.

Sifry, Micah L. and Nancy Watzman. *Is That a Politician in Your Pocket?* Hoboken, NJ: John Wiley & Sons, 2004.

Silber, William L. *When Washington Shut Down Wall Street.* Princeton: Princeton University Press, 2007.

Smith, Jean Edward. *FDR.* New York: Random House, 2007.

Stearns, Peter N. *American Fear.* New York: Routledge, 2006.

Steingart, Gabor. *The War for Wealth.* New York: McGraw-Hill, 2008.

Stiglitz, Joseph E. and Linda J. Bilmes. *The Three Trillion Dollar War: The True Cost of the Iraq Conflict.* New York: W.W. Norton, 2008.

Stiglitz, Joseph. *Making Globalization Work.* New York: W.W. Norton, 2007.

Stockholm International Peace Research Institute. *SIPRI Yearbook 2009: Summary.* Stockholm: Stockholm International Peace Research Institute, 2009.

Talbott, Strobe. *The Great Experiment: The Story of Ancient Empires, Modern States, and the Quest for a Global Nation.* New York: Simon & Schuster, 2008.

Taubenberger, Jeffrey K. and David M. Moren. "1918 Influenza: The Mother of All Pandemics." *CDC Emerging Infectious Diseases,* January 2006.

Tichon, Nicole. *Tax Shell Game: The Taxpayer Cost of Offshore Corporate Tax Havens.* Washington, D.C.: U.S. Public Interest Research Group Education Fund, 2009.

Tyler, Patrick. *A World of Trouble: The White House and the Middle East—From the Cold War to the War on Terror.* New York: Farrar, Straus, Giroux, 2009.

Uhalde, Ray and Jeff Strohl. *America in the Global Economy.* Washington, D.C.: National Center on Education and the Economy, 2006.

UNCTAD. *World Investment Report 2008* (New York: United Nations, 2008), Annex B, 257.

Unger, Craig. *The Fall of the House of Bush.* New York: Scribner, 2007.

United States Conference of Mayors. *Strong Cities. . . Strong Families. . . for a Strong America: Mayors' 10-Point Plan.* Washington, D.C.: United States Conference of Mayors, 2008.

United States Conference of Mayors. *U.S. Metro Economies: GMP—The Engines of America's Growth.* Lexington, KY: Global Insight, 2006.

U.S. Bureau of Labor Statistics. "Employment, Hours, and Earnings from the Current Employment Statistics Survey (National)." *http://data.bls.gov/PDQ/servlet/SurveyOutputServl*et.

U.S. Bureau of Labor Statistics, "The Employment Situation: June 2009." *www.bls.gov/news. release.*

U.S. Bureau of Labor Statistics. "Union Members Summary." *BLS Economic News Release,* January 2009.

U.S. Central Intelligence Agency. *World Factbook 2008.* Washington, D.C.: U.S. Government Printing Office, 2008.

U.S. Congressional Budget Office. *The Budget and Economic Outlook: Fiscal Years 2002–2011.* Washington, D.C.: Government Printing Office, 2001.

U.S. Department of Commerce, Bureau of Economic Analysis. "Current-Dollar and 'Real' Gross Domestic Product." *www.bea.gov/national/index.htm#gdp.*

U.S. Department of Defense. "Active Duty Military Personnel Strengths by Regional Area and by Country, December 31, 2007." *http://siadapp.osd.mil/personnel/MILITARY/hist.*

U.S. National Intelligence Council. *Global Trends 2025: A Transformed World.* Washington, D.C.: U.S. Government Printing Office, 2008.

U.S. Small Business Administration. *The Small Business Economy: A Report to the President, 2009*. Washington, D.C.: U.S. Government Printing Office, 2009.

Veseth, Michael. *Globaloney: Unraveling the Myths of Globalization*. Lanham, MD: Rowman & Littlefield, 2005.

Voskopoulos, George. "A European Dwarf and an American Giant." *American Chronicle*, 21 July 2006.

Wagley, John R. *Transnational Organized Crime: Threats and U.S. Responses*. Washington, D.C.: Congressional Research Service, 2006.

Walter, Andrew and Gautam Sen. *Analyzing the Global Political Economy*. Princeton: Princeton University Press, 2009.

Weisman, Alan. *The World Without Us*. New York: St Martin's Press, 2007.

Wiggin, Addison and Kate Incontrera. *I.O.U.S.A.* New York: John Wiley & Sons, 2008.

Wilper, Andrew P., Steffie Woolhandler, Karen E. Lasser, Danny McCormick, David H. Bor, and David U. Himmelstein. "Health Insurance and Mortality in U.S. Adults." *American Journal of Public Health* 99 (December 2009): 2289–2295.

Wilson, Dominic, and Roopa Purushothaman. "Dreaming with BRICs: The Path to 2050." *Goldman Sachs Global Economy Paper No. 99*, October 2003.

Wolf, Martin. *Fixing Global Finance*. Baltimore: Johns Hopkins University, 2008.

Wolff, Edward N. "Recent Trends in Household Wealth in the United States: Rising Debt and the Middle-Class Squeeze." *Levy Economics Institute Working Paper #502*. New York: Levy Economics Institute of Bard College, 2007.

Wong, Bernard P. *The Chinese in Silicon Valley: Globalization, Social Networks, and Ethnic Identity*. Lanham, MD: Rowman & Littlefield, 2006.

World Bank. "Gross National Income Per Capita 2008, Atlas Method and PPP." *http:// siteresources.worldbank.org/DATASTATISTICS*.

World Bank."World Development Indicators Database." 1 July 2009. *http://web.worldbank. org/WBSITE/EXTERNAL/DATASTATISTICS/*.

World Health Organization. *The World Health Report 2000—Health Systems: Improving Performance*. Geneva: World Health Organization, 2000.

World Health Organization. *World Health Statistics 2009*. Geneva: World Health Organization, 2009.

World Tourism Organization. "Testing Times for International Tourism." *World Tourism Barometer*, June 2009. *www.unwto.org/media/news*.

Wright, Lawrence. *The Looming Tower: Al-Qaeda and the Road to 9/11*. New York: Alfred A. Knopf, 2006.

Wright, Ronald. *What Is America? A Short History of the New World Order*. Toronto: Alfred A. Knopf Canada, 2008.

Wyatt, Derek, MP. "The Changing Role of an MP." *www.derekwyatt.co.uk*.

Zakaria, Fareed. *The Post-American World*. New York: W.W. Norton, 2008.

Zsoldos, István, and Anna Zadornova. "New EU Member States—A Fifth BRIC?" *Goldman Sachs Global Economics Paper No. 173*, 26 September 2008.

Index